Language Skills for Journalists

Language Skills for Journalists

R. THOMAS BERNER

School of Journalism
The Pennsylvania State University

HOUGHTON MIFFLIN COMPANY   BOSTON

Dallas   Geneva, Illinois   Hopewell, New Jersey   Palo Alto   London

This book is dedicated to Karen, Tracey and Amy, for
giving me the time; and to my promotion and tenure committee,
for giving me the reason.

Printed in the U.S.A.
Library of Congress Catalog Card Number: 78-69584
ISBN: 0-395-26789-7

CREDITS

Some of my sources have given me permission to use copyrighted material. They are:

CHAPTER 1 **Page 3:** Goldfinger quotation, Copyright 1976 by Newsweek, Inc. All rights reserved. Reprinted by permission. **Page 4:** Quintilian quotation, Lincoln Barnett, *The Treasure of Our Tongue,* © 1962, Alfred A. Knopf, Inc. **Page 5:** Aristides quotation, Reprinted from *The American Scholar,* Volume 46, Number 1, Winter, 1976–77. Copyright © 1976 by the United Chapters of Phi Beta Kappa. By permission of the publishers. **Page 29:** "Areas between . . . fuel sandstorms." Copyright 1977, Smithsonian Institution, from *Smithsonian* magazine, June 1977. **Page 29:** "With four . . . Island yesterday." © 1977 by The New York Times Company. Reprinted by permission. **Page 30:** "In a long . . . and frustration." © 1976 by The New York Times Company. Reprinted by permission. **Page 31:** "And while . . . his limousine." © 1976 by The New York Times Company. Reprinted by permission. **Page 31:** New York Times sentences on press conference with Jimmy Carter, © 1976 by The New York

Times Company. Reprinted by permission. **Page 31:** "The day . . . 'the bench.' " ©
1976 by The New York Times Company. Reprinted by permission.

CHAPTER 2   Page 35: "He proved . . . such things." Reprinted by permission from
Time, The Weekly Newsmagazine; Copyright Time Inc. 1976. **Page 36:** "But you . . .
shoulder blades." Reprinted by Permission, The Philadelphia Inquirer, July 24, 1976.
Page 36: "Plutonium . . . or worse." Copyright 1976 Smithsonian Institution, from
Smithsonian magazine, July 1976. **Page 36:** "Smiles . . . headed uptown." © 1976 by
The New York Times Company. Reprinted by permission. **Page 36:** "But this . . . the
freeze." Copyright 1977 by Newsweek, Inc. All rights reserved. Reprinted by permission. **Page 41:** "By mid-October . . . 48 percent." Reprinted by Permission, The Philadelphia Inquirer, Oct. 31, 1976. **Page 41:** "While ambitious . . . of the world."
Reprinted by Permission, The Philadelphia Inquirer, Oct. 31, 1976. **Page 42:** "If his
. . . the establishment." Reprinted by Permission, The Philadelphia Inquirer, Oct. 31,
1976. **Page 50:** "Gas would . . . residential markets," © The Washington Post 1976.
Page 51: "He says . . . the same." Reprinted by Permission, The Philadelphia Inquirer, Oct. 31, 1976. **Page 53:** "Worried one . . . really is." Reprinted by permission
from *Time,* The Weekly Newsmagazine; Copyright Time Inc. 1976. **Page 54:** "New is
. . . incumbent." © 1976 by The New York Times Company. Reprinted by permission. **Page 55:** "For such . . . of bankruptcy." Reprinted by permission from *Time,* The
Weekly Newsmagazine; Copyright Time Inc. 1976. **Page 55:** "These impulses . . .
tingling." © 1977 by The New York Times Company. Reprinted by permission. **Page
55:** "Using race . . . not unconstitutional." Copyright 1977 by Newsweek, Inc. All
rights reserved. Reprinted by permission. **Page 60:** " 'I know . . . and interview." ©
1976 by The New York Times Company. Reprinted by permission. **Page 66:** "Taiwan
wanted . . . its anthem." © 1976 by The New York Times Company. Reprinted by
permission. **Page 71:** Sentences by Gene Gilmore and Robert Root, *Modern Newspaper
Editing,* © 1971 by The Glendessary Press. **Page 74:** "Yet he . . . fan is . . ." © The
Washington Post 1976.

CHAPTER 3   Page 83: "These parts . . . adjectives." © 1969, Houghton Mifflin
Company. Reprinted by permission from *The American Heritage Dictionary of the English
Language.* **Page 85:** "involuntarily de-schooled," © 1976 by The New York Times
Company. Reprinted by permission. **Page 85:** "Go to . . . of baseball." © 1976 by
The New York Times Company. Reprinted by permission. **Page 86:** "It had . . .
lawyered." © The Washington Post 1976. **Page 86:** "Kelleher forbade . . . the defen-
dant." From *The Quill,* published by The Society of Professional Journalists, Sigma Delta
Chi. **Page 86:** "Couponing . . . she explains." "What makes . . . newsletter." Copyright 1977 by Newsweek, Inc. All rights reserved. Reprinted by permission. **Page 87:**
"But some . . . their beauty." © 1977 by The New York Times Company. Reprinted
by permission. **Page 87:** "Every research . . . then Carter-ized." Copyright 1976 by
Newsweek, Inc. All rights reserved. Reprinted by permission. **Page 87:** ". . . is in
. . . is normal." Copyright 1977 by Newsweek, Inc. All rights reserved. Reprinted by
permission. **Pages 87–88:** John O'Hara sentences, *My Turn,* © 1964 Random House,
Inc. **Page 88:** "His ever-burning . . . unrealized." Copyright 1977 Smithsonian Institution, from *Smithsonian* magazine, January 1977. **Page 88:** Definition of annualize, *The
Compact Edition of the Oxford English Dictionary,* Oxford University Press, 1971. **Page 88:**
"It quickly . . . gate crashed." © 1976 by The New York Times Company. Reprinted
by permission. **Page 89:** "Theismann . . . scrimmage." © The Washington Post
1976. **Page 89:** "It's known . . . blind-sided." Copyright 1977 by Newsweek, Inc. All
rights reserved. Reprinted by permission. **Page 89:** "So during . . . medical hut."
Reprinted by permission from *Time,* The Weekly Newsmagazine; Copyright Time Inc.
1976. **Page 90:** "For long . . . entire length." © 1977 by The New York Times Com-

Contents

EIGHT
Meaning

Preface

ABOUT THIS BOOK

This is a very practical book for journalists and journalism students. It provides ways of dealing with common language problems by presenting a multitude of examples from journalistic writing and many exercises for practice. My purpose in writing this book is to make you sensitive to how the English language operates so that you will use it more effectively. In short, this book is for people who think about language and love to use it to its maximum effectiveness.

My approach is functional, with lapses into the traditional. The advice of two college English professors, S. Leonard Rubinstein and Robert G. Weaver, sets the focus of this book:

> Each part of speech, each mark of punctuation, each link of grammar serves a function. Each exists because it does something only it can do. It exists not by law, not by rule—but by logic of function. Don't learn a law. Don't learn a rule. Learn the function of each as you would learn the function of a hammer or a saw. Then you will be able to say what you want to say. Syntax is the logic of function.

What good journalists and copy editors understand is function, not rules.

The divisions in the book are arbitrary. Each chapter depends on the other and should be read in the context of the others, not as a separate entity. For example, the first chapter, which is on writing, necessarily includes information on sentence structure, function, convention, modification, punctuation, spelling, meaning and usage. The chapter on writing also includes terms not explained until two or three chapters later. That is intentional. A thirsty person should not rapidly swallow gallons of water when measured sipping of the same amount will quench thirst better.

As you read each chapter, keep in mind what you have already read.

You will find some material and advice repeated because they are worth repeating or because they apply to more than one aspect of grammar. You must read this book at least once. You cannot put it on a shelf for future reference until you know what is in it to refer to.

The first thing you should do is take the language usage test on page 257. Feel free to use a dictionary to check spellings and meanings. Record your score, then take the test again after you have finished reading the book. Compare the before and after scores.

Featured throughout this book are many exercises and answers that will help you correct the problems identified in the text. The book is intended to be a self-help text, but only if you do the exercises will the book's purpose be fulfilled. Even if you have to refer to a particular section to answer an exercise correctly, you are still learning.

This book is based largely on my experiences as a journalist (primarily a copy editor) and as a journalism professor. While most of the examples come from newspapers, the major differences between print and broadcast usages are noted. I have also consulted more than 40 grammar and usage books, as much for the differences and disagreements among them as for the similarities. I have found that the interplay between conflicting opinions often offers the best solution for a particular problem.

This book will not replace a book on grammar by a grammarian. I do not discuss diagramming, although an intense study of grammar probably would. Nor is there a chapter on capitalization; those conventions peculiar to newspapers are discussed in textbooks on newswriting and in the stylebook jointly developed by the wire services, United Press International and the Associated Press.

NOT A SEXY TOPIC

Grammar is not a sexy topic. "Investigative journalism" sounds exciting; "grammar" doesn't. But grammar describes the writing and the speaking characteristics of a people. And if you, the journalist, want your stories read or listened to, you must follow your readers' and listeners' conventions of grammar.

Actually, you don't have as much to learn as you think you do. You may not be an expert on the language, but you do know grammar. You've been learning grammar since you were a child. As you learned to speak, you imitated your parents and other people close to you. You formed sentences you had never heard anyone speak—and they were, for the most part, grammatically correct. Yet nobody told you a subject is followed by a verb is followed by an object, and so on.

Your biggest problem with grammar might be that you cannot explain what you know. But you don't have to be able to label a conjunctive appositive to use one correctly. Nor for that matter is it crucial for a journalist to be able to identify gerunds and participles—*as long as the journalist uses them effectively.*

ACKNOWLEDGMENTS

I have not used footnotes, but instead refer to my sources within the text—standard journalistic practice. The bibliography contains complete reference information for all my sources—little recognition for the aid they have been. Many of the examples in the book come from newspapers, magazines and the newscasts of television stations. In order to maintain transition, I have sometimes found it clumsy to acknowledge my sources every time I use a sentence from them, but I have acknowledged every source at least once unless I was using an example of bad language usage. In addition to the sources that provided copyrighted material, these media graciously allowed me to use some of their sentences: ABC News; The Associated Press; Bend (Ore.) *Bulletin;* CBS News; *Centre Daily Times,* State College, Pa.; *The Daily Collegian,* University Park, Pa.; *Columbia Journalism Review; The Erie* (Pa.) *Times; Gannetteer; More;* NBC News; *The Pennsylvania Mirror,* State College, Pa.; *Penn State Journalist;* Reuters news service; United Press International; The Washington Post Writers Group; *The Washington Star;* The Washington Star Syndicate; WTAJ-TV, Altoona, Pa.

Also deserving of recognition are my colleagues in journalism and English at Pennsylvania State University who tolerated my unscheduled and disruptive stops at their offices as I tested parts of this book. Many of their suggestions have been incorporated without credit.

Others who have helped tremendously are Edward T. Frye of the State College (Pa.) Area School District and Francis Bogert of the Penns Valley (Pa.) Area School District, whose jobs include evaluating student performance in the use of English. Melvyn A. Topf, coordinator of humanities at Roger Williams College, Bristol, Rhode Island, contributed much, both as a friend today and as one of my early college English teachers. I would also like to thank the reviewers who gave me helpful comments on the manuscript: D. J. Cline of South Dakota State University; John L. Griffith of the University of Florida; Jack Hart of the University of Oregon; Larry Horney of Ball State University; George A. Hough, III, of Michigan State University; Terry Hynes of California State University; Elden Rawlings of Texas Christian University; and Herbert Strentz of Drake University. And I cannot say enough good about the six high school English teachers who helped shape my attitude toward the language. Rarely can a person boast of having had six good high school English teachers; I hope my children are half as lucky.

My students have also helped me write this book. To the records officer they may be nothing more than numbers; to me they are dangling modifiers, unparallel constructions, pronouns without antecedents and subjects and verbs that do not agree.

Finally, I must thank Gerry Lynn Hamilton, a former copy editor for *The York* (Pa.) *Dispatch,* who edited this book. Among other things, Gerry removed extraneous words and challenged vague statements. Where I pontificated, Gerry deflated. He also shortened my long sentences when they became tiresome. No writer is above the pencil, and it is a pleasure when one knows a good editor is reading one's copy.

R.T.B.

ONE

Writing

HOW TO WRITE BETTER

There is no easy formula you can follow to become a good writer. Good writing is difficult; it is a labor of love. Most good writers say writing is the hardest thing they do. Some good writers hate to write because it is so difficult. Fortunately, the rewards make it worthwhile. Still, words do not just fall upon a piece of paper in their clearest and most logical sequence. The writer must put them that way. The writer must be able to take two positions at the same time—that of the reporter of the event and that of the reader or listener of the report. Ultimately the reader or listener must be satisfied.

Good writing is clear, concise and interesting. Some journalists add accurate to that list; fiction writers would probably substitute believable for accurate. Clear writing demands a clear mind. You must think before you write. You must organize in your mind what you want to say. That doesn't mean a word-by-word organization. It means you must be sure of the direction you want your story to go, and it means you must be the driver at all times. If you become a back-seat driver, your direction will suffer.

ORGANIZATION AND WORD CHOICE

To write well, you must organize your thoughts, put them into the right compartments and build the compartments one after the other. Organization is a state of mind and a state of function. Usually journalists write off the top of their heads; there is no time for extensive outlines, and even rough ones seem a waste of precious seconds when a deadline is fast approaching. Still, a good journalist does not go barren of thought into a story. As the event unfolds, he or she is thinking about how to write it.

The journalist, especially, has no choice but to think about writing the story as it is happening. Time is crucial to any editor whose responsibility to get the paper out on time or the newscast on the air at the right moment transcends any feelings that may be hurt in the process. Ideally, every journalist should rewrite what he or she has written—an impossibility that can be adjusted for by thinking thoroughly before writing. Good writing, for the most part, is rewriting; the journalist has neither the time nor the energy to rewrite. That is why every thought he or she puts into a story before beginning to write it is important.

One useful way of organizing a story is according to the way it happens. However, because of journalistic writing's compacted and to-the-point nature, which is necessary for conveying the most information to the reader in the least amount of time, newswriting does not always follow that structure. The inverted presentation of information is the standard way of writing news stories today. Critics call it, with much disdain, *formula writing.* However, the detractors do not realize all writing has formulas, be it fiction, magazine or television. The formula is to tell the story according to the most efficient and understandable way for that particular story.

Organizing a story well is not the only method used to gain clarity. How you organize each sentence in the story is just as important. If you are having problems writing good sentences, or if you want to keep writing good ones, the following advice applies particularly to you.

Keep your sentences short. Use active verbs. Use plain words. Avoid clever phrases. Short sentences convey your thoughts best. Short sentences cannot become bogged down with too many thoughts. The average length of good sentences is 20 words. All sentences are kept simple. It can be very boring.

If you are having problems, start with the core of expression—the short sentence—and build up from there to complex and compound sentences and combinations of both.

Use plain words and active verbs in short sentences. If your average sentence length is 20 words, you will see that you cannot put too many thoughts or ideas into one sentence. Because of that, short sentences carry your thoughts best. But short sentences also tend to be simple sentences (subject-verb-object) and can be very boring—sometimes better for putting someone to sleep than getting an idea across.

What I have just done, for the most part, is reworked the paragraph of short and simple sentences into a paragraph of complex sentences of varying structure and length. It is easier for a writer to build from the simple sentence to the complex (and compound and compound-complex) than to edit such sentences into simple sentences. You can write short and simple sentences then edit or revise them into suitable complex, compound and compound-complex sentences. Of course, retain some simple sentences. A mix of structures is the most effective.

You will enrich your writing by keeping it simple, only this time I don't mean simple sentences but rather uncomplicated prose. Americans love their writing that way; they adore anyone who can make clear to them something complex. When Leon Jaworski, the special prosecutor of the Watergate scandal, wanted a lawyer to write the investigating team's report, he picked George Frampton, "a brilliant young lawyer with an analytical mind and *the ability to write clearly* [italics added]." When Nathaniel Goldfinger, a chief economist for the AFL-CIO, died, *Newsweek* magazine said in his obituary: "Goldfinger had a gift for uncomplicating the complicated." What an epitaph for an economist! It should be the guiding light for every writer as well.

Plain words make for clear writing. As Benjamin Franklin wrote in the *Pennsylvania Gazette:* "To write *clearly,* not only the most expressive, but the plainest words should be chosen [Franklin's italics]." Use words your readers will understand; don't use pretentious or learned words when simple and plain words will do the job. Avoid *utilize; use* is fine. *Capitulate* may make a potential enemy think twice, but if your present enemy has *surrendered,* your potential enemy will get the message. *Contusions* and *lacerations* are *bruises* and *cuts* everywhere but in hospitals. *Fractures* are *breaks,* be it of rocks or bones or broken homes (*fractured* homes!). And if you and your steady *terminate* your relationship, tell your friends you *ended* it, or better still, just say, "We broke up." Perhaps you'll say it happened because your steady became *corpulent,* which is a big way of saying *fat.* Maybe your steady had too many *vesicles* to suit you. Who will know you mean *blisters?* Some may doubt the *veracity* of your reason; others will doubt the *truth.* They'll say you're *mendacious,* and if you are, then you've been *lying.* Perhaps the way you stated your reason was not *lucid* to everyone; try again, and make it *clear.* And if you *concur* with what I've said, just nod your head or say, "I agree."

Do not write about improving *student-teacher ratio* when you want to say *reducing class size. Nourishment* may conjure up thoughts of a steak dinner, which would be misleading if the word you want is *apple,* which is more concrete than *fruit, food* or *nourishment.* According to Jack Cappon, the general news editor of the Associated Press, *presidency* is an abstraction; the president's name isn't. "A broader housing policy is an abstraction," Cappon writes. "Building 700 apartments for slum dwellers is not. . . . A health problem can be anything from an ingrown toenail to terminal cancer." Other abstractions on Cappon's list include: *confrontation, negative impact, sweeping changes, procedures, unduly alarmed.* Equally vague is *carcinogens,* which is clearer when stated as *cancer-causing agents.* Two other abstractions are *wide* as in *wide experience* and *vast* as in *vast majority.* Vague as those phrases are, they are doubly dangerous when used in broadcasting. A patient reader can study the printed word; a listener gets only one chance—and if he or she hears a word wrong, it is not possible to hear it again.

The advice of a retired journalism professor, Charles H. Brown, applies here:

> The essential problem of news writing for any medium—the newspaper, the news magazine, radio, or television—lies in making the information instantly comprehensible to large numbers of people. It is not to delight with clever phrases, to charm with the mellifluous flow of language, or to transport beyond the real world to an imagined one: the art of news communication is the art of clear writing. Whatever other values the writing may have, it is bad writing from the viewpoint of the news communicator if it is not immediately clear.

And Quintilian, a Roman rhetorician, wrote centuries ago: "One should not aim at being possible to understand, but at being impossible to misunderstand."

LEARNING FROM OTHER WRITERS

Learning to write well involves, in part, imitating others who write well. I don't mean borrowing the phrases and words of other writers the way I did as a beginning sportswriter for a very small daily newspaper. My guidance until then had come from high school English teachers who did not teach newswriting. So I turned to a large daily newspaper to learn newswriting. One of that paper's sportwriters always referred to a basketball player I also wrote about as a "carrot-topped senior" (meaning he had red hair). I leaped on the phrase; I used it everytime I could and even a few times when I shouldn't have. The lesson I missed was how sportswriters use descriptive phrases as a substitute for a person's name to avoid repetition. Instead I stole someone else's phrase (and it was trite to begin with) and made it my own. That is not imitating another's writing.

Read a lot of newspapers. I am amazed at the number of journalism students who have never seriously read newspapers until they entered journalism school and then have a hard time getting into the habit. But do not limit yourself to newspapers. Read other literature as well. See how the masters of our language used it to its best effect. Do not overlook the Bible. Its simplicity makes it one of the best written works in our culture. Its writers used no razzle-dazzle to explain the Creation

> And God said, Let there be light: and there was light. (Genesis 1:3)

or the flood that put Noah in his ark

> And the rain was upon the earth forty days and forty nights. (Genesis 7:12)

When John described the weeping of Jesus, he did not assault us with overwrought language, such as, "Tears poured quickly from the face of the Master; his face wet with the gush of his tears." John wrote:

> Jesus wept. (John 11:35)

When David killed the giant Goliath, readers of the Bible were treated to straight (that is, unemotional) reporting.

> And David put his hand in his bag, and took thence a stone, and slang it, and smote the Philistine in his forehead, that the stone sunk into his forehead; and he fell upon his face to the earth. (I Samuel 17:49)

According to Aristides in *The American Scholar,* John D. Rockefeller "wrote better prose than any political scientist I can name." Aristides explains why. "Doubtless this had to do with the fact that Rockefeller sedulously read the Bible, and suffered neither lexical impoverishment nor the hunger for innovation that is now endemic and that calls for changing one's vocabulary, like one's tires, roughly every three years."

THE CRITIC

A good critic is another important element in learning to write well. Criticism requires you to have a thick skin, but writers benefit from thick skins prodded often by a good critic. The critic doesn't have to be an editor. Use your roommate or a friend. After all, you are trying to communicate with anyone who reads. Let your friend tell you if what you have written makes sense. Don't let your critic read it and say, "It's fine." Ask your critic what you've said in your story. If you are a good writer and your critic is a conscientious reader, he or she will be able to tell you. Spouses, parents and children are good critics, too. Your family and relatives know good writing. They may not know how to write well, but they certainly know what they like and understand. Your critics don't need a portfolio of college degrees to be good critics. If you feel that way, your writing probably reflects your mistaken attitude, which the reader will grasp just before he or she stops reading.

Self-criticism is as important as a good critic. Self-criticism is the most ego-smashing thing you will ever do, this critical editing and revising of your own writing. Nothing destroys you more (or so you'll feel) than to tear apart your own work and redo it. But you cannot fall in love with what you write. Love your writing as you would your child, but correct it when it's wrong no matter how painful that may be. Don't be afraid to whip sentences into shape when wholesale revision is the only cure. Don't be bashful about changing a word or two—or even discarding some. Do it with as much self-honesty as you can muster. It is better that you put your work into the best possible shape; only you and your ego know about it and feel the pain. But when an editor needs to make frequent revisions, it reveals a careless or uncaring writer, one the editor will quickly lose interest in.

Learning to write well is like learning to type well—practice, practice, practice. Write and revise, and write some more. When writing, compose on a typewriter or video display terminal, which will give you the advantage of practicing two skills at once. As a journalist you will go to a typewriter or video display terminal better prepared for the pressure of deadlines if you have practiced extensively. If you have disciplined yourself, you can handle deadlines.

ECONOMY IN GOOD WRITING

Journalism students have a difficult time grasping the tenets of tight writing. Yet it is probably the concept most widely agreed upon among teachers of writing and good writers. They may not agree on using an adjective as a noun or whether a comma should be used in a compound sentence, but almost all teachers of writing and all writers agree tight writing is essential.

Tight writing means using no more words than necessary to give a sentence a precise meaning. Tight writing keeps the reader reading; loose, uneconomical writing loses the reader to a television program or household chores because he or she feels the wordiness of an article is stealing time from something more important.

According to Philip Knightley in *The First Casualty,* tight writing started for economical reasons. In the telegraph's infancy more than a century ago, the rate for news stories was $5 a word. "Sending a summary of a battle by telegraph meant adopting a new style: crisp, concise, and packed with facts," Knightley writes.

Every journalist, to fully appreciate tight writing, should work for a highway department. If you want to see clear messages simply stated, examine the signs highway engineers erect. The people who write these messages cannot waste words—they are limited to a relatively small space intended to be read quickly and understood immediately by any motorist. My favorite sign stands at an intersection where only a right turn is permitted. The person who wrote the message did not say NO LEFT TURN, for that would have meant a motorist could drive through the intersection, a movement equally dangerous in this instance. Instead, the sign writer produced: RIGHT TURN ONLY. Those three words convey this message: It is dangerous to turn left or drive through this intersection at all times of day and night. Violation of this sign's message may result in a bad accident or an arrest.

The second part of that sign's message is not an actual part of it. Rather, you know that to ignore a legally posted sign on a highway can result in your being arrested, fined and maybe even jailed. Your knowledge is conventional information, information about customs that every member of a society learns. And it is with conventional information that tight writing begins.

CONVENTIONAL INFORMATION

One major convention in our society is the use of a particular vehicle to transport accident victims or seriously ill persons to a hospital—an ambulance. Why report that an ambulance took an injured person to a hospital? That's something ambulances do. When something other than an ambulance is used journalists might have to report it. (Some newspapers and radio and television stations routinely mention the name of the ambulance company, particularly if it is a volunteer group, in the interest of good will.)

Furthermore, if an ambulance is involved, why bother with *taken to the hospital* at all? In place of *taken* a journalist could use *admitted* (if that is the case) or *treated*.

> Ellenberg was treated for head injuries at Cadbury Hospital.

That sentence tells the reader Ellenberg wasn't admitted, just treated. For those who disagree, they can always add *and released*.

> Ellenberg was treated for head injuries at Cadbury Hospital and released.

Journalists should provide new information for the reader-listener, not information he or she already knows. Isaac Bashevis Singer, the author, told Nadine Kofman, a reporter for the *Centre Daily Times* of State College, Pa.: "Journalism doesn't do any damage to a fiction writer. You inform people. A writer who does not inform, who tells people what they already know, is not a writer." A story filled with what people already know will not burden the reader after one or two paragraphs for he or she will have stopped reading. How much would you read of a fire story that described fire trucks or a football game story that detailed the size of the field? We already know that information, or we don't care, or the information is not important to the news. We want to know about the fire and the football game. The fire and the game are unique pieces of information; they are what is worth reporting.

NEEDLESS DETAIL

Some journalists waste the reader's or listener's time by giving more detail than needed or by giving, in essence, the same details twice. Look for that in this sentence:

> Police said the juvenile was taken to Cadbury jail where she was detained to await the arrival of her parents.

Doesn't this say the same thing?

> Police said the juvenile was detained at Cadbury jail to await the arrival of her parents.

The second example says the same thing as the first—only in fewer words. If the juvenile was detained at the jail, she had to have been taken there. A crime story produced this wordy example:

The intruder forced the resident into the basement, where she was locked inside.

No doubt the resident did not volunteer. Try this:

The intruder locked the resident in the basement.

In the following sentences the needless detail is italicized:

Manson *deprogrammed and* reprogrammed the family members.

During the trial the jury was sequestered *and kept from publicity.*

Another school bus was immediately dispatched *to take the children to school.*

The following examples—from accident and drug-smuggling stories—have to be rewritten to remove the needless detail.

Williams and Jones noticed the car along Rt. 322 near the Rt. 45 intersection. *Finding the car empty,* they *looked around and* found the victim in a ditch 60 feet away.
Williams and Jones noticed the empty car along Rt. 322 near the Rt. 45 intersection. They found the victim in a ditch 60 feet away.

Barnhart said gastric juices would destroy the swallowed condom and the cocaine *would spread through* Polsby's *body and* kill him.
Barnhart said gastric juices would destroy the swallowed condom and the cocaine would kill Polsby.

Some journalists pump stories full of needless information and detail only one or two readers might be interested in.

Described this week in *U.S. Patent No. 3,978,908,* the process greatly reduces fire and pollution hazards.

Giving the patent number adds nothing to the story.

The process, patented this week, greatly reduces fire and pollution hazards.

The reader also is not familiar with the number of every law and the number of every section in every law or policy.

The board excluded *section 6-9-10,* which deals with the number of students allowed on a bus. The section says there may be no more than five standees.

Section 6-9-10 may be important to the school bus coordinator, but it's not something the reader or listener knows or needs to know.

> The board excluded a section that limits to five the number of standees on a bus.

You can also get trapped into blow-by-blow reporting when it isn't needed.

> The commission appointed a committee last night to *write and* ask the utility not to build its proposed power line.

The reader is concerned not with the committee's method of communication, only with the communication itself.

STATING THE OBVIOUS

Some journalists state the obvious over and over again, giving them another place to tighten writing. After clearly saying the article is about a meeting of the Cadbury Sports Advisory Board and that the speaker is the gymnastics coach at Cadbury High School, does the journalist need the italicized portion of the following?

> "I would like to have a home for gymnastics *in Cadbury,*" the coach said.

Similarly, the advisory board votes on a schedule change:

> The board also agreed on a recommendation to add two girls' cross country meets *to the Cadbury High School* schedule.

Clearly the Cadbury board does not make decisions for another board. And if the Oklahoma legislature passes a law to reduce speeding, obviously the law applies only in Oklahoma; the Oklahoma legislature has no authority in other states. The logic applies to any rule-making body.

> A public hearing will precede the meeting *and testimony will be heard* on the vacation of October and Erie alleys.

Public hearings are convened to hear testimony just as power lines are built to transport energy.

> The utility wants to construct a new 230-kilovolt *power* line *to transport energy* from a substation in Cadbury to its plant in Clive.

Consider how absurd the preceding is. Can you imagine a utility wanting to construct an *old* line? And *230-kilovolt* says *power.* Along those lines is the story about the groundbreaking for a *new* store and a later sentence saying:

> The new store will be more than five times the size of the present store *when completed*.

Another sentence filled with obvious information:

> Four *additional* fire companies were called *in* to assist Cadbury firemen *fight the blaze because their efforts* were hampered by a lack of *a nearby* water *supply*.

The rewrite gets rid of 11 words, although another must be added for a smooth sentence.

> Four fire companies were called to assist Cadbury firemen, who were hampered by a lack of water.

PREPOSITIONAL PILE-UP

Prepositional pile-up, which turns sentences into incomprehensible monsters, is another place to tighten writing.

> There was a deficit to be picked up *by the committee of $97.45.*

That sentence, one of the worst I've ever read (and I did not make it up), contains two prepositional phrases (italicized). The second phrase (of $97.45) modifies *deficit* yet seven words separate the noun from its modifier. Modifiers, if they are to modify effectively, must be as close as possible to the word or words they modify, not strung along later (advice you'll hear again). For the first piece of surgery on the preceding example, convert the second prepositional phrase into a modifier and put it in front of the word it modifies.

> There was a $97.45 deficit to be picked up by the committee.

What began as a 13-word sentence is down to 12 words. And there's still more to remove. In the second operation, cut *was,* which is a linking verb, a verb that carries no force. Notice too, *there* is an ineffectual word.

> The committee must pick up a $97.45 deficit.

What started as a clumsy 13-word sentence is down to a forcefully stated 8-word sentence with no loss in meaning. If anything, the sentence has gained meaning because you're removed the obscure and weak words and put the modifier next to the word it modifies. A five-word savings may not sound like a lot until you figure how many times in a 700-word story you can eliminate unnecessary words.

Here is a sentence whose length can be halved

There is a total of $92,000 in the contingency fund.

from 10 words to 5 by writing directly

The contingency fund contains $92,000.

Don't be misled into believing that every prepositional phrase can be turned into an adjective. Consider how much you put before the modified noun, and if it's a long string of words, then you've created a monster. You could convert "Thomas Williams, a member of the board, said" into "board member Thomas Williams said"—a form broadcasters prefer—and not do damage to clarity. But if the information is lengthy, such as "Thomas Williams, a member of the Cadbury Area School Board, said," you would be better off not converting that to "Cadbury Area School Board member Thomas Williams said." The reader grasps little doses easily and chokes on anything bigger.

Sometimes the prepositional phrase belongs before the noun it modifies simply because it contains crucial information. Unintended deception results when journalists write like this:

City Council proposed a tax increase of 5.5 mills . . .

The amount of the tax increase has been hidden in a limply stated sentence. Better to say:

City Council proposed a 5.5-mill tax increase . . .

VERB-NOUN CONSTRUCTIONS

Weak verb-noun constructions can easily be turned into strong verbs. Why write *the commission gave approval* when *the commission approved* says the same thing more forcefully? What's the loss in meaning when you write *City Council will study the proposal* instead of *City Council will make a study of the proposal?* And while many organizations *hold a meeting,* they can also transact the same business when they *meet.* To tell the members of the organization they're going to meet, don't *get in contact with them* just *contact them.* And if you're going to tell them what the first order of business will be, don't say the meeting will *get under way* with a speech when *begin* or *start* reduces the number of words.

REDUNDANCY

Two plus two is always four but what may be redundant in one context is not necessarily redundant in another. A student once wrote a story about a musical group's *song lyrics,* which is clearly redundant. But the same words arranged differently may be necessary to give the correct sense to a sentence, as in:

> The lyrics of some of today's songs are unclear.

To write, in the interest of avoiding what you may consider a redundancy, "The lyrics are unclear," does not do justice to the intended meaning. Similarly, *fiscal budget* has the trappings of redundancy because most budgets are fiscal. However, if you are writing about a person's *fiscal budget* and the way the person budgets time, the distinction between the two might require you to use *fiscal budget.*

But the exceptions are few compared to the violations. Think of the many redundant phrases pushed upon readers. Careless writers tell people *to closely scrutinize the consensus of opinion,* the wordy stepchild of *to scrutinize the consensus*—all other words are redundant because they are inherent in the words used. Knowing precise meanings would have helped the writer of the following:

> Smoke rising high over the buildings billowed over a large traffic jam below.

It is the nature of billowing smoke to rise high and over something. The non-redundant version of the preceding:

> Smoke billowed over a large traffic jam.

Because we all know that heat can scorch, the following sentence from a fire story contains a redundant prepositional phrase (italicized):

> There was no damage estimate for the shed or for the main building, which was scorched *by the heat.*

Here are some sentences to study for redundant or extraneous words (the offending words are italicized):

> A *huge* throng *of people* gathered at *twelve* noon on Easter *Sunday* to debate the *controversial* issue.

> During that time *span,* a *passing* motorist saw a *flaming* inferno he knew had been started by *young* juveniles.

The widow *woman who lives* down the street is pleasant.

The family attempted to kill her *but was unsuccessful.*

In the event that our *invited* guests don't come, we will *bring to an* end our friendship with *all of* them. (Begin the sentence with *if.*)

Sen. Jones said *in a speech* last night *that* Russia's army is getting stronger *every day.*

The three will appeal to Superior Court *for a decision in their favor.*

The judge ruled that students have the *legal* right to vote in the district where they go to college.

Required *mandatory* conservation measures must be followed.

Police are not allowed to release the record of a suspect's *prior* convictions.

The treatment plant *currently* discharges its effluent into Cadbury Run.

About 3.5 million gallons a day *now* are discharged into Cadbury Run.

Also, *there are* a number of other classes *that* are larger than the administration likes.

Thomas F. Williams died of cancer in his native Wales, *where he was born.*

The tuition *fee* increase is $18 *more* a term.

Too many people look at *human* individuals as something special.

City Council plans to install *pedestrian* sidewalks in the alley.

Obviously some of what could be deleted from some of the preceding examples is not redundant, just unnecessary. Some examples, of course, would not be redundant given a different context. Talking or writing about a person's conviction in court *today* leaves you in a position of describing the person's other convictions as *prior.* Millions of redundant phrases exist and society will no doubt create more. You will have to be alert at all times. Here are some you can avoid:

REDUNDANCY	SOLUTION
remand back	remand
soothing tranquilizer	tranquilizer
is in need of	needs
could hold practice	could practice
other matters recommended	also recommended
she went on to say	she said
two separate buildings	two buildings
make an addition to	add
compromise solution	compromise
general public	public
completely destroyed	destroyed
legal contract	contract
cooperate together	cooperate

THROWAWAYS

Entire sentences are often unnecessary to news stories. Such sentences are throwaways or brick walls—sentences that stop the reader because they don't advance the story toward its conclusion. It is considered a fault of journalistic writing that such a premium is placed on advancing a story that sometimes necessary background is excluded. But good journalists are afraid to tamper with the restless reader's interest by offering even one sentence that apparently leads nowhere. Most often throwaway sentences show up as scene-setters in which the writer provides an unnecessary context. Such sentences are so static they should be bottled and sold as a cure for insomnia.

In the following, the first sentence—taken from the middle of a story—is a throwaway:

> A preliminary report on the survey was delivered by John S. Warren, regional planning director, at a meeting of the commission last night at the municipal building. [Yawn] The report recommends that housing for the elderly not be implemented on a wide scale because little need exists. [At last, the news!]

The first sentence is not really background in the sense that it provides information the reader needs to understand the story; it is part of the present story and could be said more forcefully, without putting the reader to sleep.

A preliminary report on the survey, given last night by John S. Warren, regional planning director, recommends that housing for the elderly not be widely implemented because little need exists.

Among other things eliminated were some conventional data—that the information was given at a meeting and where the meeting occurred. If necessary, they can be mentioned later in the story. The sentence is better still this way:

Little need for more housing for the elderly exists, Regional Planning Director John S. Warren said last night.

The fact that Warren is quoting a survey could be put in the next sentence or paragraph.

Basing his remarks on a survey by the regional planning staff, Warren said . . .

Here are the lead and second paragraphs of a story:

An official of the American Heart Association said today that 61.16 percent of the deaths in Cadbury last year were caused by heart-related diseases.

The announcement was made by Dr. Marian F. Williams, president of the Cadbury Chapter of the Heart Association, who released the 1975 statistics giving the origins of the heart-related deaths. The statistics are:

heart attack	257 deaths
stroke	67
rheumatic heart	10
hardening of arteries	6
other causes	21

The second paragraph does nothing to advance the story. Here is a rewrite of the second paragraph:

Dr. Marian F. Williams, president of the association's Cadbury chapter, said that 257 of the 378 deaths were caused by heart attacks. The second biggest killer was strokes, 67, followed by rheumatic heart, 10 . . .

The restructuring ties the announcement and the highest statistic to immediately give the reader some news.

Don't assume, though, that all throwaway sentences are bad. Sometimes one is necessary to provide background that cannot be subordinated harmoniously to a main clause. Then a throwaway sentence should be used because in such cases clarity is the goal and if the reader is put off by an unclear story, the journalist has failed anyway.

In the example below is a lead followed by a paragraph that is not a throwaway; it does move the story along because it gives background the reader should have.

> Hopewell County last night became the third municipality in the six-county region to adopt the comprehensive plan.
> The plan to guide growth in the region during the next 20 years has also been adopted by Pickett and Hunterdon counties. The region's remaining counties have not held a public hearing on the plan.

The second paragraph is a neat summary that explains the lead and puts Hopewell County's action in context.

In broadcasting, throwaways are not as obnoxious. Because of the lengthy or complex result, the broadcast journalist relies less on subordinating background. Instead, he or she presents the newscast in a string of simple and short sentences that will not baffle listeners. Two 10-word sentences sound better than one 20-word sentence.

ELLIPTIC WRITING

Although you may not realize it, you probably already write and speak elliptically. You do not write or say, "I am shorter than she is short," when "I am shorter than she" is clear. It is common to drop the second (even third and fourth) of parallel elements because the first element is carried over. That is elliptic writing.

> He runs to school and he walks to work.

Elliptically written, the sentence reads better without the second *he*.

> He runs to school and walks to work.

At its wordiest the following sentence could be written:

> She likes physics and *she likes* chemistry.

Such a construction takes the directness out of the sentence.

> She likes physics and chemistry.

In elliptic writing all parallel elements are not repeated. In the following sentence the italicized words are understood and did not appear in the original:

Johnstown was cut off from the world, its railroads *were* washed away and *its* bridges *were* destroyed.

The original:

Johnstown was cut off from the world, its railroads washed away and bridges destroyed.

Sometimes discardable are prepositions and articles:

The chairman of CBS Inc. said today that within the last decade the idea *of press freedom* and *the* practice of press freedom have been endangered around the world.

The sentence reads better without the italicized matter.

The chairman of CBS Inc. said today that within the last decade the idea and practice of press freedom have been endangered around the world.

There is a danger in elliptic writing, best shown in the following sign on the Ohio Turnpike:

DRIVE SLOWER WHEN WET

The first missing element is the subject of the sentence. Because the sentence is direct address, the subject *you* is understood. Also understood is the verb *are* in the second half of the sentence. But what makes the verb understood is the elliptic subject of the second half of the sentence. That subject is carried over from the first half of the sign. What the sign really says:

(YOU) DRIVE SLOWER WHEN (YOU ARE) WET

But what the sign means:

(YOU) DRIVE SLOWER WHEN (THE HIGHWAY IS) WET

While such a construction may be perfectly clear to the driver of an automobile, it would not be in print or on the air. The caution, then, is that you make sure what you are omitting has a preceding parallel element.

The pronouns (such as *who, that, which, where*) used to introduce clauses and sometimes the verbs that follow can be dropped as long as the intended meaning remains intact. Such elliptic writing is common to complex sentences (sentences containing main and subordinate clauses).

Joseph R. Jones, *who is* 75, today predicted he would live another 75 years.
Joseph R. Jones, 75, today predicted he would live another 75 years. (A broadcaster would say: Seventy-five-year-old Joseph R. Jones today predicted he would live another 75 years.)

Firemen responded to an early morning blaze *that occurred* in a shed at Smith Labs.
Firemen responded to an early morning blaze in a shed at Smith Labs.

Miss Linn was tan yesterday from the sun of Miami Beach, where she lives with her sister and *where she* swims often.
Miss Linn was tan yesterday from the sun of Miami Beach where she lives with her sister and swims often.

President Monahan, *who was* rebuffed by the House and Senate on his proposal to set fuel prices, asked key congressmen today to act as his partners in setting energy policy.
President Monahan, rebuffed by the House and Senate on his proposal to set fuel prices, asked key congressmen today to act as his partners in setting energy policy.

Any house *that is built* on a hill will provide a good view for its residents.
Any house on a hill will provide a good view for its residents.

This is a professional course *that is* aimed at improving the skills and knowledge *that are* needed for effective news work.
This is a professional course aimed at improving the skills and knowledge needed for effective news work.

You can't always drop *that*. It sometimes serves as a buffer without which a collision of words would result, giving a different meaning.

He said that last night we would study.

He said last night we would study.

The difference is between when the studying will be done (first example) and when the speaker made the statement (second example). The second example does not say when the studying will be done. Similarly, the omission of *that* in the following changes the meaning:

Paley said that at a recent general conference of UNESCO a press-restricting proposal was discussed.

Paley said at a recent general conference of UNESCO a press-restricting proposal was discussed.

The verb *feel* creates unintended meanings when *that* is dropped.

He *felt the girl* was a good student.

He felt *that* the girl was a good student.

You might argue that the reader would understand in the first example nobody is touching the girl. That is true; but it might require a second reading, which is not good, or it might raise a smile in an otherwise serious story or broadcast. A second reading might also be needed in this:

Joseph Thompson and other conservatives *warn Gov. Kellner's plan* for instant voter registration could spell doom for conservatives.

So that the plan isn't being warned, *that* is needed.

Joseph Thompson and other conservatives warn that Gov. Kellner's plan for instant voter registration could spell doom for conservatives.

Here is another sentence with extraneous pronouns, a verb and even two nouns:

Harris said he has frequently visited the area to fish with Ann's husband, Jim, *who is* a New Orleans attorney *who* Harris met while both *men* were working in the state attorney general's *office*.

To make the sentence tighter, drop the italicized words and restructure the closing prepositional phrase.

Harris said he has frequently visited the area to fish with Ann's husband, Jim, a New Orleans attorney Harris met while both were working for the state attorney general.

Still another wordy sentence:

The Department of Health, Education and Welfare, *which is* the largest department in the federal government *structure,* will be reduced *in size.*

Every italicized word and phrase can be dropped. A good copy editor will cut them—given the time. But the place to write tight is not on the copy desk; it is at your typewriter or video display terminal as you write or edit. The important thing is not to tax the copy editor's patience or waste the reader's time with extra words. Both will tire of you quickly, and while the copy editor may go on crossing out extra words, the reader is likely to look for something else to do.

TO THE POINT

If you write to the point you won't use as many words. A student turned in this sentence:

> The transcripts for the trial, which lasted 9½ months, contained 28,314 pages.

She got this back:

> The transcripts for the 9½-month trial contained 28,314 pages.

Likewise, this sentence

> At the time the strike went into effect, there was no agreement in sight.

became

> When the strike started, no agreement was in sight.

When a student wrote

> Cholesterol, she said, is not the major cause of heart attacks. Stress, sugar, coffee, cigarettes and alcohol are the main causes, she said.

a professor rewrote

> Stress, sugar, coffee, cigarettes and alcohol—not cholesterol— are the main causes of heart attacks, she said.

Another good effort reduced the total number of words in two sentences by 50 percent and one sentence.

> Up until that time, it was the longest murder trial ever recorded in American history, lasting a total of 9-1/2 months. Also, the Manson case was at the time the most expensive criminal trial.

> Until then, the Manson murder trial was the longest (9-1/2 months) and most expensive in American history.

Subordinate information that otherwise is given—without good reason—a sentence all to itself. Here is an example:

> Police reported a hot plate was stolen from G-4, Thomson Hall, March 17. *The hot plate* was valued at $64.

Get to the point.

> Police reported a hot plate *valued at* $64 was stolen from G-4, Thomson Hall, March 17.

Also:

> Another weakness Mrs. Williams discussed is the recently passed state mandate requiring a program for gifted students.

This isn't bogged down:

> Another weakness Mrs. Williams discussed is a state-required program for gifted students.

There's too much here

> In describing her reasons for running, Mrs. Williams cited her own experience with school board matters gained by attending board meetings.

but not here

> In explaining why she's running, Mrs. Williams cited the experience she gained attending board meetings.

The shortened version does not say what the experience is. But the sentence comes from an interview with a candidate for school board. It is doubtful such a candidate would discuss her experience in making apple pie or that apple pie would be the topic of such an interview.

One last example:

> The district will also hire para-professionals to aid teachers. Para-professionals are paid $2,800 yearly. Superintendent of Schools Thomas F. Williams said these steps will help eliminate classroom crowding and will cost approximately $60,000.

The author of that sentence received this:

> To help eliminate classroom crowding, the district will also hire teachers' aides at $2,800 each, Superintendent of Schools Thomas F. Williams said. The total cost will be approximately $60,000.

DROPPING THE INFINITIVE

Occasionally someone will use an infinitive where one isn't needed.

Won't unionization help *to reduce* the bureaucracy and red tape?
There's nothing wrong with:

Won't unionization *help reduce* the bureaucracy and red tape?

EXERCISES

A.   *Edit the following story.*

Cadbury University submitted a proposal to Governor Hilton S. Knapp in Capitol City today that would eliminate Cadbury's special tuition benefit to faculty and staff by the year 1984.

Cadbury employees are the recipients of a 75 percent discount in tuition payments for any course they or their dependents study in. Any employee's dependent who qualifies for the 75 percent tuition discount would pay $87.50 under the present tuition of $350 a term for a full-time student.

The discount of 75 percent has been a political thorn in Cadbury's side since the legislature earlier this year proposed the abolition of the benefit immediately.

Cadbury contends that the abolition of the benefit immediately would be unfair to employees who were hired with the full and complete understanding that they would receive a reduction of 75 percent for all dependents, including children.

Cadbury's proposal, as submitted to Gov. Knapp, would be equitable to all of its present employees, a Cadbury spokesman said, because it would ensure that those recently hired would still have an opportunity to avail themselves of the tuition reduction according to their contracts while those hired in 1984 would be hired with the full understanding that their dependents would have to pay full tuition.

The Cadbury spokesman warned that there would be problems with ending the benefit. He said that in the future persons hired to work for Cadbury University would have to be offered a higher-than-average salary to compensate for the lack of the tuition benefit. Without an increase in salary, the spokesman said, Cadbury salaries would not be competitive with other universities and colleges that offer tuition reduction benefits to their employees.

The spokesman said that the proposal to the governor to end the special tuition benefit by 1984 is a compromise Cadbury had to put into effect because the legislature wants to make sure the benefit ends next year.

ANSWER

Here is the author's version.

Cadbury University ~~submitted a proposal to Governor Hilton S. Knapp in Capitol City today that would eliminate Cadbury's special~~ *today proposed ending its* tuition benefit ~~to fac-ulty and staff~~ *for employees* by ~~the year~~ 1984. *The proposal was submitted to Gov. Hilton S. Knapp.*

Cadbury employees ~~are the recipients of~~ *receive* a 75 percent *tuition* discount ~~in tuition payments~~ for ~~any course they or~~ their dependents ~~study in~~ *themselves and.* Any ~~employee's~~ *qualified* dependent ~~who qualifies for the 75 percent tuition discount~~ would pay $87.50 under the present tuition of $350 a term ~~for a full-time student.~~

The discount ~~of 75 percent~~ has been a political thorn in Cadbury's side since the legislature earlier this year proposed ~~the abolition of~~ *ending* the benefit ~~immedi-ately.~~ *now.*

Cadbury contends that ~~the abolition of~~ *ending* the benefit ~~immediately~~ *now* would be unfair to employees ~~who were~~ hired ~~with the full and complete understanding~~ *under that plan.*

~~that they would receive a reduction of 75 percent for all dependents, including children.~~

Cadbury's proposal, ~~as submitted to Gov. Knapp,~~ would be equitable to all ~~of its~~ present employees, a Cadbury spokesman said, because it would ensure ~~that~~ those recently hired, *of* ~~would still have~~ an opportunity to *use the benefit* ~~avail themselves of the tuition reduction according to their contracts~~ (while those hired in 1984 would *not* ~~be hired with the full understanding that their dependents would have to pay full tuition.~~

The Cadbury spokesman, ~~warned that there would be problems with ending the benefit. He~~ said that ~~in the future~~ persons hired, *in 1984* ~~to work for Cadbury University~~ would have to be offered a higher-than-average salary to compensate for the lack of the ~~tuition~~ benefit. Without an increase, ~~in salary,~~ the spokesman said, Cadbury salaries would not be competitive with other universities and colleges that offer tuition ~~reduction~~ benefits, ~~to their employees.~~

The spokesman said ~~that~~ the proposal, ~~to the governor to end the special tuition benefit by 1984~~ (is a compromise Cadbury had to *develop* ~~put into effect~~ because the legislature wants to *end* ~~make sure~~ the benefit, *now* ~~ends next year.~~

B. *Turn the following into tightly written sentences.*

1. Police said that the death appears to have been from natural causes.

2. Gov. Charles said that the thing that concerns him is the rate of inflation.

3. There was discussion at earlier board meetings about the possibility of the school district borrowing up to $240,000 at low-interest rates.

4. The suspect is alleged to have pointed his weapon at the victim several times.

5. The board voted to meet with the doctor to discuss the possibility of the physician visiting the prison three times weekly for the purpose of giving physicals to new inmates.

6. The fire chief said the fire started in the engine and spread throughout the car, destroying it.

7. The accident victim was taken to the Cadbury Hospital in the Goodwill Ambulance and admitted.

8. He managed to race out the door of a Washington grocery store where he had been stopped, beginning a journey that took him away from the United States and to Buenos Aires.

9. Elderly citizens highly in need of low-income housing earn less than $5,000 a year, the survey found.

10. Williams grabbed hold of a 2–0 pitch and lofted it in a high arc over the right-center field wall for his second home run.

11. The course was divided into a number of phases.

12. Police said the passenger received an injury of the foot that was not serious.

13. The honor includes a cash award of $100.

14. The corporation made significant contributions to the alumni fund.

15. For the session last night, Thomas F. Williams, vice president of council, presided and will continue for the remainder of the year.

To fill the post of vice president, John Klein was appointed to the position.

16. Sauers was taken to Cadbury Hospital by the American Hose Co. Ambulance where he was treated for minor injuries and released.

17. State police said the arrest was the result of a lengthy investigation.

18. With the passage of time, it became more complicated to resume the project.

19. He is a friend of the Smiths, who are frequent visitors here.

20. When they hold a meeting, they discuss everything.

21. At a meeting of City Council last night, 15 citizens voiced objections to council's plans for a new street in University Heights.

22. When asked if Manson ever would be released, Bugliosi said that distinct possibility exists.

23. The dog catcher said that the matter would be handled in a routine fashion.

24. The actual facts of the case will never be known to the general public.

ANSWERS

1. Police said the death appears to have been from natural causes.
2. Gov. Charles said the rate of inflation concerns him.
3. At earlier meetings the board discussed borrowing up to $240,000 at low interest.
4. The suspect allegedly pointed his weapon at the victim several times.
5. The board voted to meet with the doctor to discuss the possibility of the physician visiting the prison three times weekly to give physicals to new inmates.
6. The fire chief said the fire, which started in the engine, destroyed the car.
7. The accident victim was admitted to Cadbury Hospital.
8. He managed to race out the door of a Washington grocery store where he had been stopped, beginning a journey that took him to Buenos Aires.

9. Elderly citizens in need of low-income housing earn less than $5,000 a year, the survey found.
10. Williams grabbed hold of a 2–0 pitch and lofted it over the right-center field wall for his second home run.
11. The course was divided into phases.
12. Police said the passenger received a minor foot injury.
13. The honor includes a $100 award.
14. The corporation contributed significantly to the alumni fund.
15. Thomas Williams, vice president of council, presided last night and will continue to preside for the remainder of the year. John Klein was appointed vice president.
16. Sauers was treated for minor injuries at Cadbury Hospital.
17. State police said the arrest resulted from a lengthy investigation.
18. Eventually it became more complicated to resume the project.
19. He is a friend of the Smiths, who frequently visit here.
20. When they meet, they discuss everything.
21. Fifteen citizens last night objected to City Council's plans for a new street in University Heights.
22. Bugliosi said the possibility of Manson's eventual release exists.
23. The dog catcher said the matter would be handled routinely.
24. The facts of the case will never be known to the public.

DETAIL AND COLOR

News stories are often dull, loosely connected paragraphs with no life or intimacy. They lack detail and color, those amplifications and descriptions that enliven a subject. The absence of these elements usually results from laziness by a reporter unwilling to observe closely or report fully. Yet the wire services and editors want color. A wire service advisory like this is typical: "After the ceremony, there will be a fresh spot lead, including major portions of the speech, the oath-taking, *color* and other activity [italics added]. And consider what Burt Blazar, the editor of the Elmira (N.Y.) *Star-Gazette,* wrote in *The Gannetteer:* "Then sprinkle in the color—a description of the scene, the quotes. Whatever. The frosting on the cake . . ."

Detail and color correctly spotted throughout a story transport the reader from the living room to city council's chambers or the White House. A journalism intern (Peter K. Jackson, then at the *Centre Daily Times,* State College, Pa.) spiced his story of a bicentennial wagon train by writing: "They flaunted fat stacks of thin programs that went for $2 apiece." An unimaginative writer would have written: "They were selling programs for $2 apiece."

Imaginative use of the language turns average writing into good writing. Gasoline fuels cars, but Farouk El-Baz, writing in *Smithsonian* magazine, knows the verb *fuel* is not limited to automobiles. He wrote:

> Areas between pebbles serve as storage areas for sand during seasons of calm winds. When the winds increase, sand is lifted *to fuel* sandstorms [italics added].

I had never thought of sand like that before.

Do not overlook the possibility of using simile, as in this sentence from a *New York Times* story by Fred Ferretti:

> With four sleek Navy yawls leading the way and dozens of tiny sailboats *darting like gnats amid a caravan of lumbering brigantines and antique sloops,* a 100-craft Parade of Sail rounded the tip of Manhattan Island yesterday [italics added].

The imaginative journalist takes us to the scene by using relevant direct quotations, an indication of real people. The journalist makes sure those direct quotations have names with them, not vague attribution tags like *a member of the audience* or *someone in the crowd.* Search out the nameless and get their names.

In addition to quoting people, you can describe them. We once had in Pennsylvania a political candidate who walked across the state dressed in clothing associated with the outdoors. A student reporter who covered the candidate's appearance at her university saw fit to describe the candidate. "Dressed in white jeans, a plaid hunter's jacket and hiking boots" was the way she began a sentence that went on to quote the candidate on his travels across the state. If the student had followed the description with the candidate's comments on foreign policy, it wouldn't have been appropriately used. Detail and color can't just be plopped into a story; they must fit logically. That is not the case in this sentence:

> Baugh, *who recently left Cadbury Hospital after undergoing treatment for a back ailment,* declined to elaborate on his dismissal last month of Andrew E. Nichols, who had been the department's second-ranking official.

Baugh's medical problems have nothing to do with the dismissal. Similarly, the following provides incongruous detail:

"It was terminal. Well, that's what they told my wife," said MacArthur, *who has a son and a daughter by a previous marriage* [italics added].

A student not as wise as the one who reported on the candidate dressed for the outdoors coupled unrelated information to produce this incongruous sentence:

The chairman of the Senate Environmental Resources Committee from 1971 to 1973, Heller said it is "necessary for the federal government to take an active, aggressive role to stimulate the economy in these times."

The same assignment brought out the best in another student.

Shaw, a teacher in Cadbury schools for 17 years, said public school funding needs revising.

The student who wrote the preceding could have mentioned the teacher's experience anywhere in the story; wisely, though, the student waited until the sentence where the experience gave context to a statement by the teacher.

A good journalist will not overlook the mannerisms of people. Nan Robertson of *The New York Times* was alert when she wrote a story on Taylor Caldwell, an author who is deaf.

In a long and rambling monologue, *while a grandfather clock she could not hear chimed the quarter-hours,* she spoke of a life whose early years were fraught with bitterness and frustration [italics added].

Of course, the italicized portion of that sentence could have been deleted without damaging the story. But it's not a question of what damage a removed phrase might do; it is a question of what a little detail will *add* to a story. It's the difference between programs being sold for $2 and "fat stacks of thin programs" being sold for $2. One student accurately began a story:

As a small group of human rights advocates shifted restlessly in the audience . . .

Some editors might delete such an opening because it is newsless, but the story would be poorer for it. Likewise, a story on Gerald Ford shortly after he lost the 1976 presidential race to Jimmy Carter would not have been as revealing if it had not contained this sentence:

And while at one point Mr. Ford appeared tempted to cross the street to shake hands with people in the crowd, he then seemed to shrug off the idea and instead smiled, waved and got into his limousine.

For one moment the candidate in Ford took hold, and then he overcame it. Lena Williams of *The New York Times* noticed it and, more importantly, reported it.

The editors at the *Times* obviously look for such reporting because their paper contains a lot of this kind of detail. Other editors might have deleted the details in the example below because they aren't relevant to the story, which is about a press conference with a 1976 presidential contender.

Mr. Carter's words were occasionally drowned out by the noise of a plane that was spraying nearby cotton and peanut fields. At one point, his daughter's Siamese cat strolled in front of him as he spoke. . . .

Later, during his stroll through Plains, Mr. Carter stopped in every store along Main Street, buying his 9-year-old daughter Amy a comic book and an ice cream cone, and eating an ice cream sandwich himself as he strolled.

Note the understatement. The journalist who wrote those paragraphs did not belabor his description. He could have written:

A loud, noisy plane was spraying nearby cotton and peanut fields, making it sometimes difficult to hear Mr. Carter.

Detail and color can establish a scene, especially when it is done in as few words as possible.

With squash racket in hand, John C. Pittenger said good-bye to the University's Board of Trustees yesterday.

The state secretary of education, a squash enthusiast, was presented the racket by the board as a token of its appreciation for his work on the board.

Detail also serves as explanation. It is the difference between saying a house damaged by a tornado is a mess and saying that and giving a description of the damage. A slow day in court provided this example:

The day moved slowly. Jurors stretched, stared at the ceiling, rubbed their eyes or scratched the backs of their necks as testimony was punctuated by objections and requests for the lawyers in the case to "approach the bench."

An explanation cannot be put off for later telling. It means nothing if it is not given where it will do the best job, as in the preceding example, where the second sentence is an explanation of the first.

What you have to remember is that your job is reporting, not interpreting, an event. Just clearly describe the event and the reader will take care of the interpretation. That happens with the following excerpt from a story by Paul Carpenter of the Associated Press:

> Meanwhile, the chair waits in undignified squalor at Rockview.
>
> It must be pulled out of an unlit cell to be seen. It is still intact, with heavy leather straps for the legs, arms, chest, waist and lap.
>
> The stained oak instrument packs a 2,200-volt, 11-to-15-ampere whallop. A tenth of an ampere could be fatal.
>
> The current runs from an electrode attached to an individual's shaved head to one attached to his left ankle. The current is left on about two minutes.
>
> The back and leg brackets are adjustable, but the chair was not built for comfort. As you sit in it, you have the feeling you could fall forward if not held in place. There is a patch of dark residue on the center of the seat.

A virtually emotionless description that made me shudder when I read it. Such is the stuff of detail and color.

TWO

Sentences and Paragraphs

THE SENTENCE

The thread of every story is the sentence. There is no room for a false stitch in sewing a story together; your sentences must proceed logically one after the other until your story is finished.

It is far easier to tell you what sentences do than to tell you what they are. In *Understanding English,* Paul Roberts says that definitions of sentences number more than 200, that the short definitions "are either untrue or impractical or both," and that "English sentences are too complicated to be encapsulated in a definition." Roberts titled the chapter he devotes to sentences "Something That Ends with a Period."

TRADITIONAL AND
NON-TRADITIONAL SENTENCE PATTERNS

Traditional sentences contain at the minimum a subject and verb, often thought of as the actor and the action. *She smiles* is an example. Sentences also have a subject-verb-object (or object of action) pattern. That is the way people talk, which makes it the ideal pattern for broadcast and print journalists.

       s   v   o
The boy struck the ball.

Another pattern is subject-linking verb-complement, in which the complement modifies or describes the subject.

     s lv   c
She is smart.

A sentence is a logical pattern reflecting the order in which people usually think. People do not separate one idea into sentences. A person who watched a Little League baseball game would not report one of the player's success at bat by saying:

The boy.
Struck.
The ball.

The reporter would instead put together all the related elements of the player's success into one sentence.

The boy struck the ball.

If the reporter wanted to explain more, perhaps what happened to the ball, he or she would tell that in the same sentence, because what happened to the ball is the result of the boy striking it.

The boy struck the ball, which bounced over the pitcher's head and into centerfield.

The reporter would not say the preceding in two sentences. He or she would not say:

The boy struck the ball.
Which bounced over the pitcher's head and into centerfield.

That is not logical. Yet that is the way some students write. They fail to perceive the logic of an action or thought. They disjoint logic by separating major and subordinate ideas into separate sentences. Often one of the elements cannot stand by itself because it is a *dependent clause*—a clause that depends on a main clause to give it meaning. The disjointure is a *sentence fragment* (italicized in the preceding). Editors and professors scorn sentence fragments; good writers avoid them.
    Another sentence fragment typical of students:

> Because the person with a college education will understand dimensions others may miss.

Because is a conjunction that shows a relationship, and that relationship is best shown within one sentence. What follows *because* in the preceding relates to a prior thought. The thoughts should be joined.

> A college education gives a person a fuller life because the person with a college education will understand dimensions others may miss.

Bad fragments typically have nothing to stand on, nothing to relate to. A sentence fragment is akin to taking a newborn child away from its parent and expecting the child to survive on its own. Such an expectation is illogical; survival is impossible. Do not disjoint the logic of a sentence. Do not use sentence fragments.

Despite what you have just read, you may have seen sentence fragments in newspapers or heard them on news broadcasts. Your eyes and ears are fine. You may have read or heard sentence fragments in a question-and-answer structure in which the answer was not the traditional sentence structure of subject-verb-object. For example:

> So which gift package did the housewife who has everything pick? *The one with the appliances she doesn't need.*

There are other examples, most of which come from the typewriters of movie reviewers, columnists, magazine and feature writers, not from the typewriters and video display terminals of everyday journalists who write hard news. Regardless, the exceptions are worth mentioning so when the time to use them arrives, you will know you aren't violating any strict law of grammar. As you study these, note there is some logic to them, that they are not like the disjointed fragments scorned earlier. The first example comes from a movie review by Jay Cocks in *Time* magazine. (All italics are added.)

> He proved his mettle and finally became one of the tribe by enduring all manner of tests and initiation rites, including a ceremony in which he was strung up by his pectorals. *Manhood through pain and all that.* The Sioux apparently set great store by such things.

Here is another, this one from a sports column by Bill Lyon of *The Philadelphia Inquirer:*

But you check him out and he doesn't breathe through gills.
His feet aren't webbed. *No dorsal fin between his shoulder blades.*

Despite the absence of a subject and verb (in that case, *There is*) the
reader carries the thought to completion without any labor. The reader
does the same thing in the following, written by Peter Gwynne in
Smithsonian magazine:

> *Plutonium. The stuff of bombs. Intensely radioactive for hundreds of
> thousands of years.* For many Americans, the very word invokes a
> dread akin to botulism or anthrax or worse.

That is the opening paragraph of Gwynne's article. Notice how he
builds up the length of each sentence—one word, four words, eight
words—before he uses traditional sentence structure. Good writers recognize that people do not always act in full sentences and the writers use
fragments to show this. From *The New York Times:*

> *Smiles. Proclamations. An exchange of gifts. Thank yous. More small
> talk. Warm goodbyes.* The whole thing was over in 10 minutes,
> and then Mr. Plimpton climbed into his limousine and headed
> uptown.

A very short fragment at the end of a sentence or paragraph serves well
for emphasis or humor, as these three examples show:

> Some of the Volunteers will sit in the stands come autumn. *In-
> voluntarily.* (Ron Bracken, *Centre Daily Times,* State College,
> Pa.)

> But this year, the westerlies veered sharply southward early in
> the autumn and have remained on the same course pretty much
> ever since. *Hence, the freeze.* (*Newsweek*)

> Back in December Penn State was a floundering wrestling team,
> one that was given little chance of beating the likes of Navy and
> Lehigh. *Especially Lehigh.* (Dennis Gildea, *Pennsylvania Mirror,*
> State College, Pa.)

Using sentence fragments as special effects can be overdone to the point
of creating a defect. The fragment is effective because it is used spar-
ingly. Back to basics.

From the traditional patterns explained at the start of this chapter
flow an infinite number of variations called simple, compound, complex,
and compound-complex, important more in function than label.

EXERCISES

A. *Underline the subject(s) and verb(s) in these sentences.*

1. The article explores an area of journalism and advertising not previously explored.

2. Rye and corn replaced sugar and peaches as the staples on the family's table.

3. Walking slowly on a warm day keeps him cool.

4. The kidnappers called Williams between six and nine times Monday.

5. Cadbury residents last night asked City Council to hold the line on taxes.

6. Tomorrow will be a partly cloudy to mostly cloudy day.

7. So tonight the network tries again with five comedies—four of them new.

8. Ms. Tyler's current series is in its ninth and final season.

9. About one-fourth of all the turtles in the world live in North America.

10. Scientists emphasize research.

11. Exhibits of historic and contemporary photographs and a lecture series will highlight History of Photography Week.

12. The destroyer pulled out of the harbor and headed toward Africa.

ANSWERS

1.	article, explores	7.	network, tries
2.	rye, corn; replaced	8.	series, is
3.	walking, keeps	9.	one-fourth, live
4.	kidnappers, called	10.	scientists, emphasize
5.	residents, asked	11.	exhibits, series; will highlight
6.	tomorrow, will be	12.	destroyer; pulled, headed

B. *Which of the following are sentences of traditional structure and which are fragments?*

1. Not a show of defiance, but more a release of emotions during a rare win.
2. Flowers for display in competition at the fair.
3. Williams prepared to resume the radio commentary he had interrupted to seek the nomination.
4. Because both sides where required to secure counsel from someone other than their solicitor.
5. Where we find a clear spot is where we'll camp for the night.
6. The indictments are expected to come under a broad charge of conspiracy to defraud consumers.
7. A place where local veterinarians can refer animals with special problems.
8. The case, in part, originated with the construction of Cadbury Junior High School.
9. Which lacks traditional room construction.
10. Ran 15 miles.
11. Five years ago Dallas Barnes and Robert Delinger were on opposite sides of the law.
12. The hunter and the hunted.
13. The man who jumps in first.
14. Anyone who knows how to fix cars is welcome to work on mine.

ANSWERS

1. fragment	8. sentence
2. fragment	9. fragment
3. sentence	10. fragment
4. fragment	11. sentence
5. sentence	12. fragment
6. sentence	13. fragment
7. fragment	14. sentence

THE SIMPLE SENTENCE

The best of the lot is the simple sentence. It sticks to one idea or action.

The boy struck the ball.

That doesn't mean, though, that a simple sentence is necessarily short. Using connectives and a variety of modifiers, a simple sentence can become quite long. First, a connective, which creates a compound object:

>   The boy struck the ball *and* the rock.

And now a prepositional phrase:

>   The boy struck the ball and the rock *at the same time.*

And another:

>   The boy *in the blue trousers* struck the ball and the rock at the same time.

And with some modification in front of the subject (in this case, an adjective):

>   The *tall* boy in the blue trousers struck the ball and the rock at the same time.

The sentence can be made longer still with a *compound predicate* (the verb and all its complements and modifiers), a pattern not to be confused with a compound sentence.

>   The tall boy in the blue trousers *struck the ball and the rock at the same time and fell.*

In an early version of this sentence the connective *and* was used to create a compound object, *the ball and the rock.* Now *and* has also been used to create a compound predicate. A five-word sentence becomes one of 19 words. But despite its length, it's still a simple sentence. Here is a simple sentence of 30 words, its length reached through the addition of two verb (in this case, *gerund*) clauses.

>   The clean air bill also covers other air pollution sources, generally giving industrial areas more time to meet standards while offering added protection for areas that now have clean air.

Here's the breakdown:

BASIC SENTENCE	The clean air bill also covers other air pollution sources,
GERUND CLAUSE	generally giving industrial areas more time to meet standards
CONNECTIVE	while
SECOND GERUND CLAUSE	offering added protection for areas that now have clean air.

The preceding is atypical of broadcast journalism because of its length and complexity. A broadcast journalist would convert to two sentences.

> The clean air bill also covers other air pollution sources. Generally, the bill gives industrial areas more time to meet standards while it offers added protection for areas that now have clean air.

Such an approach is easier on the ear; the listener can grasp the information more readily.

THE COMPOUND SENTENCE

The compound sentence relates at least two ideas or actions of equal importance. A compound sentence consists of two closely related sentences that could also be written as separate sentences—that is, both ending in a period. Compound sentences are joined with connectives (often called *coordinating conjunctions*) such as *and, but, or, nor, while, yet.* Another connective is the semicolon (;).

> It wasn't the subfreezing playing conditions or a matter of being outplayed; the game was decided by puck luck.

The use of compound sentences avoids tedious writing. When correctly structured, they take the place of two simple *but related* sentences.

> The president is waiting for the bill but the House has not yet acted on it.

With some revision that sentence could have been written as two sentences.

> The president is waiting for the bill. The House has not yet acted on it.

But to write that as two simple sentences would make for tedious writing.

As before, the length of a sentence has nothing to do with what type of sentence it is. Compound sentences can be short

> John hit the ball and Marty caught it.

> He likes the swim in the ocean; she likes to swim in a pool.

or long

> The substance of the Panamanian talks was not made public, but Panama's minister for canals took part in them.

By mid-October Williams had moved up to 42 percent, the un-decideds had dropped to 10, but Monahan held firm at 48 percent.

While ambitious men contend for high office, while the British pound falls to another new low and while the people on the Jersey shore dream of casinos, there lives quietly in our midst in Levittown the yo-yo champion of the world.

even too long

Hundreds of off-duty policemen, protesting work schedules and delayed pay raises, picketed Monday at nearly all of Cadbury's 52 station houses while representatives of the Fraternal Order of Police sought, once again without success, to persuade the mayor to agree to their demands for better working conditions.

The best thing to do with an awkwardly long compound sentence is separate it into shorter sentences.

Hundreds of off-duty policemen, protesting work schedules and delayed pay raises, picketed Monday at nearly all of Cadbury's 52 station houses. At the same time, representatives of the Fraternal Order of Police sought, once again without success, to persuade the mayor to agree to their demands for better working conditions.

Sentences with compound subjects or compound predicates may look like compound sentences, but they are not. Here is an example of each:

COMPOUND SUBJECT   *John and Marty* ran to the cabin.
COMPOUND PREDICATE   The revolution *was called "Helter Skelter" and was considered started with the first slayings.*

THE COMPLEX SENTENCE

Not every idea or action in a sentence is as important as another. A secondary idea or action is subordinate to the main idea or action. The important idea or action appears in the independent or main clause, independent because it needs no help in conveying an idea. For example:

The tall boy in the blue trousers struck the ball and the rock at the same time.

That is an independent clause. By itself it has meaning. But the idea or action in a subordinate clause does not have meaning by itself; subordinate clauses depend on main clauses for their meaning. Standing alone they are the much scorned fragments mentioned earlier.

To subordinate a clause or clauses, use *that, which, who, because, after, where, although, though, when, if.* (Remember, though, that through elliptic writing the pronouns that lead off subordinate clauses are sometimes discarded. The sentence, however, is still labeled complex.) Here is a complex sentence:

> *When the first pitch was thrown,* the tall boy in the blue trousers struck the ball and the rock at the same time.

The subordinate clause is italicized. It makes no sense by itself. Here are other examples of complex sentences:

> John Smith, *who is 61,* makes a good living predicting the outcome of political campaigns.

> *If his well connected Republican staff members were called upon to lead the investigation,* they would undoubtedly end up looking into activities of fellow Republicans and other members of the establishment.

One of the most frequent complex sentences in journalism begins with an attribution tag.

> He said *Williams could do the job.*

Such a structure defies the conventional definition that a subordinate clause cannot stand by itself because it has no meaning. In journalism, however, the distinction is that the unattributed sentence is the opinion of the writer and writer's opinions are not allowed in news stories. The preceding complex sentence could also be written:

> Williams could do the job, he said.

The failure to use complex sentences is the failure to perceive complex relationships.

> Williams criticized Monahan for not mentioning the O'Hara-Wentzel bill. The bill would provide jobs for all Americans who want them. Monahan once endorsed the bill.

Three simple sentences do not convey the essence of Williams' criticism. The first simple sentence says nothing; left out is the crucial explanation of what the bill would do and the significance of Monahan's silence. The following two simple sentences suggest that Williams' criticism, what the bill would do and Monahan's prior endorsement are separate ideas. They are not. There is a very important relationship that must be stated—and a complex sentence is the proper vehicle.

Williams criticized Monahan for not mentioning the O'Hara-Wentzel bill, which would provide jobs for all Americans who want them and which Monahan once endorsed.

One of the pitfalls of subordination is subordinating the wrong thing or something incongruous with the main clause.

The wrong thing:

An 81-year-old Minnesota man was hunting *when he died of a heart attack early today.*

The key point of that sentence is italicized. The news has been subordinated to a less important piece of information. There should be no subordination; the sentence should read:

An 81-year-old Minnesota man died of a heart attack while hunting early today.

Now the key point is in place; it is no longer hidden.

Incongruous:

The judge rejected the Blacks' request for $2,500 in damages *although he estimated that a horse drops an average of 24 pounds of manure daily.*

The italicized portion of that sentence has nothing to do with the sentence's main point—the judge rejecting the claim. If you remember a sentence is a logical pattern, that everything in it is logically related, you won't subordinate incorrectly.

Complex sentences do not have to be long.

When I am hungry, I eat.

If I were you, I'd leave.

In fact, complex sentences can be made very long by compounding the subordinate clauses, which was done in the Williams-Monahan sentence. Here are the opening two sentences from a column by David S. Broder of *The Washington Post.* In addition to noting the differences in length, also note the compound predicate and the effect Broder achieves by following a very long sentence with a very short one.

If you are James Reston of the New York Times and you're moved to celebrate Queen Elizabeth II's silver jubilee, you hop the Concorde to London in the morning, chat with the Chancellor of the Exchequer and the Leader of the Opposition in the afternoon and file an utterly definitive column on the state of

her Majesty's realm in plenty of time for a nap before theatre
and a late supper with the Times' London bureau chief, Johnny
Apple, at his mansion in Belgravia. If you are not James Reston, however, you have a problem.

It is important that you remember that a subordinate clause (or
clauses) needs a main clause in order to function clearly. The following
sentence, based on one from a newspaper, is an example of a missing
main clause:

> Thomas F. Williams, the son of David and Mary Williams, 100
> Schuylkill Ave., Cadbury, who graduated from Louisiana State
> in May with a BS degree in agronomy, who had been serving as
> president of Alpha Gamma Rho fraternity.

Without a main clause, there's nothing to make that sentence go.

EXERCISES

*Decide which are main clauses and which are subordinate clauses. Un-
derline the main clauses.*

1. Monahan, who says he would have had more trouble in the West
    if Williams had chosen O'Hara instead of Sen. Shaw as his run-
    ning mate, scheduled a speech today in San Francisco.

2. Despite crowds that established records for high attendance with
    each passing year, the county event is quieter and more serious.

3. Several universities, because they annually have good football or
    basketball teams, lead the nation in the number of people apply-
    ing for admission.

4. Harrison had stated earlier that he wished to serve only one term if
    elected.

5. And now the middle-aged high-school dropout, a maintenance
    employee at a small college, was reminiscing about the golden
    moment two months earlier when he surprised everyone by passing
    the entrance examinations at the school where he worked.

6. If for any reason the customers wish to discontinue direct deposit or wish to redirect their check to a different financial institution, it is a simple procedure to make that change.

7. Dr. Stanton urged the graduates to be alert in defending their liberties, which he said "are as precious as life itself."

8. The United States announced today it will exchange diplomats with Cuba for the first time in 16 years.

9. Although formal relations may be a long way off, the diplomats will be in charge of a full range of activities between the two countries.

10. When demand for electricity is high during the 24-hour period, the water will be discharged from the reservoir into Cadbury Dam and will turn turbines to generate power.

ANSWERS

The main clauses are italicized; the subordinate clauses are not.

1. *Monahan,* who says he would have had more trouble in the West if Williams had chosen O'Hara instead of Sen. Shaw as his running mate, *scheduled a speech today in San Francisco.*
2. Despite crowds that established records for high attendance with each passing year, *the county event is quieter and more serious.*
3. *Several universities,* because they annually have good football or basketball teams, *lead the nation in the number of people applying for admission.*
4. *Harrison had stated earlier* that he wished to serve only one term if elected.
5. *And now the middle-aged high-school dropout, a maintenance employee at a small college, was reminiscing about the golden moment two months earlier* when he surprised everyone by passing the entrance examinations at the school where he worked.
6. If for any reason the customers wish to discontinue direct deposit or wish to redirect their check to a different financial institution, *it is a simple procedure to make that change.*
7. *Dr. Stanton urged the graduates to be alert in defending their liberties,* which he said "are as precious as life itself."
8. *The United States announced today* [that] it will exchange diplomats with Cuba for the first time in 16 years.

9.   Although formal relations may be a long way off, *the diplomats will be in charge of a full range of activities between the two countries.*

10. When demand for electricity is high during the 24-hour period, *the water will be discharged from the reservoir into Cadbury Dam and will turn turbines to generate power.*

POSITIONING FOR CLARITY

Subordinate clauses can appear in various parts of sentences: the middle of a main clause, before a main clause, at the end of a main clause.

The tax bill, *which is long and complex,* will be voted on to-morrow.

The president, *who is eager for a rest,* will begin his vacation next week.

You could edit both of those clauses in the interest of tight writing. Broadcast journalists especially would do that in order to keep the subject and its verb together. In broadcasting, you do not insert long or confusing phrases between subjects and their verbs.

The long, complex tax bill will be voted on tomorrow.

The president, eager for a rest, will begin his vacation next week.

The second sentence could also be written:

Eager for a rest, the president will begin his vacation next week.

Even though the modifying clauses were edited and moved from behind the word they modify to in front, they were still kept as close as possible to what they modify. But you would not shift the clause in the first sentence so the sentence would read:

The tax bill will be voted on tomorrow, which is long and complex.

The subordinate clause now modifies *tomorrow.*

There are many sentence patterns in which the modification can appear at the beginning, middle or end of a sentence and the reader will understand what it modifies. But you should avoid such a loose approach to sentence structure. The writer of the following did not:

I have never been sick a day in my life, excluding my childhood years.

What is wrong is that the qualification of the main clause is not given first as a warning or tip-off to the reader. It violates truth in writing. The example sets up the reader to believe one thing, then qualifies it. It's like this sign in a clothing store:

½ OFF
ALL LEISURE SUITS
(except some national brands)

Placing the modifying phrase first immediately gives the reader the qualifications or modifications of the main clause. There is no misleading the reader in this:

Excluding my childhood years, I have never been sick a day in my life.

Sometimes the related clause must appear first lest what it explains is not clear.

Nations have responded negatively to the president's statements on human rights because of increased nationalism.

The question is, were the statements made because of increased nationalism? No—and the proper stress makes that clear.

Because of increased nationalism, nations have responded negatively to the president's statements on human rights.

Remember, though, that because the beginning of a sentence is a good place for vital information, it ought not be wasted on trivia. Unless you are concerned with transition, don't place a time element at the start of a sentence, especially a lead such as this:

At last night's Cadbury City Council meeting, city manager Thomas F. Williams presented a draft of a construction contract.

Another element whose placement you must consider is the attribution tag. In some instances, print journalists place the attribution tag at the end of a sentence because they want to give the news first then follow it with the source of the news. They believe the news is more important or of more interest than the source.

The United States will enter into a unique trade agreement with Russia, *a State Department spokesman announced today.*

Some editors prefer the source first so the reader knows immediately who is speaking. Broadcasters demand the source first because it represents the natural speaking pattern. People, when they speak, don't put attribution tags at the end of their sentences.

> *A State Department spokesman announced today* that the United States will enter into a unique trade agreement with Russia.

No one can lay down a rule that covers every situation. Once newspaper or magazine journalists have quoted someone with full identification, they will shift later attribution tags to the middle or end of a sentence, again because of the feeling that what is being said is of more importance or interest than who said it. Suppose a story began with the source, as in the case of the trade agreement announcement. The second paragraph, a direct quotation, might be written like this:

> "The agreement will allow the two countries to exchange goods heretofore banned in both countries," Assistant Secretary of State Thomas F. Williams said.

Attribution consistently used at the beginning of a sentence can get clumsy.

> *Monahan said* that, if necessary, the government should have the right to enforce mandatory conservation methods.

Also, such a structure uses a strong position (the beginning) for the attribution tag. Bury the attribution tag and a better sentence results.

> If necessary, *Monahan said,* the government should have the right to enforce mandatory conservation methods.

Just as important as qualifying phrases are subordinate clauses that provide a context for a direct quotation. When they follow the direct quotation, they force the reader to back up to see what the direct quotation means.

> "That kind of hits us where it hurts," Councilman Thomas F. Williams said when told the cost-plus fee would be used for housing outside the city.

A better sentence would not make the reader back up; it keeps the reader moving along.

> When told the cost-plus fee would be used for housing outside the city, Councilman Thomas F. Williams said: "That kind of hits us where it hurts."

Now you have a context for the direct quotation; now it means some-thing. But the sentence's structure suffers because it violates the journal-istic practice of not beginning a sentence with a dependent clause. Broadcasters do not allow sentences written for the ear to open with dependent clauses. Newspaper editors, communicating in a different medium, prefer that sentences open with the main thought followed by any subordinate thought. The advice is good. But like any other advice or rule, you should ignore it when logic says otherwise. Many of this book's sentences begin with dependent clauses because of my feeling that giving qualification first enhances overall sentence clarity.

Here are four sentences, each one structured a different way. Which sentence is the best?

> Dr. Lewis Thomas said last night that man must consider the influence of all life on the separate parts of life *if he is to survive.*

> Dr. Lewis Thomas said last night that man—*if he is to survive*—must consider the influence of all life on the separate parts of life.

> Dr. Lewis Thomas said last night that *if man is to survive,* he must consider the influence of all life on the separate parts of life.

> *If man is to survive,* Dr. Lewis Thomas said last night, he must consider the influence of all life on the separate parts of life.

The fourth sentence functions well. The qualification or context is first, the attribution tag is buried, and the main clause follows. The commendable feature of the second sentence is that it sets off the qualifi-cation with dashes, which give emphasis. However, some might see that sentence as choppy because of the abruptness. They, no doubt, would pick the third or fourth sentence.

One stress that should come at the beginning of a sentence is the sig-nal that tells the reader that what is to follow contradicts or clashes with what he or she has just read. The transition marker *however* is sometimes placed at the end of a sentence to the detriment of meaning.

> The planning commission proposed a four-lane link between the two bypasses. Planner James Dugan said that building the link would cost an extra $20 million, *however.*

However—the tip-off that what is to follow is not in accord with what has just been said—belongs at the start of the second sentence or near the start.

The planning commission proposed a four-lane link between the two bypasses. *However,* planner James Dugan said that building the link would cost an extra $20 million.

The planning commission proposed a four-lane link between the two bypasses. Planner James Dugan said, *however,* that building the link would cost an extra $20 million.

Some writers would never put *however* at the beginning because they feel it hangs there too limply to be effective. William Zinsser suggests placing *however* as early as is reasonable (a natural break in the sentence, as in the second of the two preceding examples) so that "its abruptness then becomes a virtue." It's up to your ear or your editor.

Here, for side-by-side comparison are sentences structured differently for different stress.

The House, when it reconvenes, will pass the tax-reform bill. After that is done, the congressmen will review legislation on food stamps. Even though both proposals are good ideas, opposition exists in the two parties' caucuses. Our congressman opposes the tax-reform bill because it does not actually reform our tax laws.

When the House reconvenes, it will pass the tax-reform bill. The congressmen will review legislation on food stamps after that is done. Opposition exists in the two parties' caucuses even though both proposals are good ideas. Because the tax-reform bill does not actually reform our tax laws, our congressman opposes it.

It is not a question of which one is better. What you should observe is the difference in stress—and remember the importance of that difference when writing.

THE COMPOUND-COMPLEX SENTENCE

A compound-complex sentence contains at least two related ideas or actions and at least one subordinate idea or action.

MAIN CLAUSE	Gas would be piped ashore from the sites,
SUBORDINATE CLAUSE	which are between 47 and 92 miles off the coast,
CONNECTIVE	and
MAIN CLAUSE	pipelines would carry the gas from the coast to the country's most lucrative industrial and residential markets.

Note that the subordinate clause adds amplifying information to the first main clause. In this case, the subordinate clause could be dropped without doing harm to the main clause. However, that particular subordinate clause is an example of giving detail at the right moment. Here is one more compound-complex sentence:

> He says the election could be closer because the incumbent is closing the gap, but he says it's going to be Tommy Williams just the same.

Like any other sentence of great length or complexity, the compound-complex sentence does not function well in broadcasting.

EXERCISES

A. *Collect from newspaper stories, columns and editorials examples of simple, compound, complex and compound-complex sentences.*

B. *In the margin identify these sentences as simple, compound, complex, compound-complex.*

1. Warren, who was not present at the 25-minute hearing, was convicted May 20 by a jury of trying to impede a federal grand jury probe of an influence-peddling scheme involving the sale of admissions to state-operated medical and veterinary schools.

2. The legislature passed the law July 2 and it took effect early this month.

3. The measure, which passed in the last legislative session and must be approved again this year, would have the attorney general run for office every four years during the presidential election.

4. The Republican commissioner, whose successor will be named by county Judge F. Thomas Williams, told the two Democratic commissioners that another reassessment of property values would be a "hard apple to bite," but that the time has come to conduct the reappraisal.

5. A similar arrangement was made between the American and Egyptian governments prior to their resumption of diplomatic relations in 1974.

6. Thirty-one other states have some form of postcard registration.

7. When Dallas made retirement mandatory at 65, those already working for the Sanitation Department were exempted.

8. Monahan was in California; Williams in Colorado.

9.   One proposal that has surfaced recently is to use the water of Cadbury Dam to generate electricity.

10. Eight of the indicted guards and civilian employees were charged with other criminal acts as well, including the sale of confidential inmate records, the fencing of stolen property, the arranging of auto-insurance frauds and brutality against one inmate.

11. On her way from the airport Monday, the movie star was mobbed by an enthusiastic crush of children, and the prime minister stopped their car briefly.

12. This book is interesting, but that book is better.

13. Tractor-drawn wagons, with guides, will leave from the horticulture and agronomy farm headquarters every 45 minutes to one hour.

14. Barnhart said that the best way to remove the cocaine would be surgery because gastric juices would eventually eat through the condom.

15. The Yankees are a good baseball team, but the Cincinnati Reds are the best, which is why they won the World Series in 1976.

16. The weather shrank the number of guests at an outdoor dinner party at the governor's home from more than 400 to fewer than 30 and forced them inside.

17. The Nevada Assembly Friday defeated the Equal Rights Amendment by a vote of 24–15.

18. Though Gibson has said he has some ideas about ways to negotiate a settlement, aides say he plans mostly to listen rather than try out his own conceptions.

19. British diplomats will work out of the Swiss embassy while Russian officials will be in the Bulgarian embassy.

20. Knapp has strongly opposed the amendment, but he cannot legally veto a constitutional amendment.

21. "This was highly prejudicial to the defendant, and he is at least entitled to a new trial," Linn said.

22. In the coming week, incoming students will meet the president of the university, the dean of all the colleges and the head of every department to hear their ideas and suggestions on college life.

ANSWERS

1. complex   3. complex
2. compound   4. complex

5. simple	14. complex
6. simple	15. compound-complex
7. complex	16. simple
8. compound	17. simple
9. complex	18. complex
10. simple	19. compound
11. compound	20. compound
12. compound	21. compound-complex
13. simple	22. simple

SENTENCE VARIETY

While you construct sentences, you must give thought not only to main and subordinate clauses but also to variety. Variety in sentences—both in structure and length—makes for good writing. To write all sentences in the same structure makes for tedious writing. To write all sentences in the same structure makes for tedious reading. To vary your sentence structure and length is good.

The lack of structural variety in the last three sentences is poor—especially when you want to keep the reader reading. You already know that subordination of a minor idea is one form of sentence structuring, one way of creating variety. Inverting normal word order is another.

The most infamous inverter is *Time* magazine, whose style Theodore M. Bernstein calls "walking-on-the hands school of writing." He objects because it distorts natural emphasis and disorients the reader by its repeated use. Inverts *Time:*

> Worried one top aide when the campaign was finished: "I'm afraid some people will start wondering how straight a guy, how nice a fellow the president really is."

Actually the magazine's style has changed since Bernstein criticized it, but its poor imitators remain.

> Contained in the bag was a .32-caliber revolver.

Written in the normal pattern, the sentence is stronger because an active verb replaces a linking verb (*was*). The sentence is also tighter.

> The bag contained a .32-caliber revolver.

Here is another poor imitator, this one a headline found in a 1946 edition of a magazine.

FROM DECK TO DESK MOVES MEMBER

Decades later the problem persists:

> New is an attack, delivered with Springer staring straight into
> the camera, on James McMichael, the Conservative-Republican
> incumbent.

Then there is the *wringing of the hands* way of speaking, which should
not be imitated by print or broadcast journalists.

> Four wars our people have gone through.

Normally structured, the sentence reads and sounds better.

> Our people have gone through four wars.

A student in a beginning newswriting class produced this:

> Found 60 feet from his car in a ditch near the intersection of Rt.
> 322 and Rt. 45 was Thomas F. Williams.

Said I to the student:

> Confused is the reader when backwards run sentences.

Sometimes, though, inversion is the lesser of two sins.

> The residency of the State Ballet at the main campus during the
> summer, the Invitational Film Festival for film critics in No-
> vember, a photographic exhibit by the National Endowment for
> the Arts, and the purchase of video casette equipment for the
> Graduate Center will be funded by the money alloted for the
> support of cultural activities.

Part of the problem with the sentence is the passive voice, which is discussed later. The sentence could be rewritten in the active voice or it
could be inverted. Inverted it would read:

> To be funded by the money allocated for the support of cultural
> activities will be the residency of the State Ballet at the main
> campus during the summer, the Invitational Film Festival for
> film critics in November, a photographic exhibit by the Na-
> tional Endowment for the Arts, and the purchase of video ca-
> sette equipment for the Graduate Center.

Sometimes inversion serves as transition.

> City council postponed action on a proposal to plant trees in the
> city's parking lots. *Also postponed was* action on a plan to install
> street lights in Celtic Circle.

The italicized portion of that sentence gets the reader from one unrelated topic to another by linking them through the postponed action. Too much of that, though, spoils a story.

Consider also that you can sometimes invert sentences to change the stress. This is not a change in word order; functionally, the order is the same—noun-modifier-verb-modifier-object—or whatever the case is. In leading into the discussion on *Time* style, I wrote:

> Inverting normal word order is another {way}.

But I could have written:

> Another way is inverting normal word order.

Short sentences, better than long ones, lend themselves to such changes. The reader or listener won't lose the thought or miss the stress in a seven-word sentence. In a longer sentence let clarity dictate.

Another device for achieving variety is to change a negatively phrased sentence into a positively phrased one. But that has its pitfalls, too, as these examples show:

> For such reasons, a lot of the country was *not un*happy to watch New York City in the past tottering like a Charlie Chaplin drunk on the brink of bankruptcy.

> For such reasons, a lot of the country was happy to watch New York City in the past tottering like a Charlie Chaplin drunk on the brink of bankruptcy.

Just because the people were *not unhappy* doesn't mean they were *happy*. Such are the subtleties of the language, a point reinforced in three more examples that cannot be changed from negative to positive:

> "We're not going to not do it," the city manager said.

> These impulses abolish the pain signals; the only sensation remaining is a not unpleasant tingling.

> Using race as the primary criterion in drawing legislative boundaries is not unconstitutional.

Usually, in changing a negative sentence into a positive one, you merely need a different verb.

> The gymnastics team's coach asked for a new gymnasium because the gymnastics team *has no* adequate facilities.

To get onto the positive track, you might write:

> The gymnastics team's coach asked for a new gymnasium be-
> cause the gymnastics team *lacks* adequate facilities.

In converting the negative sentence to a positive one, I also replaced a
meaningless verb (*has*) with a meaningful one (*lacks*).

SENTENCE LENGTH

After World War II the wire services asked readability experts to examine their stories in an effort to improve them. Briefly, the experts determined that, on the average, short sentences (17 to 20 words) of short or
common words built around active verbs are the best. What resulted was
the popular idea that all sentences could be no more than 20 words.
Many people ignored the word *average*.

The *Philadelphia Inquirer* and *The New York Times* provide a contrast.
The average length of sentences on one front page of the *Times* ranged
from 30.7 words a story down to 21.5. Such a range is intolerable. Some
of the sentences in the *Times* were 40 to 50 words long, including one
lead of 44 words!

An *Inquirer* front page contained, on the other hand, staff-produced
stories whose average sentence length ranged from 17 to 21.3. Another
page included a staff-written story with an average sentence length of
25.8 words. In the same edition were two Associated Press stories—one
averaging 16.75 words; the other, 27.45. The average sentence length
of the *Inquirer*'s lead editorial was 25.5 words. But here's the difference
between the staff-written story that was 25.8 words and the editorial:
The staff-written story's longest sentence was 38 words; the editorial's
was 49. Likewise, the longest sentence in the AP's average-sentence
story of 27.45 words was 39 words; its shortest was 7.

Keeping stories to an average sentence length of 20 words is not practiced by the wire services only. The *Centre Daily Times* of State College,
Pa., produced three Page One local stories averaging 21, 20.8 and 13.1
words a sentence. The 13.1 average was a story written for children,
most of whom were just beginning to read. The writer of the story, a
high school student, knew his audience.

From *The Bulletin* in Bend, Ore., comes still another example—a local
story with sentences averaging 18.6 words. The writer, Dave Swan,
achieved that by writing only 10 of 37 sentences longer than 20 words.
Here are four unrelated paragraphs to show some of Swan's pace:

Henry "Hank" Bostleman, 532 NW Riverside, Bend, has been blowing glass for 25 years. He is now 70.

Bostleman is a neon sign blower. He works for the Carlson Co., 1605 NE Forbes Road.

"I really enjoy having something to do," he said. "A lot of people my age don't have enough to keep them busy."

"The new modern equipment has quite a few refinements on it," he said. "But I've used this for years and it still works. In fact, I just had a sign come back in for repair that has been working for over 17 years. I think that's pretty good!"

What should not escape you—whether you are in print or broadcast journalism—is that some of the most effective sentences are direct quotations. People don't talk in long sentences. A sentence is too long if it can't be spoken in one deep breath. And I'll even add—a heavy smoker's short breath. If your sentences make people gasp for air between the beginning and end, they are too long. How would this sentence read in a newspaper or sound on the air?

Fraught with more personal problems than he knew what to do with and on top of that burdened with some of his in-law's problems [gasp], a Cadbury man who was considered a shoo-in for mayor in next year's election [gasp] fired the person many people thought would be his speechwriter because the writer [gasp] wrote too many long sentences which the Cadbury man could not read in one breath [gasp], the resultant overbreathing killing him just after he fired his speechwriter [a very deep gasp of relief].

Naturally, when you're writing against a deadline, you cannot measure the length of your sentences. The secret is learning to write sentences of the right length before deadlines become a part of your life. Compute the average length of your sentences. If the average is high, find ways to reduce it.

Look at what you write; do you go on and on without putting in periods while at the same time ignoring commas, semicolons and other devices that might make reading your sentences easier or do you spot natural breaks in your long sentences and stop the sentences before they get out of hand? The preceding sentence is 53 words. To make it read comfortably, change it to three sentences.

Look at what you write. Do you go on and on without putting in periods while at the same time ignoring commas, semicolons and other devices that might make reading your sentences easier? Or do you spot natural breaks in your long sentences and stop the sentences before they get out of hand?

The paragraph has been reduced to an average of slightly more than 17 words a sentence simply by inserting punctuation marks that indicate full stops—periods and question marks—rather than punctuation marks that merely slow the reader down—commas and semicolons. One sportswriter still hasn't learned the trick. He produces sentences like this, column inch after column inch:

> Old Glory football practice is just a day old, so it can't really be said that Old Glory's quarterback question, if there ever was one, has been settled, but on Saturday Eddie Wolf spoke as if he's pretty certain who will be calling the signals for the Flag Wavers when the season opens Sept. 11 against Buckingham.

There are 56 words for you to grasp in one breath. A period instead of a comma between *settled* and *but* would have made the preceding marginally digestible. Sometimes a writer—but not a broadcaster—will produce a long sentence because he or she wants to insert additional information about the subject of the sentence. But in this sentence, the additional information only increases the sentence length; it doesn't have anything to do with the story.

> Williams, *who never has to wait longer than 1.9 seconds at a checkout counter anywhere in the world because his first act after replacing Dave Dillon as chairman of the committee was to order seats installed for the Legislature's checkout counter clerks,* again is risking his reputation as an amateur oddsmaker by making a list of predictions for next year's professional football season.

Trying to say too much at once creates long sentences, as evidenced by these examples from a student's paper:

> Bugliosi, a former deputy district attorney for the Los Angeles County District Attorney's office, made the statement in response to a question from the audience after his speech on the Tate-LaBianca murders for which he successfully prosecuted Charles Manson and four members of his family.
>
> Although he had been called in 1967 to prepare a search warrant for Sirhan's car, Bugliosi said he had no further involvement with the case until late 1975 when one of the bystanders

accidentally shot during the RFK assassination petitioned to have the murder weapon test-fired again.

More importantly, a number of individuals who were present at the hotel where Kennedy was shot in the hours and days after the killing, among them hotel employees, Los Angeles police officers and a former FBI agent, say that bullets were found there which were never mentioned in the state's case.

My advice to the student: Provide more bam-bam-bam and less plod-plod-plod-plod-plod. Here's a rewrite; it begins one paragraph later than the original because the first paragraph in the original is a throwaway:

Bugliosi, who in 1967 prepared a search warrant for Sirhan's car, said he became involved in the case again when a bystander at Kennedy's assassination asked to have the murder weapon test-fired again. The request was made in late 1975.

More importantly, Bugliosi said, some of the witnesses and investigators contend bullets were found at the scene of the assassination but never mentioned in Sirhan's trial. Among those making that claim are a former FBI agent, some Los Angeles police officers and some hotel employees, Bugliosi said.

The rewrite's longest sentence is 33 words; the original's shortest is 45 (the throwaway sentence). And while some of the rewrite's brevity was reached by eliminating extraneous or redundant information, the main work of shortening the sentences came by not cramming too much between periods. Note that the date of the request rates a sentence to itself as does the explanation of who said there were unmentioned bullets.

Transitional areas in sentences provide ideal places for windy writers to insert periods. Make sure, however, that you're not putting a period in an unnatural spot. Don't, for the sake of brevity, punctuate this sentence

He drank 15 gin and tonics and 17 glasses of beer at the fraternity house party and then passed out.

like this

He drank 15 gin and tonics. And 17 glasses of beer at the fraternity house party and then passed out.

when what you could do is

He drank 15 gin and tonics and 17 glasses of beer at the fraternity house party. And then he passed out.

And be careful when you're dealing with *not . . . but* constructions, which cannot be separated between two sentences.

> What you need is not a profound knowledge of the terminology of the English language's grammar, but a sensitivity to how the language operates.

To replace the comma (which some writers would not use anyway) with a period would foul the meaning of the sentence by creating two very fuzzy fragments.

While you're working on reducing the length of your sentences, you must also vary their length. It is not enough to vary structure; you've got to work on your pace too. If you stick to one main thought a sentence, you will vary your sentence length naturally. Here are sentences of virtual unvaried length:

> He said a president should lead this country and that right now there is a lack of leadership.
>
> "Never has a president vetoed so many bills since the Civil War," Monahan said.
>
> Williams defended himself, saying the vetoes have saved millions of dollars in deficits.
>
> Of the 56 bills Williams has vetoed, Congress has sustained 42, Williams said.
>
> Earlier this year Williams vetoed a $3.7 billion appropriations bill for public works jobs.
>
> He said the extra billions were not enough to make jobs where the jobs really are.

The length of those sentences is 18, 14, 13, 13, 14, 16, which is hardly variety. The lack of variety is readily apparent when you look at the sentences. Each is virtually the same length; each ends around the same place in a line. Sight alone indicates there is a problem. As an exercise, rewrite those six sentences with a more varied structure. The secret: tighten and subordinate.

Students aren't the only ones to write impossible sentences. Here is a 37-word sentence from a newspaper:

> "I know I'm not supposed to speak out, but I do it anyway," the 71-year-old Cree, whose German surname was adopted by an Ojibwa great-grandfather in honor of a white benefactor, said in an interview.

What brought that sentence to my attention was the distance between the subject (*Cree*) and the verb (*said*). The first time I read the sentence,

I couldn't find the verb; it had been overwhelmed by the clause (*whose . . . benefactor*). The clause, like one appearing on page 58, has nothing to do with the main idea of the sentence so it can be dropped and made into a sentence of its own. That would solve the problem of length.

Finally, here are two sentences whose combined length is less than 20 words. Simple as they may be, they're good sentences.

> It was the second test in the robot's organic molecule analyzer.
> The first was negative.

EXERCISES

A. *Compare the average sentence length of news stories in various newspapers. Study, too, the length of sentences in one newspaper, breaking down your study by sections in the paper, such as Page One, lifestyle (or whatever it's called), editorial, sports, business.*

B. *In news stories with long sentences, rewrite the sentences so they are shorter and easier to read —either for print or on the air. Remember, though, your audience is an adult one.*

C. *Reduce the length of these sentences by inserting periods where they fit naturally. Slight editing may be necessary.*

1. Under the student regulations, in effect in a student government election for the first time, the cost of all on-campus campaigning for all student candidates is paid entirely from the student activities fund and no personal contributions are permitted, except for a limited amount channeled through committees recognized by the Undergraduate Student Government.

2. Last April the commissioners held a meeting with hospital officials to discuss a list of possible Elmbank uses, and, with a few exceptions, the hospital officials approved the list before agreeing to further negotiations.

3. A Soviet spokesman initially reported that the jet had been seized by five gunmen but later said that three were involved—one carrying a Somalian passport, the second carrying an Ethiopian passport and the third carrying a Moroccan travel permit.

4. Clifford has come under mounting pressure from students, lawyers, and more recently, alumni of the school, to appoint an impartial group to investigate allegations of a cover-up at the school where faculty members have testified that more than half of last year's engineering class of 250 students could have been involved in collaborating on a take-home test last April.

5. Notices will be sent to about 150 school superintendents—the first superintendents to leave their positions since the state's financial crisis forced reductions in the public school system but in some instances the superintendents will be pushed to lower-paying positions than they had; in others, they will be let go altogether.

6. The society said the highest number of species reported by a group in this country was 221 turned in at Des Moines, Iowa; 62 other groups in communities from Virginia to Washington listed 125 or more species.

ANSWERS

1. Under the student regulations, in effect in a student government election for the first time, the cost of all on-campus campaigning for all student candidates is paid entirely from the student activities fund. No personal contributions are permitted, except for a limited amount channeled through committees recognized by the Undergraduate Student Government.

2. Last April the commissioners met with hospital officials to discuss a list of possible Elmbank uses. With few exceptions, the hospital officials approved the list before agreeing to further negotiations.

3. A Soviet spokesman initially reported the jet had been seized by five gunmen. But the spokesman later said three were involved—one carrying a Somalian passport, the second, an Ethiopian passport, and the third, a Moroccan travel permit.

4. Clifford has come under mounting pressure from students, lawyers, and more recently, alumni of the school, to appoint an impartial group to investigate allegations of a cover-up at the school. Faculty members there have testified that more than half of last year's engineering class of 250

students could have been involved in collaborating on a take-home test last April.

5. Notices will be sent to about 150 school superintendents—the first to leave their positions since the state's financial crisis forced reductions in the public school system. In some instances the superintendents will be pushed to lower-paying positions than they had. In others, they will be let go altogether.

6. The society said the highest number of species reported by a group in this country was 221 turned in at Des Moines, Iowa. Sixty-two other groups in communities from Virginia to Washington listed 125 or more species.

SOME SENTENCE FAULTS

Mistakes made in structuring sentences are easy to avoid provided the writer keeps a clear mind at all times. Discipline yourself to think clearly as you write—no matter what the pressure on you. If you must stop while you're constructing a sentence to see where you've been so you can decide where you're going, fine. Sometimes you'll discover that the end and the beginning don't match and you'll begin anew.

Read the following and think about what you might have changed to make it clear:

> The charges were brought by Cadbury police in connection with an incident in which a pedestrian was hit by a vehicle on South Mahanoy Street Saturday night and then left the scene of the accident.

First, realize that the sentence says "a pedestrian was hit . . . and then left the scene of the accident" when what really happened was that the car left the scene. You could change the connective *and* to the pronoun *which* to at least make it clear that the car did the leaving.

When the writer neared the end of the sentence, he had forgotten the beginning. Go to the beginning. The first problem appears in the first four words—the passive voice (*were brought*) of the main clause's verb. Avoid passive voice wherever possible; it's a backward way of saying things. Switching to the active

> Cadbury police *brought* the charges . . .

I drop two words (*were, by*). Now to prune more

> . . . after a car hit a pedestrian . . .

eight more words by the wayside.

. . . and left the scene on South Mahanoy Street Saturday night.

Four more words dropped; in addition, I placed the car's actions (*hit* and *left*) closer together. By separating them too much, the writer sent the reader backwards looking for the verb's subject when the reader should have been going forward. By changing to active voice, I produced a better sentence.

Cadbury police brought the charges after a car hit a pedestrian and left the scene on South Mahanoy Street Saturday night.

Errors in sentences are mostly a byproduct of length. The longer the sentence the more opportunity there is for error. The writer of this sentence tried to cram so much into 28 words that he shifted the subject and never made it clear when he returned to the sentence's original subject:

She was admitted to the psychiatric ward of a hospital where her family was permitted to visit her and was to be transferred to a district hospital today.

The subject of *to be transferred* should be *she,* but as the sentence is constructed, it's *family.* Two sentences would correct the error.

She was admitted to the psychiatric ward of a hospital where her family was permitted to visit her. She was to be transferred to a district hospital today.

Here is a shorter sentence that is still constructed poorly enough to be confusing:

The statements by both candidates were in answer to questions from the Arms Control Association, a private disarmament study group, and published Monday.

The last three words confused me because it is not clear what the subject of *published* is. You have two options—a rewrite or two sentences.

Published Monday, the statements by both candidates were in answer to questions from the Arms Control Association, a private disarmament study group.

The statements by both candidates were in answer to questions from the Arms Control Association, a private disarmament study group. The statements were published Monday.

The placement of a time element can sometimes confuse a reader, although its misplacement usually causes mirth, not confusion.

> William Monahan's opposition *seized yesterday* on his addition . . .

That is not what Saul Bellow meant when he wrote his novel *Seize the Day.* Transpose the verb and the time element to eliminate the smile on the reader's face.

> William Monahan's opposition yesterday seized on his addition . . .

PARALLEL CONSTRUCTION

A more serious error is violating parallel construction without good reason. Obviously you cannot write stories containing nothing but 20-word sentences. So, as you vary your sentences among simple, compound, complex and compound-complex, you must be aware of parallel construction. The problem develops when you list items in a series, be they nouns, verbs or entire clauses. You should maintain the same form or function for all coordinate elements within a sentence. This sentence does not violate parallel construction:

> He likes *books, birds* and his *car.*

Parallel construction is not a matter of singular and plural number, but of consistent form or function. Thus, if you were to put prepositional phrases into a series you would not be limited to the preposition that begins the series.

> He can sleep *at* night, *during* the day and *in* the evening.

Verbals in a series are maintained in parallel construction.

> The wildest onslaught of tornadoes and violent storms this year erupted in the midlands Wednesday, *killing* at least four persons, *injuring* scores and *leaving* hundreds homeless.

Here is a sentence in which the first verbal needs a parallel:

> He ordered them *to keep* their farm reasonably free from manure and *the removal* of the manure piled next to the Williams' property.

The second italicized phrase should function the same way as the first.

> He ordered them *to keep* their farm reasonably free from manure
> and *to remove* the manure piled next to the Williams' property.

The following sentence does not violate parallel construction, although the parallel functions are not repeated in their entirety:

> Taiwan wanted *to compete* as the Republic of China, *fly* its flag
> and *play* its anthem.

That sentence has been shortened through elliptic writing. Written out fully, it would be:

> Taiwan *wanted to compete* as the Republic of China, *wanted to fly*
> its flag and *wanted to play* its anthem.

Most editors would prefer the first sentence because it is shorter and less demanding on the reader. However, don't be lulled into believing that all elliptic writing is clear or desirable. In the following the writer dropped the preposition *by,* whose absence changed the meaning of the sentence:

> Evidence of the controversy was exhibited *by* last month's peti-
> tion from residents protesting the continued development of the
> tract and the presence of several residents at last night's meet-
> ing.

Do you know where the second *by* belongs? The prepositional phrases piled one atop the other make the meaning of the sentence unclear. Prepositional phrases adhere to the closest noun (or verb, if that's what they're modifying), which means you reach an area in the sentence that seems to say:

> . . . the continued development *of the tract and the pres-
> ence* . . .

At first reading I thought *tract* and *presence* belonged to *of* and that the full phrase modified *development.* In other words, what was being developed was *the tract and the presence.* Only after three readings did I realize what was meant.

> Evidence of the controversy was exhibited *by* last month's peti-
> tion from residents protesting the continued development of the
> tract and *by* the presence of several residents at last night's meet-
> ing.

The writer, in attempting to be compact, was inexact. Two sentences might have solved the problem—two sentences totaling 33 words instead of the 28-word mess that resulted.

> Evidence of the controversy surfaced last month in a petition from residents protesting the continued development of the tract. The evidence reappeared last night with the presence of several residents at the meeting.

Dr. Robert L. Butler, a professor of biology at Penn State, found the following barbarism in an advertisement by an engineer:

> My system is practical to use in breeding fish, biological laboratories, and for use in fish farming, the industry of the future, for a good source of protein, very much needed throughout the entire world to help eliminate starvation and for better health.

Among other things, the advertised system breeds not only fish but also biological laboratories. Parallel construction was violated because the writer attempted to put too many unrelated ideas into the sentence— a fault Butler has appropriately named *shack building*.

Compound predicates are trouble spots when the writer, for no apparent reason, changes tense.

> Williams said the sign *was* unattractive and *detracts* from the building's appearance.

The writer started in the past tense (*was*) then moved into the present (*detracts*) without good reason. In that sentence, the present tense should have been used because the sign was still standing when the story was written; it existed at the time of the sentence. As far as Williams is concerned, the standing sign *is* unattractive and *detracts*. Had the sign been removed prior to Williams' comment, past tense would have been correct.

> Williams said the sign *was* unattractive and detracted from the building's appearance.

Clauses in a series should be parallel, as they are here:

> He said that was the way to repair it, that there was no other way, and that it was the way he wanted the work done.

> "We should be vigilant for those who want too much power concentrated in one place, who want to silence an unpopular

minority, who want to jail a reporter or throttle a television station, who want to deny teachers the freedom to teach and students the freedom to learn," Dr. Stanton said.

Here is a sentence that needs parallel clauses:

The receivers tell firemen *when there is a fire* and its location.

The sentence is not as awkward when parallel construction is followed.

The receivers tell firemen *when there is a fire* and *where it is lo-
cated*.

If you think as you write and edit closely when you're finished, you
won't violate parallel construction. Remember what you've done, how
you began a sentence, which this writer didn't:

Williams suggested *closing* the loopholes for the rich and . . .

As soon as the writer reached the connective, he should have doubled his
guard for parallel construction. He didn't.

. . . *rejection* of salary increases for government officials.

Rejection has to be recast as a gerund to fit with *closing,* also a gerund, or
the sentence can be rewritten. In the interest of parallel construction the
writer should have said:

Williams suggested *closing* the loopholes for the rich and *rejecting* salary increases for government officials.

Here is another violation:

The suggestions included the possibility of *hiring* an additional
teacher for Park Forest and the *transfer* of a part-time teacher
from Panorama Village to Radio Park.

Correctly structured:

The suggestions included the possibility of *hiring* an additional
teacher for Park Forest and *transferring* a part-time teacher from
Panorama Village to Radio Park.

Sometimes correcting the problem is not a matter of form but of
reconstruction.

The party leader said he *was* upset by the vote and will go to
New Mexico in an attempt to change it.

> The addition *will provide* the 92 students with four teachers and *follows* the recent hiring of a teacher for the fifth and sixth grades.

Some editors might argue that while those two sentences violate parallel construction, there is good reason. But those who don't like the sentences can right the violation by subordinating.

> The party leader, who said he was upset by the vote, will go to New Mexico in an attempt to change it.

> The addition, which will provide the 92 students with four teachers, follows the recent hiring of a teacher for the fifth and sixth grades.

Sometimes there is good reason to violate parallel construction.

> The other six *were killed* and their murders *remain* unsolved.

A change in the tense of either verb would change the meaning. You can't subordinate because the sentence is compound, unlike some of the previous examples that merely had compound predicates. In those, the subject remained the same. That doesn't mean compound sentences should not be parallel; it does mean there are exceptions. The logic of time should dictate in those cases, not the convention of parallel construction.

EXERCISES

Make the following parallel.

1. In other business yesterday, City Council approved plans for reconstruction and landscaping the McAllister Street parking lot.

2. To walk, running and flying are my favorite forms of exercise.

3. To find the business, take the first turn to your right, you'll cross the street and walk one block.

4. Proof that he was human came when he walked in here and talks about his pain.

5. If for any reason customers wish to discontinue this plan or want their checks redirected to another bank, they may do so.

6. The association recommended that the board consider adding two basketball games to the schedule, which increases it to 22 games, and to extend the girls' cross-country schedule to include two meets with Smethport.

7. Williams said he was proud of his role in authorizing the break-ins and feels he had an obligation to authorize them.

8. It would also abolish the service's board of governors, make the agency's chief subject to confirmation, providing an extra $2.3 billion in subsidies, and bar any rate increases or substantial cutbacks in service until next year.

9. As part of its study, the commission traveled through the state holding public hearings, took testimony from parents, teachers and administrators, and observing school activities.

ANSWERS

The italicized portion has been corrected.

1. In other business yesterday, City Council approved plans for *reconstructing* and landscaping the McAllister Street parking lot.
2. *Walking,* running and flying are my favorite forms of exercise.
3. To find the business, take the first turn to your right, cross the street and walk one block. (*You'll* deleted; it was future tense. The others are present.)
4. Proof that he was human came when he walked in here and *talked* about his pain.
5. If for any reason customers wish to discontinue this plan or *to have* their checks redirected to another bank, they may do so.
6. The association recommended that the board consider adding two basketball games to the schedule, which increases it to 22 games, and *extending* the girls' cross-country schedule to include two meets with Smethport.
7. Williams said he *is* proud of his role in authorizing the break-ins and feels he had an obligation to authorize them.
8. It would also abolish the service's board of governors, make the agency's chief subject to confirmation, *provide* an extra $2.3 billion in subsidies, and bar any rate increases or substantial cutbacks in service until next year.

9. As part of its study, the commission traveled through the state holding public hearings, *taking* testimony from parents, teachers and administrators, and observing school activities.

FALSE SERIES

Similar to parallel construction fault is what Bernstein calls "series out of control" and what H. W. Fowler calls "bastard enumeration." From a student paper comes this example:

> Peanuts appears in 700 newspapers in the United States, 71 newspapers abroad, and is translated into a dozen languages.

Insert another *and* and the problem is corrected.

> Peanuts appears in 700 newspapers in the United States *and* 71 newspapers abroad and is translated into a dozen languages.

Gene Gilmore and Robert Root say the problem can also arise with a surplus verb. Their example:

> He is a determined golf player, a collector of antique clocks and often reads a detective story at night.

Their cure:

> He is a determined golf player and a collector of antique clocks. He often reads a detective story at night.

TRANSITION

Not even an apprentice bricklayer would think of building a house without using cement to keep the bricks together. Similarly, no journalist should put together a story whose sentences are not cemented together. The cement is the transition from one sentence to the next. Commonly used transition words are *meanwhile, but, still, nevertheless, for example, however, also, for, and, on the other hand, next, similarly, again, consequently, as a result, in other words.*

But before continuing, look over the preceding paragraph to see how I linked one sentence to the next. What I did was repeat words or variations of words so that the idea was continued. I first used the word *similarly,* which told the reader an analogy was coming. To make sure the analogy was there I not only used a similar idea, I also repeated two of the words in the idea—*cement(ed)* and *together*. In sentence three I repeated the word *cement* and then used for the first time the word *transition,* which I then repeated in sentence four. That's transition—clearly linking past ideas to the present and future. You do it in sentences all the time, using the connectives mentioned in the first paragraph in addition to others.

Within sentences the two most common transition words are *and* and *but*.

> Councilman Williams said the proposal was faulty *and* he announced plans to modify it.

In that sentence two related actions were linked by *and*.

> Government officials said the hijackers ordered the plane to turn west to Hawaii, *but* the pilot told them he did not have enough fuel *and* he continued on to Los Angeles.

That sentence shows a contrast between two actions. *But* means, among other things, *on the contrary* or *however.* Its purpose is to tip the reader that what is about to be read will disagree, contradict or modify what has just been read.

But should not be thought of in terms of internal sentence transition only. As noted earlier, when your sentences get too long, a period before *but* is a good place to start shortening them. Whether you use *but* to carry from one part of a sentence to another or from one sentence to another depends largely on readability. Your guide is how much you want to make the reader swallow before you give a break. In this example the writer chose to make two sentences:

> Britain demanded the meeting and proposed that it be held today. But Lebanon proposed a delay until Wednesday afternoon, and Britain agreed.

Because both sentences have two actions (*demanded, proposed; proposed, agreed*), the writer was on safer ground not tying them together in one sentence. It would have been too much to understand.

(Be careful with *but* and its synonyms. Because it sets up a contrast, *but* is not a substitute for *and,* which joins related ideas. Failing to appreciate *but,* one sloppy journalist wrote: "Father Kenney has been a quiet, unassuming priest, but loved and respected by Catholics and non-Catholics alike." There is no contrast; *and* is correct.)

Here are three consecutively written paragraphs that lack transition:

Lee exhibited her "Children Before Dogs" t-shirt, created for her most widely known campaign, to "Scoop the Poop" in New York City.

Toxicariasis, a disease transmitted primarily by contact with dog feces, especially affects children who often play where dogs are "curbed."

Lee said she likes dogs but predicted a day when dogs will be banned because owners do not adequately control or care for them.

One possible transition from the first to the second paragraph might have been:

The campaign is aimed at fighting toxicariasis, a disease transmitted primarily by contact with dog feces. The disease especially affects children.

The key to that transition is to repeat the word *campaign*. For the same assignment another student wrote the following as consecutive paragraphs:

Government health agencies, Lee said, pressured doctors and television networks into promoting the vaccine, although it was untested.

The FBI was called, Lee said, when she received threats on her life following an attack on dog owners who place their pets before people.

What is lacking is something early in the second paragraph to advise the reader that the subject has changed. A third student did this to change the topic:

In a discussion on oral sex, Lee told the female members of the audience that the virus—herpes simplex—causes blindness and is incurable, in addition to being very painful.

Likewise, the following short news story from Reuters news service, reports on two topics. Those words that serve as transition from one topic to the other are italicized.

China confirmed today that Hua Kuo-feng, the Communist Party Chairman, has a wife and family.

The disclosure came in a front-page article in Jenmin Jih Pao, the party newspaper, which said that Mr. Hua's daughter graduated from Middle School 166 in Peking in 1974. It gave her name as Hsiao-li, or Little Li.

At the same time the Chinese press made its strongest attack yet on Mr. Hua's opponents, declaring that they should be shown no mercy.

"Being benevolent to them would be a crime against the people," newspaper articles said.

Little is known about the personal background of most Chinese leaders. But since Mr. Hua's appointment as successor to Mao Tse-tung last month, the press has gradually told the Chinese people more about the new chairman.

The Jenmin Jih Pao article, attributed to teachers of Middle School 166, described Miss Hua as Mr. Hua's youngest daughter and said that like millions of other educated Chinese teenagers she had been "sent to the countryside" to help national development.

Adding to the personality cult that is apparently being built around the burly chairman, the article said that Mr. Hua had walked from his office to attend a parents' meeting at the school instead of using an official car. He modestly did not announce his arrival, it added.

Besides the italicized portions of the story, there is one more transitional device—the fifth paragraph. It eases the reader through the topic change.

Transitional devices between paragraphs are not necessarily placed at the beginning of a sentence. They do, however, come early enough to bridge the action.

The change in academic standards was cited by the accrediting team as proof the department was no longer performing its mission well. Members of the department and the dean of the college, *on the other hand,* said standards were not the only thing that should be used to measure quality.

Repeating words is a valid transitional device.

Yet he somehow finds time for his favorite novelist, Agatha Christie.

Another Agatha Christie fan is . . .

"The flow of international news has been impeded rather than advanced," Paley said, citing censorship and *attempts* at censorship throughout the world.

One *attempt* occurred when UNESCO's General Conference . . .

Sometimes transition is not a matter of existing or not existing, but rather is a matter of degree. The following example shows a transition that is not bad. But it could be made better.

> On the committee are Curtis Boyer of Pickett County, Barry O'Hara of Clive County and Joseph Holt of Orange County. Boyer said a new line could be built parallel to the old one.

The degree of improvement comes in moving *Boyer* to the end of the series of committee members so his name appears back to back.

> On the committee are Barry O'Hara of Clive County, Joseph Holt of Orange County and Curtis Boyer of Pickett County. Boyer said a new line could be built parallel to the old one.

Transition can exist on the continuity of the action alone.

> High moral standards are required for Cadbury police officers, according to Chief Bernice T. Showman.
> Showman said last night she insists on those standards so that respect for the police is maintained.
> "Police officers have to be just a little bit better than anyone else in society so that they won't be looked down upon," she said.

To get from the lead to the second paragraph, the writer repeated the police chief's surname. To carry the story to the third paragraph, the writer used a direct quotation that explains the second paragraph.

You will discover as you edit that you can remove some transitional devices without doing harm to the story. Often the story's action carries the reader and it is not necessary to help the reader beyond that. A question-and-answer format overcomes any lack of relationship on the strength of the questions alone. Curiosity on the reader's part is the transition. However, questions made up by a journalist within a normally written news story are a cheap device and show a lack of imagination. For example:

> Will Kaplan and his associates get out of prison when they become eligible for parole in April next year?

Paragraphs can serve as transitional devices—as in the Hua story. At the end of a city council story a journalist might want to add a list of unrelated actions. To take the reader from the main action to the list, the journalist might write:

In other action, the council:

Or the journalist could shorten that to:

The council *also:*

In a complex story, paragraphs are often necessary to get the reader from one topic to another. For instance, journalists covering a debate of political candidates might focus on two opponents at the expense of others. When the time comes to report on the others, the journalist might use this transitional device:

> Also on the platform for the debates were Patrick Neuman, a Democrat, and Mary Agee, a Republican, who are opponents in the local legislative district contest.

The story would then continue by reporting what Neuman and Agee said. Unfortunately, the transitional sentence is virtually a throwaway, which some editors would accept only reluctantly. Here's a better example:

> Lee pointed out that the discoverer of the swine flu told her he wouldn't let anyone take the immunization shot. Numerous cases of paralysis have resulted from the shots.
> Lee, executive director of the "Children Before Dogs" organization, also talked on the diseases children contract from the worms in dog feces.
> The larvae of the worm get into the child when he kisses the family pet or plays on the carpeting, she said.

What makes the transitional paragraph in the Lee excerpt superior to the one in the political story is that it is not a throwaway sentence. It presents something more concrete than just identification of two people as political opponents.

This paragraph functions the same way—giving background information (italicized) to keep the reader clear:

> Also discussed was the proviso of in-patient psychiatric service, *which Colina Jordan said she has urged in Centre County for more than 20 years.*
> Mrs. Jordan was told that when Mountainview is expanded, mental health care would be a primary concern.

Be careful your transition does not commit you to something you might have no control over later. Keeping in mind that make-up editors sometimes have to cut stories to fit a hole and that they usually do so by chopping from the story's end, paragraph by paragraph, consider this transition near the end of a student's story:

> "The flow of international news has been impeded rather than advanced in the past decade," Paley said.
> He cited *three examples* of attempts to censor events in certain countries as efforts to restrict the free press.
> *One example* is . . .

Of course, the student also cited examples two and three. But if the story had been cut and example three was among the missing, imagine how stupid the newspaper would look. To avoid a problem, dump the *three examples* paragraph entirely.

> "The flow of international news has been impeded rather than advanced in the past decade," Paley said.
> *For example,* in India . . .

Now if any examples are cut, the reader will be none the wiser.

Time elements can serve as transition and can be critical to clarity. When the time changes, the reader should be told immediately. If you change the time but don't tell the reader, you will create confusion. Here are three paragraphs in which the time changes, and the time element serves well as transition:

> *Earlier this year* Feldman warned that the agency would halt virtually all development unless the legislature agreed to set strict auto emission standards.
> Lawmakers ignored the threat and defeated the measure twice. *Yesterday,* the Environmental Review Committee also voted, 9–3, to reject the anti-emissions proposal.

Whichever transitional device you use, make sure it is real. Don't force it, the way a television newscaster once did.

> (Film of local fire is shown. Film ends; anchorman speaks:)
> "While there were no injuries in that fire, the death toll in an earthquake in Guatemala has risen to 3,000."

Linking a local fire of little consequence to a tragic earthquake is absurd. Such contrivances are justifiably scorned.

PARAGRAPHS

Those who have the perseverance to define a paragraph agree that unity plays a key role. Completeness, order and coherence are other sure signs you have a paragraph in hand.

A paragraph should not drift away from the main thought like a ship sailing for Europe that suddenly splits in half and also sails for South America. Because of the different ideas in these two sentences, the following should be two paragraphs:

> The Clive-Cadbury series goes back to 1900 and the record is fairly even at 14–13–2, with Clive leading as it always has. Quarterback Dave Dillon leads the Cadbury offense in both passing and rushing.

Because the second sentence has nothing to do with the first, it should be placed in a separate paragraph.

Theme-writing rules aside, two general rules for newspaper paragraphs stand out.

The first is: Usually write one-sentence or very short paragraphs because they will put more white space (also called air) into your gray-appearing story and make it easier on the eye—that is, more legible in print. Newspaper columns are getting wider, but the increase is hardly enough to justify increasing the length of paragraphs. Column widths range from 9½ picas (six picas equal one inch) to 14 and 15 picas. But in a couple of nationally known newspapers checked for paragraph length, the width of the column of type had no apparent effect on the number of sentences in a paragraph. Most of the paragraphs were one sentence long no matter what the column width.

The second rule is: Don't bury "quotes" (direct quotations) at the end of paragraphs. If there is a quote a journalist wants to use, he or she should display it. That is why a copy editor would break the following into two paragraphs after the first sentence:

> Malta's newspaper criticized a reported British plan to use the offer of assistance to win concessions in talks on the future of naval bases on the island. "It appears that some British diplomats have been on the lookout for opportunities to use aid as a public relations gesture," one newspaper said in an editorial. "This may do for panty-hose makers, but it is hardly becoming of a nation like Great Britain."

However, getting a quote out front in a paragraph can lead to confusion when the person being quoted is also being mentioned for the first time. When you change speakers or characters, tell the reader immediately, which did not happen in this example:

> The Phillies have lost 11 of their last 12, scoring a total of 13 runs in their last nine games. Pirate pitcher Jim Rooker went the distance on a nine-hitter Wednesday night.
>
> "I don't know, I really don't know," Phillies Manager Danny Ozark said in his team's hushed lockerroom. "But I think we're going to snap out of it. We should, and I feel we will win."

At first reading it appears the writer is quoting Jim Rooker because Rooker is the last person mentioned before the quote. In such a situation, start the new paragraph with attribution so the reader knows immediately who is speaking. Perhaps this is even better:

> In his team's hushed lockerroom, Phillies Manager Danny Ozark said: "I don't know . . ."

In any case, don't make the reader scramble back and forth in a story to find out what he or she wants to know. Keep the story clear always.

POINT OF VIEW

One day my family was preparing to leave for Grandma's. The 3-year-old spoke:

"Can I bring something to Grandma's?"

"Take," I corrected her.

"Can I bring something to *take* to Grandma's?"

That's point of view: the way you look at something. Do you view the world as a 3-year-old or her father? Neither. As journalists, you should assume a modest omnipotent point of view by not identifying with anyone—the people you are reporting on or the people you are reporting for. That doesn't mean that you don't care about these people; it means you don't mix identities with them. If, for example, a speaker says: "We must do our best to improve conditions in this country," you, the journalist, might paraphrase that as:

> The people must do their best to improve conditions in the United States, Williams said.

When paraphrasing quotations, shift the pronouns (*I, you, we, our,* and so on) to third person pronouns or nouns (such as the speaker's name, or, as in the preceding example, *the people*).

Had the person who wrote this headline—HOW WE GOT IN TROUBLE IN VIETNAM—been thinking like that, he or she would have substituted *U.S.* for *we.* The use of *we* outside direct quotations in news stories leads to confusion when the reader then turns to the editorial page and reads an editorial that says: "We believe the president . . ." In that phrase, it is the editorial *we;* it belongs only on the editorial page.

Despite the plea for an omnipotent point of view, newspapers must face the reality of where they exist. A New York City newspaper reporting the visit of someone to that city would write:

> King Tut of Egypt *came* to New York City today from Washington, D.C., where he had been visiting for three days.

When you're in New York City, you can't *go* there. But if you're in Washington and you're writing about the same event for a Washington newspaper, your point of view shifts.

> King Tut of Egypt *went* to New York City from Washington, where he had been visiting for three days.

Some newspapers are more provincial about point of view than others. The story is told of a day when Great Britain was covered by a thick fog. Ships dared not sail from the island to Europe and vice versa. Who was cut off from whom? Reportedly, one London newspaper headlined its story on the fog:

CONTINENT FOGGED IN

What the European newspapers wrote is unrecorded.

This provincialism extends to newspapers circulated in a very wide area. Often a major newspaper's headline on a story distant from its base will include words such as upstate, downstate. UPSTATE MAN WINS HONORS may be fine for the people *downstate,* but what about the people who live in the vicinity of the story? Will they pass over it because they believe *upstate* means upstate from them? Better to use the points of a compass or the name of a town than to confuse the reader.

Editors of newspapers that are sold in more than one community are acutely aware of how a slip in point of view might be taken by readers of one community after the editor has spent a lifetime telling all communities that none is favored above another. One Pennsylvania newspaper covers an entire county that includes a university. When someone at the university dies, its public information office writes an obituary that invariably includes the phrase, "He *came* to the university in . . ." From that writer's point of view, *came* is correct. But from the point of view of the newspaper's audience, which includes people not connected with the university, the point of view has to be changed. After all, the reader does not necessarily identify with the university and his or her livelihood does not necessarily derive from the university. Hence, the newspaper edits that phrase to say: "He *went* to the university in . . ."

However, if someone born in another county becomes a resident of the newspaper's county and dies there, the paper writes: "He *came* to Centre County . . ." If the person is a native of the county but dies elsewhere, the paper writes: "He *went* to Miami in . . ." Clearly, the paper has a county point of view. Thus, when one reporter whose beat covered only one community wrote: "The Cadbury Fire Co. expects delivery of its new truck *here* Tuesday," the editor ordered *here* cut from the story. To the editor, *here* meant the entire county, which wasn't what the writer of the story meant.

In the same vein, a wire service story datelined Pittsburgh included this phrase: "Before *coming* to Arkansas in 1973 . . ." The correct word for that Pittsburgh story is *going*. If you remember come *here,* go *there,* you shouldn't have problems.

The principle behind point of view requires journalists to remember not how their words read or sound to them but how the reader-listener will interpret the words. Maintaining the audience's point of view is extremely critical in journalism because point-of-view misuse can create ambiguity or indicate to the reader-listener an unintended bias that could interfere with the main point of the news. If you keep your audience in mind at all times, you probably won't have problems with point of view.

THREE

Function

PARTS OF
SPEECH—THEN AND NOW

At one time traditional grammarians taught eight parts of speech—no more, no less. Those teachers said English contained nouns, pronouns, verbs, adjectives, adverbs, prepositions, conjunctions, interjections. Students were required to memorize the definitions of those parts of speech. "What is a noun?" the teacher would ask. And the students would reply: "A noun is the name of a person, place or thing."

The belief was that you could not use a noun in any other function except a noun function. Dictionaries determined what nouns (and other parts of speech) were. Such blind faith, though, creates problems. One dictionary says *football* is a noun, as in "He threw the football" and "The football is next to the bench." Very clearly *football* is used as a noun in those sentences. But what is it in this sentence?

The football field isn't large enough for three teams.

A very strict teacher would say the sentence is incorrect because *football* is a noun and nouns do not function as adjectives. Adjectives modify nouns; they do not serve as nouns. But *football* does modify something—*field*. The teacher might win the debate by saying that *football field* is perceived as one concept; that both words are nouns. True. But the dictionary also says *field* is a verb ("Iowa *fields* good football teams") and an adjective ("He is a *field* hand at the Smith farm"). It should be apparent, then, that it is impossible to define a part of speech without seeing how it is used. That's functional grammar.

Grammar today is classified according to the way it is studied: traditional, structural or transformational. Other descriptions include generative, which some no doubt would call degenerate. But no matter what it's called, our grammar is still the study of the conventions of contemporary language usage and not the study of some rules set down in the eighteenth century and adhered to blindly ever since. We must concern ourselves with how words and phrases function today and label them accordingly.

Generally speaking, the parts of speech can be divided into four very broad categories: nouns (including pronouns), verbs, connectives and modifiers. No matter what you want to say about, for example, a clause (relative, dependent, independent), your primary concern is how it modifies a noun or a verb or another clause. When you talk about the number and tense of a verb in a clause, you do it in the context of how that clause modifies another part of a sentence. Journalists care only that their sentences and punctuation are conventional so their stories can be understood by their readers; hence, they are concerned with function, not some esoteric study of grammar.

More enlightened dictionaries, while still labeling words as noun, verb, adjective, and so on, qualify themselves. *The American Heritage Dictionary of the English Language,* after advising its readers that its entries are traditionally labeled, says:

> These parts of speech are not to be regarded as perfectly exclusive categories. Many nouns in English, for example, can be used to modify other nouns in the manner of an adjective but nevertheless lack other essential characteristics [form] that would require their classification as adjectives.

The opposite is also true. Today we think nothing of using as nouns what once were only adjectives, such as *the local* when we mean *the local division of an international union,* or *the international* when *the international union* is understood. The sales pitches that interrupt our television viewing are *commercial messages* yet we refer to them as *commercials.* Editors write *editorials,* which are really *editorial opinions.* The verb intensifier *must* also functions as a noun ("This story is an advertising department *must"*) and as an adjective ("The president views the environmental bill as *must* legislation"). The verb *hires* is also used as a noun in some newsrooms ("The last three *hires* at our newspaper came from the same university"). Some people consider the usage incorrect, although *hires* has had that noun usage since the Bible was written. Similarly, *cancels* is listed as a noun in dictionaries of all ages, although its noun usage is common among philatelists only ("The Postal Service will offer a new plan for obtaining first-day *cancels"*).

One verb that many will not accept as a noun is *think.* Perhaps the noun usage became popular after A. A. Milne, describing an action of Winnie-the-Pooh, wrote:

> He took his head out of the hole and had another *think* . . .
> [italics added].

The word *hedge* was once a noun meaning shrubs; today it's also a verb ("He *hedged* on the bet"). The word *dare* at one time was most commonly used as a verb; today, though, we also use it as a noun ("He took the *dare"*). An adverb, *out,* has gained respectability as a noun ("He looked for an *out"*), and *physical,* an adjective, also functions as a noun ("The soldier reported for his *physical* at 9 a.m."). There are a lot of words in American English that function at least two ways, such as:

attire	*gasp*	*nick*
bag	*guard*	*note*
bend	*halt*	*outlaw*
benefit	*honor*	*parallel*
blank	*hub*	*pass*
cart	*hurl*	*rake*
damage	*inch*	*scheme*
deal	*insert*	*scorn*
flank	*knight*	*visit*
flow	*lead*	*warp*
gain	*model*	*whine*

In addition to using the same word in two or more ways, we convert nouns into modifiers by changing their form (*Congress, congressional; fish, fishy; disease, diseased*) and adjectives into nouns through a similar process (*sweet, sweetness; pure, purity*). Add *en* to an adjective and you have a verb (*black, blacken; white, whiten; red, redden;* although *blue, bluen* doesn't work). Before a noun *en* or *em* creates a verb (*code, encode; power, empower*). Nouns also become verbs by adding *ed* (*chair, chaired; author, authored*), although some editors won't accept those two because they don't fill a void in the language—a test you should make a new word pass before using it.

Further conversion of nouns occurs when we prefix them with *de, re* or *be*. Some people want to *de-sex* the language although I've never heard of anyone trying to *sex* it. Margot Hentoff once referred to children kept out of school against their will as being "involuntarily de-schooled." The instructions on a light tell the user how to put in a new light bulb by advising:

> To relamp, pull down on glass.

Imagine the cowboy outfitted with two pistols being described as a "bepistoled terror," an example based on a syndicated columnist's description of a very famous American general. And a *New York Times* book reviewer once advised his readers:

> Go to Yankee Stadium with the sportswriter whose books are said to have *bejeweled* the game of baseball [italics added].

Sometimes, when we use the same form of a word to function as a noun, adjective or verb, the result can be confusing, as in the following headline:

LEBANESE FERRY WOUNDED

In my first reading I took *ferry* for a noun when it was really functioning as a verb. Various forms of verbs do function as nouns and adjectives with less confusion than the preceding example—a pattern explained in Chapters 4 and 5.

OTHER EXAMPLES OF
FUNCTIONAL GRAMMAR

Some professors will tell students they've used a word incorrectly by saying, "That's a noun," where the students used a noun to function as a verb. The professors are usually right but for the wrong reason. The issue is not whether a word is a noun or a verb or an adjective, but whether the word is clear and necessary in a particular function. It is not necessary to say:

The driver *ignitioned* the car.

What's wrong with:

The driver *started* the car.

On the other hand, a new word may be created to encompass a broader phrase. Joan Ryan of *The Washington Post* once interviewed Dick Schapp, at the time the editor of *Sport* magazine. Schapp was talking about a story (described as a "scandal-tinged feature") he had written about a well known football coach. Schapp said about the story:

"It had to be *lawyered*" {italics added}.

The first reaction of any stuffy grammarian would have been to scream, "That's not a verb!" And the dictionary would have supported the grammarian. The word is not listed as Schapp used it. But does that matter? Look at the word again. Does it not say the story had to be legally laundered or legally cleaned or the libel had to be removed by a lawyer? I think it does, and I believe its use is legitimate.

Another creation not found in old or new dictionaries comes from *The Quill*. Referring to a federal judge, the magazine reported:

Kelleher forbade all note-taking except by *credentialed* news reporters, the attorneys involved and the parents of the defendant {italics added}.

I have heard it said that proposals passed from one committee to another and then another have been *committeed* to death. Of course, people who don't know what it's like to deal with committees may not appreciate the phrase, so its use is confined to those familiar with committees. But most of us are familiar with a lot of small taxes slowly depleting our wages—a process known as being *nickeled and dimed* into poverty.

As the times change, so do the functions of words. People who collect supermarket discount coupons, according to *Newsweek*, call their action *couponing*, as in

"Couponing is an addiction," she explains.

and

What makes couponing a business is the newsletter . . .

The usage is not as strained as you might believe. More than 150 years ago anything bearing coupons was said to be *couponed*.

Sometimes creating a new word is not a matter of, say, changing a noun into a verb but of using a contrasting or opposite word. The verb *moonlight* gave Eric Pace of *The New York Times* such an opportunity.

> But some, including George Plimpton, New York's fireworks commissioner, who *daylights* as a writer, emphasize that fireworks' charm also stems, more innocently, from their beauty [italics added].

During the Democratic National Convention of 1976, the party felt it had in Jimmy Carter a candidate who could win the presidency. To make sure all was well within the party, a platform suitable to Carter was adopted. Almost anything Carter didn't like was reworded, diluted or removed. It was the year of party harmony, and the platform was quickly adopted at the convention with barely a murmur of protest. Howard K. Smith of ABC News told his audience there had been no fight over the platform because it had been *Carterized* before it was presented. That one word—in the right context—says what took me four sentences to say. What makes the word so good is that is it evocative; it conjures up for the interested viewer all that went into Carter's rise to national prominence. Two months later *Newsweek* told its readers what Carter's staff was doing with background material for the candidate.

> Every research paper and memo is alphabetized, categorized— and then Carter-ized [*Newsweek*'s hyphen].

The second time around I didn't like it; the novelty had disappeared.

Newsweek also reported that at Duke University the faculty uses the phrase *to Parkerize,* which "is in honor of 69-year-old professor of history Harold T. Parker, and it means to teach many more sections than is normal."

Novelist John O'Hara created a word in the same vein as *Carterize* and *Parkerize.* Knowing that most of his readers were familiar with Walter Mitty, the shy man who dreamed of performing heroic deeds, O'Hara wrote in one of his newspaper columns:

> It is, of course, the spot every professional politician sees himself in at one time or another. If you pitch four innings for Gibbsville High School, you cannot fail to *mittyize* yourself as the hero of the World Series, and it's a dream to live on because

the chances are so great against its ever coming true [italics added].

Walter Mitty also gave us a modifier, as in this sentence from *Smithsonian* magazine:

His ever-burning Mittyish great actor ambition was unrealized.

Carterize, Parkerize and *mittyize* might lead you to believe you can take any noun and add *ize* to make a verb. Forget it. Can you imagine memorandums for President Dwight D. Eisenhower being *Eisenhowerized?* It's too much. The *ize* treatment doesn't always work (*doorize*) or it sometimes sounds pretentious (*formalize*)—which journalists shouldn't. At the same time, an *ize* word can be unnecessary.

A summary of rate increases resulting from this filing, based on *annualized* revenues as of . . .

Perhaps the writer of that partial sentence from a business report was trying to say the company's long-term earnings had been computed on an annual basis rather than monthly. But what I really suspect is that the writer meant *annual*—and that's what should have been used. If *annualize* has any meaning, it is this definition (labeled *rare*) from the *Oxford English Dictionary:* "to write for, or contribute to, an annual (publication)."

From a story in *The New York Times* comes another example of functional usage:

It quickly appeared that every rolling stone in town was showing up. Those invited brought guests. Others *gate crashed* [italics added].

That phrase did not appear in what is traditionally known as a straight or hard news story. While that shouldn't matter, it is true that journalists have more freedom with the language when writing or broadcasting feature stories or columns than they do when writing or broadcasting news stories. *Gate crashed* is strained and forced and serves no purpose for which there aren't other phrases. What's wrong with

Others crashed the gate.

It is more conventional, and because of that, it doesn't make the reader stop and take note. It doesn't shout, "Hey! Look at me! Aren't I cute!"

When your usage interrupts reading or sidetracks listening, you have done the reader-listener a disservice.

That could happen with this sentence, which is derived from an editorial:

> Can you imagine a disease striking *conventioning* members of the American Legion and nobody else?

There's nothing wrong with saying "members of the American Legion convention."

Sports fans, no doubt, probably wouldn't stop reading after seeing this sentence in *The Washington Post:*

> Theismann bounced right up after a wicked hit when he was *blind-sided* and sacked early in the scrimmage [italics added].

To the fan (and the quarterback) *blind-sided* means to be tackled from an approach the football player can't see—his blind side. The verb has also entered the language of politicians. Sen. Gary Hart once complained to *Newsweek* about not being dealt with candidly, then said:

> "It's known as being blind-sided."

Some functional usages need to be explained, as was done in this quotation from a United Press International story:

> "I can't see any excuse for this unless the officials were improperly trained or they were guilty of *homering* (favoring the home team). . . . I doubt very much if the officials were *homering*" [italics added].

Some functional usages may sound strained or contrived. *Time* magazine produced this sentence:

> So during some friendly horse-play, he literally lassoed a ten-year-old Korean boy and *lollipopped* him into the medical hut [italics added].

Lassoed doesn't bother you but *lollipopped* (meaning he lured the boy with lollipops) may have made you read twice. However, before you go out on the linguistic limb and condemn *lollipopped* while accepting *lassoed,* be advised that *lasso* entered our language as a noun. Usage made it a verb we accept without question today. Perhaps *lollipopped* will reach that status. Perhaps we'll never see it again.

It is doubtful, though, that the following usage from *The New York Times Magazine* will go away—unless we stop building dams.

> For long stretches, the river shore is undeveloped and forested, but nonetheless the Mississippi has been dammed and *leveed* and diked along its entire length {italics added}.

Here are some more examples; the italics are mine:

> For 42 yules *New Yorker* writer Frank Sullivan saluted friends and celebrities in a full-page poem, *nutmegged* with his gentle wit and redolent rhymes. (*Time*)

> The program from China was *satellited* to other countries. (CBS)

> I shouldn't be surprised if Raymond Chandler and Stephen Crane get strong *showcasing* in Volume Two. (*The Philadelphia Inquirer*)

> The offbeat television comedian, 33, is planning to marry Jacqueline Carlin, 27, an actress and model who does TV commercials—including some that have run on "NBC's Saturday Night," the show that *showcased* Chase until he bowed out last month. (*Newsweek*)

> Sen. Daniel P. Moynihan consulted with members of such a panel before recommending that Carter not replace three respected Republican-appointed U.S. attorneys in the state—including Robert Fiske in the *showcase* Southern District in Manhattan . . . (*Newsweek*)

> In two months, Hoge has *housecleaned* the veteran Washington staff of the Sun-Times, dismantled the Daily News's respected foreign service and—in a weekend burst of energy at his kitchen table—restyled the News's make-up and news coverage. (*Newsweek*)

> Councilman Richard Wion countered that it would be illogical to ask the county *to sidewalk* its property and not make a similar request of the Union Cemetery Association. (*Centre Daily Times*, State College, Pa.)

I thought I had another example when I heard a sportscaster, Jim Simpson of NBC, describe a football field with artificial grass as being artificially *turfed*. I found *turfed* in a 1949 dictionary but not in a 1969 dictionary. Few dictionaries list the word *tenure* as a modifier.

> She is a *tenured* faculty member at UCLA.

If not common to the country at large, it is a very common word among college professors. Less common is this usage:

> The president of the university stopped *tenuring* research faculty in 1970.

That word also is not listed in any dictionary. And no dictionary I know of lists the following usage from *Newsweek:*

> The proposal was *back-burnered* and ultimately forgotten . . . [italics added].

Dr. Alex Comfort, an expert on sex and aging, was quoted in *The New York Times* as saying:

> "We tend to *childrenize* old people, and they will tend to react in kind" [italics added].

A headline on a *Times* story about installing fixtures produced a non-existent but clear usage.

FIXTURING UP A LOFT

A gown with a V-neck (also V-neckline) was described in an advertisement as:

> A fabulous *V'd* gown with a deep front slice and lace doing a beautiful job [italics added].

Joseph Durso, in a sports column in *The Times,* wrote:

> When they *gavel* themselves to attention Monday morning, they will be trying to make some sense out of a scenario filled with intrigue, plots, subplots, feuds, lots of money and a cast of thousands [italics added].

At one time *gavel* was a verb, but not with the meaning Durso gave it. Modern dictionaries list it as a noun only.

Young children, not yet ingrained with the grammatical prejudices of elders, are fertile with examples of functional usage. Perhaps because she likes to get to the point quickly, my younger daughter (then 3) said

> Watch me *batoning*.

which is shorter than saying

> Watch me twirling my baton.

She also once advised two of her dolls who were wearing cowboy hats to play cowboy by saying:

> You two go *cowboying*.

Equally to the point, my older daughter (then 6) got into the backseat of the family car, her safety first in mind, and demanded:

> I want to be *seat-belted*.

There was no doubting what she meant, even though she had taken a noun and converted it into a verb.

An anonymous 3-year-old once told his mother that the wind had stopped by saying, "It has stopped *wind-ing*," a usage that would not work in writing without the hyphen, but would have no problem over the air waves.

Red Smith, a *New York Times* sports columnist (an understatement, if there ever was one), once wrote:

> They said that if the standard contract did not bind the player to his employer from cradle to grave, players would be *gypsying* across the map in greedy pursuit of the top dollar [italics added].

Some dictionaries list *gypsy* as a verb, but Smith told me he learned his definition as a child.

> To gypsy, to travel from place to place schlepping family, household goods, horses and maybe a dancing bear, has been a part of the language familiar to me since, as a child in Green Bay, Wis., I saw gypsy caravans answering that description— and ran indoors lest they kidnap me and sell me into slavery, as all right-thinking boys knew to be the gypsy custom.

Smith closed his letter:

> As to converting nouns into verbs, we do it often, of course. We sin instead of committing a sin. But I have my own limits. I will not *host* you unless you will *guest* me. If you *author* a textbook, I will not *reader* it.

And syndicated columnist George F. Will has complained about Americans' "perverse national genius" for turning "respectable nouns into disagreeable verbs." Three examples Will would no doubt dislike come from computer specialists, whose language some editors and teachers prefer we ignore.

They know where they can *input* information.

Curricula must *interface* with other colleges' curricula.

The researchers are exploring the possibility that such subsets can provide laymen with a convenient method of *accessing* information in *formatted* data bases without learning a formal computer language.

Maybe it depends on how sensitive or defensive you are about the language that determines where you stand on *Carterize, mittyize, blind-sided, lollipopped, back-burnered, lawyered, host,* and so forth. Whether or not you agree with some of these usages depends on how you learned the language. I prefer to be flexible, perhaps because I do not view functional usage as an ominous and permissive force that will destroy the language. For despite the language's flexibility, it also has its limitations, as Langacker explains:

> Since a language is used primarily for communication, a speaker is not free to innovate without limit; his linguistic system must remain similar enough to the systems of the people around him to enable them to understand him.

Because clear communication remains the prime goal of language usage, most unclear usages don't stand a chance.

EXERCISES

As a user of words you should be keenly aware of innovative language usage and sloppy abuse. Examine the italicized words in the following sentences to determine if they are used well. Then look them up in two dictionaries not published by the same company or at the same time. Indicate in the margin which words are correctly used—based on the dictionaries—and which are not.

1. For two centuries, Americans were driven by the urge to *wester.* (*The American Legion Magazine*)
2. Her own memory is especially *sieved* regarding the sequence of events in 1936 and 1937. (*The New York Times Book Review*)
3. But after the phone call an agreement was reached that if and when Kissinger writes his book Meredith will *agent* it. (*More*)
4. In "The Intelligent Coed's Guide to America," Mr. Wolfe *anatomizes* the American intellectual's dogged attempt to deny the fact

that, politically and economically at least, some things are looking up in the United States. (*The New York Times*)

5. He has written authoritative books, first *serialized* in The New Yorker. (*The New York Times Book Review*)

6. The University of Southern California, whose next assignment will be a Rose Bowl date with Michigan, posted its 10th straight victory today by holding off Notre Dame, 17–13, on the 50th anniversary of one of college football's most *storied* rivalries. (*The New York Times*)

7. The child's mother *humored* her with a balloon.

8. The inventory shows we have some extra pencils; will that be the case when we *inventory* again in six months?

9. From the outside it looks like one of those television commercial homes, where the sun slants through *curtained* windows into a bright kitchen and a smiling family is eating breakfast so cheerfully that the aura of good will is overpowering. (*No-Fault Marriage*)

10. Maybe it's the black jerseys we wear or the team logo (an eye-*patched* pirate). (UPI)

11. If you *roughen* the surface, nobody will walk on it.

12. We can assume he was smart enough not to *hymn* praises to the Christmas tree's notoriously dropsical leaves or petals. (*The New York Times Magazine*)

13. After Smith returned to England, the princess became *detribalized* and married John Rolfe, the tobacco planter. (*The New York Times*)

14. Members of the party *caucused* for five hours.

15. No mumbo jumbo would *voodoo* Trumbo. (*The New York Times Book Review*)

16. The remains of five victims were flown from Spain to the Dover Air Base for *casketing* before being escorted to relatives, a spokesman for the base said. (AP)

17. He *quieted,* or at least forestalled, some premonitory rumblings of displeasure on the Hill. (*Newsweek*)

18. The president, *weekending* in Denver, Colo., said today . . . (CBS)

19. There are also some sheep in the area where the horses are *stabled.*

20. Because I drive to work on a country road, it is a good *commute.*

21. The mayor *essayed* a poem whose merits may be judged by the opening couplet. (*The New York Times Book Review*)

22. If we *weather* this crisis, we can stand anything.

23. Everything has to be *vouchered.* (*Centre Daily Times,* State College, Pa.)

24. Every time the professor *critiques* my work, I learn something.

25. The couple *backpacked* through the Adirondacks.

26. The big idea behind the San Francisco Bay Area Rapid Transit system was to *one-up* the automobile. (*The New York Times*)

27. The other was Hamilton Jordan, 32, the good-old-boy South Georgian who *blueprinted* and managed the president's campaign—and whose hopes for high station seemed to friends now to be in danger. (*Newsweek*)

28. Byrd, by contrast, is a master technician who built his authority on hundreds of small favors performed—and *index-carded*—during six years as party whip. (*Newsweek*)

29. After an education major is *certified,* he is allowed to teach.

30. Some people *muscle* their way through a crowd the way some people *barge* into a party uninvited.

31. The winds will *gust* up to 40 miles an hour tonight.

32. Anne Rupert, after *interning* with Jack Anderson and with Philadelphia Magazine, is on the news staff of the Asbury Park (N.J.) Press. (*Penn State Journalist*)

33. Picked to *helm* it as "editor-in-chief," with Barbara Howar and Charles Kuralt as on-air colleagues, was the obviously "rehabilitated" Rather. (*TV Week*)

34. A boat *crewed* by men and women will be entered in the rowing competition.

35. In the *siting* of sewage treatment plants, an electric power line, sludge disposal facility, or a variety of other agency decisions, what mechanisms are best for obtaining public input?

36. When the Navy creates a new command, it seeks good officers and enlisted men to *staff* it.

37. It has led to a 22 percent cutback in military manpower below the pre-Vietnam level, chronic recruiting difficulties, and a drift toward a heavily black army *officered* mostly by whites. (*The New York Times*)

38. Here—as Kate and Harvey try to *dialogue* with each other and break the need cycle—is a sampling of the fallout of their marital crisis. (*Newsweek*)

39. As the sand grains *avalanche* down the steep slope, they sometimes generate a high-pitched musical sound or a roar, and the dunes are thus termed "singing" or "booming" dunes. (*Smithsonian*)

40. Mario Andretti, the race car driver, is beyond *compare.*

41. On the eve of his ouster, Bhutto, 49, was *partying.* (*Newsweek*)

FOUR

Conventions

NOUNS AND PRONOUNS

As you learned in the last chapter, defining what a noun is can be tricky. Adhering to the traditional definition (*name of a person, place or thing*) leaves little room to maneuver words into a necessary function. If we accept *football* as a noun only, how could we economically describe the field on which the game of football is played?

Linguists say that a word is a noun when it can be used in certain areas of a sentence, such as the subject of a verb or as the object of a verb or a preposition. Break down the preceding sentence according to function, with stress on which words are nouns, and we would probably agree on every one. Here is the sentence again—with all nouns italicized:

> *Linguists* say that a *word* is a *noun* when it can be used in certain *areas* of a *sentence,* such as the *subject* of a *verb* or as the *object* of a *verb* or a *preposition.*

Now consider what influence some of those nouns had on other parts of the sentence. For one, the noun serving as the subject of the sentence influenced the verb. *Linguists* is plural (that is, more than one), so the verb must agree in number and person. *Person* used to be a confusing label in grammar, especially when applied to verbs. Traditionalists say there are six persons:

PERSON	SINGULAR	PLURAL
1	I say	we say
2	you say	you say
3	he, she, it says	they say

While there are six persons, there are only two verb forms you have to concern yourself with. Most verbs in the English language follow the same pattern—you add an *s* to form the third person singular, present tense. Disregarding for the moment irregular verbs and other tenses, you need to recognize only two forms: third person singular and all others. The only time you have to worry about a verb ending being influenced by a noun is when the noun is third person singular, present tense. Had *linguist* (meaning only one) been used in the example, the verb would be *says*.

Another word influenced by a noun in the sentence on linguists is the word *it*. Called a *pronoun* (*I, you, he, she, it, they,* for example), *it* takes the place of a noun. The noun determines whether a pronoun is singular or plural and masculine, feminine or neuter gender.

Carnegie Building is old; *it* was built early in this century.

In that sentence the pronoun refers to *Carnegie Building,* which is singular. Thus, so is the pronoun. The noun that influences the pronoun is called its *antecedent.* If the antecedent is plural, so is the pronoun.

Leaders of the hospital union said yesterday *they* would defy a restraining order obtained by the city.

They refers to *leaders.* The pronoun agrees with the noun. The most common pronoun error is not having the pronoun agree with its antecedent.

The girls' cross-country *team* has had difficulty in finding competition because of *their* winning record.

Their should be replaced by *its* to be correct.

The girls' cross-country team has had difficulty in finding competition because of *its* winning record.

Similarly:

T. Roger Smith of Cadbury told the *commission* the power company will take advantage of *them.*

The correct pronoun is *it.*

> T. Roger Smith of Cadbury told the commission the power
> company will take advantage of *it.*

However, because *it* is neutral and impersonal, some writers use the
word as little as possible. To avoid *it,* some writers would change the
sentence to:

> T. Roger Smith of Cadbury told commission *members* the power
> company will take advantage of *them.*

A plural noun allows the use of the plural—and more personal—*them.*
Another:

> Each little community had to have *their* own newspaper.

Correct:

> Each little community had to have *its* own newspaper.

An incorrect pronoun can be funny, as an advertisement from an X-
rated movie attests:

> Take *your* lover to see this film . . .
> Before *they* take someone else!! [Italics added.]

A long sentence gives rise to pronoun error because the writer often
forgets what he or she is referring to.

> The combination of renovation costs at Elmbank, a feared lack
> of control over operations and dwindling confidence in dealing
> with Willow Community Hospital officials finally prompted the
> Cadbury Medical Services Authority to put Elmbank behind
> *them* and build a new medical center in Cadbury.

Them was meant to refer to *Authority* (5 words back), but because *them* is
plural, it really refers to the last plural noun, which is *officials* (12 words
back). The wrong pronoun changes the meaning of the sentence. To be
correct, *it* should replace *them.*

Sometimes pronouns are used in a sentence other than the one in
which the antecedent appears.

> Among those rescued was *Mary Storms,* a 22-year-old secretary
> who had served as a volunteer at the post and married one of the
> defenders. *She* lost a leg and broke an arm during the bombing.
> *She* was several months pregnant but lost *her* child. *Her* husband
> has been killed.

Note, too, the pronoun agrees with its antecedent in gender (male, he; female, she; neuter, it). In that example all of the pronouns are female because they refer to a woman.

Sometimes pronouns refer to a noun ahead instead of back:

> When *they* got to the stream, the *campers* took off their boots.

Although a pronoun can refer to a noun in another sentence, the situation gets confusing when there is a noun in the same sentence as the pronoun but the noun is not the pronoun's antecedent. From *The Gannetteer,* a magazine published for employees of Gannett Co. Inc.

> A helicopter put Pribble on board. Because of *his* size, one of the crewmen had to make the flight to the hospital on a runner outside the bubble.

The writer intended the pronoun *his* to refer to *Pribble,* but *his* really refers to *one* in *one of the crewmen,* which caused Gordon V. Metz, the assistant news editor of the San Bernardino (Calif.) *Sun-Telegram,* to comment: "We put the crewman on the runner because of HIS size; we meant Pribble's." There is no sin in repeating a word when it will remove an ambiguous pronoun.

> A helicopter put Pribble on board. Because of Pribble's size, one of the crewmen had to make the flight to the hospital on a runner outside the bubble.

In fact, because listeners of radio or television news broadcasts have nothing in front of them to refer to, broadcast journalists use as few pronouns as possible. They favor repeating a word over using a pronoun. Given these two sentences

> President Monahan said he would announce his proposals on energy conservation later today. *He* said the proposals would make everyone unhappy.

broadcast journalists would write

> President Monahan said he would announce his proposals on energy conservation later today. *The president* said the proposals would make everyone unhappy.

Pronouns are used frequently in attribution tags because the writer does not want to repeat a person's name to the point of monotony. The caution is: Don't use too many pronoun attribution tags. Return occasionally with the person's name or some other clearly identifiable tag so the reader doesn't forget who's speaking. And if two direct quotations are separated by a paragraph that does not refer to the speaker, use the speaker's name in the paragraphs where he or she is quoted. It is disconcerting to meet a pronoun too far removed from its antecedent.

Also keep in mind that pronouns refer to the nearest noun. Confusion often results when another noun intercedes between an antecedent and its pronoun.

> Britain has agreed to sell to Egypt a highly advanced radar air defense *system* to double *its* holdings of ground-to-air missiles.

Such a sentence might make the reader reread to determine if *its* refers to *system* or *Egypt* (or, remotely, *Britain*). *Its* belongs to *Egypt*.

> Britain has agreed to sell to Egypt a highly advanced radar air defense system to double Egypt's holdings of ground-to-air missiles.

There could be ambiguity in these sentences because of the pronoun in the second sentence:

> The program allows students to spend three years at Houston in a liberal arts and pre-engineering program and two years at Texas State in specified engineering programs. *They* will receive degrees in the appropriate area from each school.

At first reading *they* seems to refer to *programs*. But *they* really refers to *students* near the beginning of the first sentence. The clearest way to begin the second sentence:

> The students will receive . . .

Similarly, a story about a person who died from gunshot wounds included the person's obituary. But the writer opted for a pronoun where the name of the victim should have been used to make clear who was being written about.

> Coroner Williams is awaiting the results of toxicology tests before making a ruling in the death.

> *He* was born in Cadbury . . .

He refers to the coroner, but the writer meant the victim.

Make sure the pronouns you use do have antecedents. Nothing can be quite as confusing as a pronoun with no clear antecedent.

> Breslin is on the list, he said, because he voted against a federal strip mine bill. Breslin said he did that because he feels *it* is a state, not a federal, function.

What *it* refers to is unclear. Even in the context of the story, the pronoun's antecedent was absent. I'll hazard a guess to make the sentence clear.

> Breslin said he did that because he feels regulating strip mines is a state, not a federal, function.

The second example:

> Both oppose right-to-work laws in Michigan; Simpson because she says *it's* unconstitutional, Williams because he doesn't believe *it* is a problem.

It's, because it is singular, apparently refers to the phrase *oppose right-to-work laws.* Opposing the laws is not unconstitutional nor is it a problem. If the writer had used the plural pronoun *they,* the reference to *laws* would have been clear.

> Both oppose right-to-work laws in Michigan; Simpson because she says they are unconstitutional, Williams because he doesn't believe there is a labor problem.

The second *it* has nothing to do with anything in the original sentence.

Overworking a pronoun—that is, using the same pronoun several times to refer to different nouns—can be confusing.

> According to police, Dennis, 21, got the cocaine into this country by putting *it* into a condom, tying *it* shut, and swallowing *it.*

To make clear there's been a shift in antecedents, repeat the new antecedent.

> According to police, Dennis, 21, got the cocaine into this country by putting it into a condom, tying the condom shut, and swallowing it.

A similar example:

> Such was the case last week when Mr. and Mrs. Thomas F. Williams of Pine Street filed suit against *their* neighbors, Mr. and Mrs. Donald Black, seeking to have *their* horse farm declared a public nuisance.

Dropping the second *their* in favor of using the possessive form of the antecedent makes the sentence clearer.

> Such was the case last week when Mr. and Mrs. Thomas F. Williams of Pine Street filed suit against their neighbors, Mr. and Mrs. Donald Black, seeking to have the Blacks' horse farm declared a public nuisance.

Equally confusing is this:

> Jones, only 5-feet-2, convinced his followers *he* was Christ, *he* said.

The pronoun in the attribution tag refers to the speaker the reporter is quoting. Maybe the reader will understand the *he* in *he said* does not refer to Jones. Then again, maybe the reader won't.

Too many pronouns spoil the flavor, especially if there is no antecedent because the writer used a pronoun to begin with.

> Acting under Jones' implied orders, *they* killed not because *they* had a fear of what Jones might do to *them* if *they* did not but because *they* had a pre-existing hostility toward society.

The sentence would be clearer if it had started like this:

> Acting under Jones' implied orders, *his followers* killed . . .

Pronouns can make murderers out of murder victims.

> Post-mortem stab wounds in the *victims* show that *they* killed with gusto.

> Post-mortem stab wounds in the victims show that *the killers* killed with gusto.

Still another problem with pronouns is using them indefinitely when it isn't necessary. Here is an example of a common usage:

> It will be cloudy and warm today.

Of course, there's nothing wrong with:

> Today will be cloudy and warm.

But some writers refuse to be direct, and they fall back on the indefinite pronoun, which creates vague sentences.

> It was figured the pay increases will total $232,131 a year, based on average salaries.

What does *it* refer to? What does *it* mean? What's wrong with

Pay increases will total an estimated $232,131 a year, based on average salaries.

Likewise, *there* (which is not a pronoun) is overused.

There was some snow in Arizona.

You can write

Snow fell in Arizona.

and

There has been a general increase in the number of reported rapes and attempted rapes at the university during the past three years.

What's wrong with:

The number of reported and attempted rapes at the university this year has increased during the past three years.

Finally:

It used to be that home fire warning devices were available only as part of extensive and costly fire alarm systems.

The *it* does nothing positive; get rid of it.

Home fire warning devices used to be available only as part of extensive and costly fire alarm systems.

Antecedents are not restricted to nouns alone. A phrase or clause can be an antecedent, which is the case in the following:

Imagine if *the error is made in the lead?* Here are two leads where *that* happens.

The italicized phrase in the first sentence can be substituted for the pronoun in the second.

Here are two leads *where the error is made in the lead.*

As you can see, it's more economical to use a pronoun in the second sentence.

PRONOUN FORMS

The form pronouns take depends on how and where they are being used in a sentence. Learning the various forms so that you do not write *hisself* for *himself* is a matter of rote. The personal pronouns used as the subjects of verbs are:

PERSON	SINGULAR	PLURAL
1	I	we
2	you	you
3	he, she, it	they

When used as objects, pronouns take these forms:

PERSON	SINGULAR	PLURAL
1	me	us
2	you	you
3	him, her, it	them

In their possessive form, pronouns look like this:

PERSON	SINGULAR	PLURAL
1	my (mine)	our (ours)
2	your (yours)	your (yours)
3	his (his)	their (theirs)
	her (hers)	
	its (its)	

The forms in parentheses are used in elliptic writing when the object referred to is known.

Is this your book?
No, it's hers. (No, it is her book.)

The apostrophe is not used to create the possessive form. That is a major exception to the convention of making the possessive form by adding *'s*. If you remember that possessive pronouns are possessive to begin with, you won't add *'s*. You don't have to make possessive what already is.

Reflexive pronouns reflect a noun already used to emphasize the noun.

The president *himself* will attend the security meeting.

Reflexive pronouns take these forms:

PERSON	SINGULAR	PLURAL
1	myself	ourselves
2	yourself	yourselves
3	himself	themselves
	herself	
	itself	

Relative pronouns—pronouns that relate a subordinate clause to a main clause—are: *who, which, that, what.*

The student *who* loves writing will write all the time.

The college, *which* already offers 100 majors, is considering adding another one.

This is the house *that* Jack built.

I see *what* you mean.

Only *who* changes form according to pattern. As a subject it is *who;* as an object, *whom,* and in the possessive, *whose. Whom* is losing favor and some consider it pretentious.

Who do you believe?

Old-guard grammarians prefer:

Whom do you believe?

Any time you are unclear if it should be *who* or *whom* in an interrogative sentence, recast it as a declarative sentence and see the function *who* takes.

You do believe who.

In that sentence *who* functions as an object and the standard form is *whom.* But it is a form slowly disappearing and the choice between *who* and *whom* now appears to be more dependent on who your editor is, not your grammarian.

The last set of pronouns, called *demonstrative,* are *this* and *that* with the plural forms *these* and *those.* Generally, *that* refers to something already mentioned and *this* refers to something coming up. (Distance is another criterion; something close takes *this;* something farther away takes *that.*) The best example of this-that usage comes from former President Richard M. Nixon. When asked a question at a news conference, he often began his response:

Let me say *this* about *that* . . .

This stood for his response to come; *that* for the question already asked.
That is overused or misused when *it* would carry the meaning.

He said that *that* is a good proposal.

Change the second *that* to *it* both to avoid the *that that* construction and because *it* satisfies the meaning. The remaining *that* can be deleted in the interest of economical writing.

He said it is a good proposal.

Underline the correct form of the pronoun so it agrees with its antecedent.

1.   Anyone who has ever attempted to wend *his* or *her/their* way through football traffic knows how difficult the experience can be.

2.   The Spanish press, snarled by a web of restraints on what *it/they* can publish, faces new problems following the arrest of two journalists three days ago.

3.   Council decided to increase *its/their* budget.

4.   The horse by the fence is a trotter. You will never see *him/her/it* with a saddle on.

5.   Wanamaker's will display *its/their* new fall fashions at a special preview Saturday.

6.   The board of trustees held *its/their* first public committee meetings Thursday and Friday.

7.   The school board canceled its June 16 meeting. *It/They* will meet June 23 to give the budget final approval.

8.   Williams had predicted the shutdown would fail and he blamed the news media for promoting *it/them*.

ANSWERS

1.	his or her	5.	its
2.	it	6.	its
3.	its	7.	It
4.	it	8.	it

NOUN OVERUSE

One of the most distracting abuses in our language is noun overuse, that piling up of noun after noun after noun to function as one noun. There are various explanations for its cause. Jacques Barzun says it is a "by-product of scientific writing" based on the scientist's attempt "to remain impersonal and detached." Writing in the language quarterly *Verbatim,* Bruce D. Price suggests noun overuse is an attempt to fuzz meaning, not improve it—similar to the Newspeak described by George Orwell. Price, who has dubbed it *Nounspeak* in his article "Noun Overuse Phenomenon Article," says the result has created a "clunk-clunk" sound in our language.

We readily accept nouns in pairs, although functionally what we have are an adjective and a noun. Some—such an *air bag, aircraft carrier, space ship, authorization procedures, budget analysis*—are fairly easy to swallow. They are perceived as one word. But when we get to three words and more, the overuse becomes abrasive: *budget appropriation procedures, world-food problem, core curriculum innovation package, space ship booster rocket ignition system.* The paired nouns, for the most part, are really converted nouns plus prepositional phrases: *a bag of air, a carrier for aircraft, a ship for space, procedures for authorization, an analysis of the budget.*

In the interest of economical writing, writers turn many noun-prepositional phrase combinations into paired nouns. The problem arises when writers have what they feel are too many prepositional phrases: "The U.S. Air Force's course in the mechanics of equipment in aircraft fuel systems." Instead, this writer creates (courtesy of Price): "U.S. Air Force aircraft fuel systems equipment mechanics course." What the writer has really created is a monster, a noun overuse that defies comprehension. The writer even ignores the possessive form of Air Force, which compounds the abuse.

Before you put nouns in front of other nouns as modifiers, make sure there is not an acceptable adjectival form that would function better. Don't write *Congress budget* when *congressional budget* is better. Don't be charmed by noun upon noun upon noun upon noun. Two nouns in a row are not likely to be unclear; but when you get to three and more, problems will arise. Given such monstrosities to deal with, journalists should break them down for the reader, not repeat them. Chapter 8, which is on meaning, provides more examples of noun overuse and its related fuzziness. Here are a few examples:

market-economy developing
  countries
age-status system
public-achievement ratio
boat topping paint
watch, quarter, and station bill
amphibious assault ships
nuclear-powered guided missile
  cruiser
medical school entry
public work project employment
death instinct concept
group hospital expense policy

premiums disability benefit policy
automatic premium loan option
marital interaction processes
middle-class divorce rates
peer group permissiveness scales
additional living expense insurance
business risk and insurance
  planning
family purpose doctrine
mercantile open stock burglary
  policy
community problem areas

Some of those might be acceptable because not every word in them is a pure noun. But what seems to be an infinite number of words preceding any noun is pollution enough for me.

And, if you believe that only scientists, sailors, sociologists, insurance companies, lawyers, educators and bureaucrats are guilty, I leave you with this example—from a sports story:

> suicide squeeze bunt single

It would have been better if the batter had struck out; the writer did.

VERBS

Verbs make sentences go; all other parts of speech are secondary to the verb. The noun alone carries little in a sentence; the verb, everything. You can write about cars, trucks, councils and Congress, but what readers or listeners want to know is: What happened? The verb tells them. Nouns are meaningless without verbs. *Congress* tells us nothing. *Congress approved* or *Congress didn't approve* has meaning. Verbs generate an action no other part of speech can. Verbs (defined in their broad sense to also include *verbals,* derivatives of verbs) do a tremendous amount of work in our language. Look at the verbs in this sentence:

> Although reporters have been *imprisoned* in the past, they have almost invariably been *charged* with specific violations of rules *imposed* on the press.

Here is a verbal acting as a modifier:

The carefully *worded* statement said that the protest note, delivered last Sunday in Rome, does not allege a threat on the aide's life.

Do not mistake *delivered* for a verbal; it is a verb. What you have is elliptic writing in which the subject and auxiliary verb are understood. Written in full the sentence would include this construction:

. . . protest note, *which was* delivered . . .

By deleting the pronoun *which* and the auxiliary *was,* we get a more economical sentence.

Once you understand the structure of verbs you will understand verbals, which will in turn expand your knowledge of functional grammar. The principal parts of a regular verb are:

PRESENT TENSE	PRESENT PARTICIPLE	PAST TENSE	PAST PARTICIPLE
treat	treating	treated	treated
wound	wounding	wounded	wounded
impose	imposing	imposed	imposed

The present participle is formed by adding *ing* to the present tense (drop the final *e,* if there is one); the past participle is the same as the past tense.

The present participle, when used as a verbal, is called a *gerund* ("*Running* for office is a chore"); the past participle is called a *participle* ("*Improved* conditions help"), while a third verbal is called an *infinitive* ("*To play* well is reason enough *to play*").

Here are some verbals functioning as nouns:

To impose on others is not a good habit.

Imposing on others is a sign of bad manners.

The *wounded* were taken to a hospital.

As modifiers:

The *wounded* soldiers were taken to a hospital.

The *imposing* mountain left us no choice but to detour around it.

The *inspired* soldiers regrouped and fought off the *invading* troops.

Examine your writing for possible verbals buried in uneconomically written sentences, such as:

The soldiers *who were wounded* were taken to a hospital.

By transferring *wounded* to before the noun, you can reduce the length of the sentence and increase its force.

The wounded soldiers were taken to a hospital.

Don't bury strong words in weak clauses.

VERBS AND AGREEMENT

First, let us review how verbs agree with their subjects in number and person. Remember that while there are six persons, there are only two verb forms in the present tense.

PERSON	SINGULAR	PLURAL
1	I write	we write
2	you write	you write
3	he, she, it writes	they write

You may believe that even if a verb does not agree with its subject, the meaning of the offending sentence is still clear. That is not true. Note that the meaning of the following sentences is determined by the number of the verb which is determined by the subject of the sentence (italicized).

Racing *cars* are fun.

Racing cars is fun.

Here are some troublesome constructions.

Singular subjects linked by *and* or commas and *and* (which creates a compound subject) usually take a plural verb.

The Senate and the House *debate* different bills at the same time.

According to the party chairman's letter, the date, time and place of the county committee meeting *have* yet to be set.

However, if each noun is considered as an individual, then a singular form of the verb is used.

Each bill and resolution before Congress *needs* the approval of both houses.

Every boy and girl in the playground *is* where he or she *wants* to be.

The tip-offs are *each* and *every*. They tell you if the idea of individuals is being conveyed.

Singular subjects connected by *and* but referring to the same person or thing take a singular verb.

The governor and state party leader *is* thinking about new rules for primary elections.

The Thomas Paine Cottage and museum in New Rochelle *contains* a smaller, square tombstone representing Paine's original burial site.

In the first sentence the governor is also the party leader. In the second the cottage and museum are the same building, not two buildings. The cottage is a structure that houses the museum.

Or, nor and *but* are connectives that signal the singularity, not the plurality, of your subjects.

The Senate or the House *finds* fault with every proposal the president has.

Neither the president nor his secretary *is* accepting telephone calls today.

Not only the president but his wife as well *likes* to watch television.

In *either-or* and *neither-nor* constructions, the subject nearest to the verb determines the number of the verb.

Neither the president nor his *advisers were* available for comment.

Neither the advisers nor the *president was* available for comment.

Some editors would require rewriting because of the awkwardness of the form.

The president and his advisers were not available for comment.

Rewrite cautiously, though, because emphasis can be changed—as is the case in my rewrite.

Confusion results when the subject appears plural because of a modifying phrase attached to it.

The House in addition to the Senate *is* in session.

The City Council, along with the Planning Commission, *makes* decisions on zoning.

The houses in addition to the land *were* sold.

Formerly chief executive officer of Merritt, Wolfson—together with other members of his family and associates—*controls* about 40 percent of the conglomerate.

These constructions again are examples of what some editors might convert to compound subjects. Again the caution is that rewriting might change a desired emphasis. If you stick with these constructions, the way to determine the number of the verb is to drop the modifying phrase so it is clear what the subject of the sentence is.

The way to keep boys happy is to feed them lots of ice cream.
The *way is* to feed them lots of ice cream.

One of our members conducts herself improperly.
One conducts herself improperly.

Seventh Army officers believe that the use of hard drugs and marijuana has been reduced.
Seventh Army officers believe that the *use has* been reduced.

The sentence about the Seventh Army comes from a newspaper. It had to be corrected for use in this book. The error is very common, usually made with a singular subject modified by a plural prepositional phrase. Although not as common, the reverse construction also causes problems.

Members of the Department of Agriculture's Soil Testing Group *was* at the field today.

Correctly written, it would be:

Members of the Department of Agriculture's Soil Testing Group *were* at the field today.

Collective nouns take a singular verb when considered as one unit and a plural verb when considered by their individual parts. Five such nouns are jury, family, faculty, majority, and number.

The majority of the country *supports* the president. (One unit)
The majority of the voters *are* undecided. (Individuals)

The jury *is* out. (One unit)
The jury *were* divided on the verdict. (Individuals)

My family *meets* once a year at Posties Grove. (One unit)
My family *disagree* on whether to hold the reunion on a Saturday
or a Sunday. (Individuals)

Some people (myself among them) find plural verbs with singular-sounding nouns to be strange. Thus, wherever the plural is called for, we write:

Members of the jury were divided on the verdict.

That makes the subject clearly plural.
   The word *number,* according to H.W. Fowler, usually follows this rule: If it is preceded by the definite article *the,* it takes a singular verb; preceded by the indefinite article *a,* a plural verb.

The number of people who live in the West Ward is high.

In that sentence the stress is on *number* not *people.* But if the stress was on the prepositional phrase, then the verb would be plural.

A number of people who live in the West Ward are Welsh.

To be sure, substitute the word *numerous* for *number of,* and if the sentence makes sense, go with the plural verb.

Numerous people who live in the West Ward are high.

That is nonsense. But:

Numerous people who live in the West Ward are Welsh.

that makes sense.
   Plural numbers when considered as a unit take singular verbs.

Five million dollars *is* all that *is* needed to finish the project.

Nearly $1 million *was* lost in a similar asparagus strike.

Forty hours of work *keeps* Brewer busy but 50 *isn't* enough for Kellner.

Two years *is* the longest time we can go without that new highway.

He said the wealthiest 1 percent of the population gets 25 percent of the tax benefits and the wealthiest 14 percent *gets* 53 percent of the benefits.

Three percent *is* hardly much of a pay raise.

Singular verbs also follow *everybody, nobody, somebody, anyone, anybody.*

Government officials are careful to avoid creating a feeling that *anyone* but the terrorists *is* responsible for the bombings.

Any and *none* march to a different drummer and can take a plural or a singular verb. At one time *none* always took the singular, the convention being that it meant *not one* or *no one.* Now the convention calls for a singular or plural verb, depending on what the writer wants to indicate. *The New York Times* tells its reporters that if they want to indicate the idea of one, use *not one* or *no one* but not *none.*

It always takes a singular verb regardless of the verb's *complement* (the word or words that follow a verb to complete a predicate construction).

It *is the mistakes* that bother her.

On the other hand, the verb number that follows *there* is determined by the complement.

There *are* 50 *reasons* why Jewells won't; there *is* one reason why Jewells will.

There *has* been a steady *increase* in promotions.

There *have* been many *promotions.*

There *are* still serious *problems.*

There *are* also new *problems* for river communities that used to aid each other in fighting fires but now have nowhere to cross.

Some words that look plural because they end with *s* are really singular and are treated as such. They include: *economics, phonetics, news, mathematics, linguistics, semantics, energetics, pedagogics, aesthetics.* Still others, such as manners, are always plural. A dictionary tells when a plural-looking word takes a singular verb. A dictionary will also tell you which *s*-ending words can go either way, such as *acoustics.*

Acoustics *is* a subject I don't understand unless I'm in a classroom where the acoustics *are* bad.

You might also want to follow Philippines with a plural verb. To remember that the word is singular, keep in mind the country's full name is Republic of the Philippines. Thus, this headline, referring to the government, is correct:

PHILIPPINES, GIVING NO EXPLANATION,
DENIES RE-ENTRY TO AP BUREAU CHIEF

The following sentences show other plural-sounding and plural-appearing words that are usually treated as singular.

The United Mine Workers represents miners.

Sears sells many products, from bedclothes to toggle switches.

Paramount Studios releases seven films a year.

The United Steelworkers bargains for job security.

Metro-Goldwyn-Mayer was a big movie studio at one time.

There are also some Latin words whose plurals are not formed by adding *s* and therefore their plural forms appear singular. Perhaps the commonest of them is *media,* as in *news media.* Often a journalist (who should know better) will incorrectly write or say:

The news media *is* now a national business of concentrated ownerships.

That usage is becoming more acceptable, but if you are strict, it should be:

The news media *are* now a national business of concentrated ownerships.

The singular form is *medium.* Another:

The larvae of the worm *gets* into the child when the child kisses the family pet.

Larvae is plural and the sentence should read:

The larvae of the worm *get* into the child when the child kisses the family pet.

The singular is *larva.*

Then there is a Latin word that does not follow the preceding pattern—*datum, data.* Although plural, *data* is being used more as either plural or singular.

The data are ready.

The data is ready.

A dictionary will usually settle any doubt about words with unusual plural and singular forms.

PRONOUN-VERB AGREEMENT

A pronoun, as you already know, agrees with its antecedent. Likewise, any verb should agree with the pronoun's antecedent. The disagreement results because not all pronouns have plural forms.

> The provost instructed the vice president for undergraduate studies to initiate a study of the effectiveness of the university's so-called service courses, which *includes* English composition.

The error is in the italicized verb. The antecedent of the pronoun *which* is *courses,* which is plural. Thus, the verb must be plural.

> . . . courses, which *include* English . . .

In the following sentence, locate the italicized pronoun's antecedent and then determine if the verb agrees.

> His explanation was that journalism education often inspires a high ideal among students *that* gradually disappears the longer students work in the real world.

The antecedent of *that* is *ideal* and the verb *disappears* does agree. Examine this sentence for the same problem.

> Her book was written for the intelligent student and layman *who does not have a background in the basics of psychology.*

What you first have to determine is what the italicized clause modifies—*student and layman* or just *layman.*

> Her book was written
> for the intelligent student
> and {for the}
> layman who does not have a background in the
> basics of psychology.

The clause modifies *layman* only. Had it modified *student and layman,* the correct verb would be *do.* Elliptic writing caused the initial confusion and should be avoided in ambiguous situations. Had the writer used the bracketed phrase, ambiguity would have been avoided.

Keep the pronoun's antecedent clearly in mind at all times. Sometimes a word, phrase or clause intervenes between the antecedent and the pronoun. The intervening clause in the following is italicized:

Maybe it's the black jerseys *the football team wears* that make it appear formidable to its opponents.

That refers to jerseys, which is plural and which makes the verb following the pronoun (*make*) also plural.

Then there are those sentences in which the noun at the end of a prepositional phrase, not before it, serves as the antecedent of the pronoun. For example:

Murder is one *of those horrors* that causes trusting people to lock their doors at night.

If you are confused about what the pronoun refers to, dump the phrase.

Murder is one that causes trusting people to lock their doors at night.

That sentence makes no sense because the pronoun's antecedent is missing.

Murder is one of those horrors that cause trusting people to lock their doors at night.

As you look at the full sentence again, you can see the pronoun *that* refers to *horrors,* not *one.* Thus, the verb is plural. Sometimes the correct solution isn't clear-cut. Sentences 6 and 17 in the following exercises test the problem.

EXERCISES

Underline the correct number of the verb.

1. The president and the pope *is/are* meeting today.

2. A moderate number of deficient students *was/were* well distributed among school facilities in the area.

3. Neither of the two men *has/have* met before.

4. There *is/are* millions of fish in the sea.

5. It *is/are* the problems of grammar that *interests/interest* us.

6. This is one of those sentences that *serves/serve* to show two things—relative pronouns and agreement.

7. There *is/are* less to complain about in the recent assessment than there *was/were* in the previous one.

8. A number of the survivors *was/were* taken to the closest hospital.

9. The cost of the project is $5 million; *it is/they are* going to be hard to raise.

10. News *is/are* what reporters are always seeking.

11. Books *is/are* more popular today than they ever were.

12. Neither the lamb nor the mice *is/are* aware of the rain.

13. Neither the mice nor the lamb *is/are* aware of the rain.

14. Their efforts to hide the facts from the public *is/are* disappointing.

15. Williams said that current academic policy plans and projects of educational policy *was/were* evaluated.

16. A group of Johns Hopkins University scientists *is/are* studying human arteries to see whether arterial patterns can contribute to disease.

17. If you *is/are* one of those students who *wants/want* an extra writing course, this is your chance.

18. He doesn't know that the subject and verb *doesn't/don't* agree.

19. He is being closely watched because, to a considerable extent, the future of Quebec and of Canada, *hangs/hang* on his success or failure as leader of the French Canadian majority.

20. On a purely practical level, a number of scientists *has/have* complained about the time and talent that *has/have* been wasted in futile efforts to replicate fraudulent or shoddy experiments.

ANSWERS

1.	are	7.	is, was
2.	were	8.	were
3.	has	9.	it is
4.	are	10.	is
5.	is, interest	11.	are
6.	serve	12.	are

13.	is	17.	are, wants
14.	are	18.	don't
15.	were	19.	hangs
16.	is	20.	have, have

VERBS—TENSE

Tense means time. There are six tenses in the English language: present, past, future, present perfect, past perfect, future perfect. None are hard to understand and learn.

Present tense deals with today or with conditions that exist when a news story is written and will continue to exist even if the subscriber doesn't read the paper for 10 hours after the story was written. For example:

> A geographer said yesterday that public schools no longer teach students the effect climate can have on a country's economy.

Some news stories (usually analyses, in-depth articles and features) are written in the historical present, which provides both a sense of immediacy and continuity to a story. Present tense gets the nod in broadcasting because the viewer or listener sees or hears the news report. Most newspaper stories, on the other hand, are written in the past tense because most news is past; it happened before it was reported.

> Three cars *collided* at the intersection of Broad and Centre streets today, Cadbury police said.

The headline on the preceding would be written in the historical present because one purpose of a headline is to give immediacy to a story. Thus, the headline might say:

3 CARS COLLIDE
AT INTERSECTION

A major problem between present and past tenses results when the unthinking journalist puts too much stress on past tense at the expense of logic. Clearly, when you are quoting someone who spoke at a meeting, the speech or attribution tag (usually *said*) is in the past tense. After all, the speaker said it—past tense, once and done. But what if the speaker was talking about an on-going project?

> "I don't like the way the bypass is coming," Williams said; "it looks as if it will ruin our environment."

Would you change the direct quotation to the past tense? Of course not. You know Williams is speaking of his position on the bypass; his position is unlikely to change unless the bypass changes. The problem arises when the journalist paraphrases a speaker. Perhaps the journalist has a grammar book that says when a writer converts direct discourse (as it is called in grammar books) to indirect discourse, the tense of the verb should be changed one degree (e.g., from present to past). Following that rule would give us:

> Williams *did* not like the way the bypass *was* coming because, he said, it *looked* as if it would ruin the area's environment.

By changing the tense, you have changed the meaning. The italicized words must be present tense: *does, is, looks.* Using past tense where logic calls for present tense could confuse the reader.

> Williams *believed* the bypass was a good project until the federal government became involved.

My immediate reaction is, doesn't he believe that anymore? If Williams still believes that, you've done him and the reader a disservice. (It is safer, by the way, to write: Williams *said* he believes . . . Who really knows what or how anyone believes?) Here's another:

> Secrecy in the American system of justice *was* dangerous, he said.

> Secrecy in the American system of justice *is* dangerous, he said.

The standard example on this problem is the paraphrased or indirect quotation of this:

> "The world is round," Williams said.

> Williams said the world *was* round.

If you remember that absurdity, you will be able to apply the logic to other occasions.

The tense problem also comes up when journalists are writing about reports and studies. The incorrect tendency is to write:

> The study *said* housing for the elderly is not needed for a majority of the region's senior citizens.

But long after the story appears, the study will be saying the same thing. If the study is superseded, then the superseded one no longer rates present tense treatment. That belongs to the current study.

Journalists favor the historical present when writing in-depth articles. The logic is they are quoting long-standing positions on issues, positions not likely to change as soon as the ink is dry on that day's newspaper. However, if you begin an in-depth article in the present tense, do not shift to the past without good reason. If you mix the tenses, you'll confuse the reader because you will have mixed the time. Don't write in one sentence

Jones *says* government is important to all people.

and in another

Jones *said* people are important to government.

The reader will want to know if the past tense of the second statement means Jones no longer believes that. If that is the case, state it clearly.

Similarly, this example from a newspaper story raises doubts:

Both the current president, Lawrence E. Walsh, and the lawyer who succeeds him this week, Justin A. Stanley, *had* those credentials.

How the two attorneys lost *those credentials*—if that was the case—was not made clear in the story. That is probably because they didn't lose *those credentials*. Correctly written, the sentence is:

Both the current president, Lawrence W. Walsh, and the lawyer who succeeds him this week, Justin A. Stanley, *have* those credentials.

When a condition is unlikely to change between the time a statement is made and the time it appears in print, use the present tense. In the following sentence the italicized words should be *are, has*.

Miller noted further that the two cities' museums and operas *were* comparable, but that Des Moines *had* nothing equivalent to Munich's gardens.

The past tense of *be* (*was* and *were*) is a popular but erroneously used form, especially in accident stories. Reading such a story, the reader learns that five people were injured. Preceding the list of the names of the injured is:

They *were:*
—Mary Sue Harper, 22, 213 Mountain Ave . . .

By using the past tense the journalist has made the accident a fatal one. If it had been, the journalist wouldn't have written:

Dead *were:*

The past tense of *be* is also sometimes misused in political stories where a vote is reported.

Opposing the senator were five of his colleagues. They *were:*

The first *were* is correct; it indicates a past action. The italicized *were,* alas, sounds as though the five colleagues are dead (perhaps for opposing the senator?).

Journalists are haphazardly aware of the *are-were* problem. In one paragraph of a news story appeared:

The pressmen charged with rioting, inciting a riot and destruction of property *were* [followed by their names]. All except Mr. —————, who *lives* in this city, *are* from . . .

A marvelous resurrection if there ever was one.

Journalists also use the past tense in some instances that might suggest the present. In an obituary the journalist might write:

Funeral arrangements *were* incomplete.

That tells the reader that at the time the obituary was written, the funeral arrangements were incomplete, but they might have been completed between the time the story was written and read later in the day. On the other hand, the survivors of a dead person still exist and should be so treated.

There *are* six survivors.

Present-past tense misuse also occurs in the caption of a photograph. Captions are written in the present tense because they are describing a photograph the reader can see as he or she reads—just like film in a television newscast. Sometimes, though, a caption writer mistakenly adds a past time element to the present tense sentence, leaving:

> Councilman Thomas F. Williams *discusses* taxes with Mayor
> Harry J. Anderson *yesterday.*

The *yesterday* saps the present tense of its immediacy. Better to find
another sentence or a subordinate clause (in the past tense) for the time
element. A sentence by itself:

> The discussion *occurred yesterday.*

A subordinate clause:

> Councilman Thomas F. Williams discusses taxes with Mayor
> Harry J. Anderson, who *yesterday opened* his office to unscheduled
> visits by councilmen.

What you want is a construction that puts a past tense element with a
past tense verb while preserving the present tense immediacy of the
caption.

Similar to incomplete funeral arrangements, a hospitalized person's
condition does not rate the present tense. If a hospital reports a person's
condition at 10 a.m. for a story you write at 11 a.m. but will not be
read by most people until 5 p.m., the present tense can trip you.

> Williams *is* in good condition, a hospital spokesman said.

What happens if between 10 a.m. and 5 p.m. Williams' condition turns
critical? Or, worse still, what if he dies? To cover yourself, use the past
tense *and* a time element.

> Williams *was* in good condition at *10 a.m. today,* a hospital
> spokesman said.

Some journalists might also write:

> Williams *was* in good condition, a hospital spokesman said at
> 10 a.m. today.

The future tense is used to write about events that are going to happen.

> The president *will address* Congress tomorrow night.

In American idiom, the present tense is sometimes substituted for the
future.

> Tomorrow *is* Sunday. (Tomorrow *will be* Sunday.)

> The Steelers *play* the Packers tomorrow. (The Steelers *will* play the Packers tomorrow.)

> Cadbury City Council *meets* tonight to discuss taxes.
> (Cadbury City Council *will meet* tonight to discuss taxes.)

Two more examples, the first one from a story published on a Tuesday:

> The tuna-porpoise issue is at the top of the agenda as the House *returns* Wednesday from a five-day Memorial Day recess.

> On Thursday, lawmakers *turn* their attention to the president's proposal for a Department of Energy.

This example is based on a story written for Thursday afternoon use:

> Hogan *concludes* his 10-day visit to South America Friday and *flies* to Mexico for an overnight stop and more talks with Mexican leaders on the oil situation. He *returns* to the United States Saturday.

The major problem with future tense arises when it is misused in the conditional mood, a matter I will explain presently.

The past tense can also be used to refer to the future, as in this sentence from L. M. Myers:

> If you tried in Phoenix tomorrow, you could probably find one.

While there is a future sense to the sentence, it comes from *if,* not the verb. It is idiomatic. Most editors would probably change the sentence to:

> If you try in Phoenix tomorrow, you can probably find one.

The present perfect tense is used to describe an action that begins in the past and continues to the present or almost to the present. The present perfect is also used to refer to an indefinite time in the near past. The present perfect is identified by the auxiliary verbs *has* and *have,* which are singular and plural respectively, placed before the past participle.

> The Interior Department *has estimated* that the total quantity might be as high as 9.4 trillion cubic feet, about 40 percent as great as the largest discovery on Alaska's North Slope.

The sense of that sentence is similar to the historical present tense. While the Interior Department may have made the estimate only once, it is a continuing estimate that will probably be restated if someone asks. The estimate was made in the past but continues through the present.

> The prime minister said the hijackers confessed their mission was ordered by the militant rebel leader whom the king *has accused* of waging a campaign of subversion against his regime.

When that sentence was written, the king had not retracted his accusation, so it was assumed the accusation was a continuing feeling on the king's part.

Here is another sentence showing action that occurs over an indefinite time:

> In the five years Thomas F. Williams *has been conducting* the Famous Symphony Orchestra, it *has increased* in size and quality.

The first verb is written in the progressive form (identified by the *ing* ending). The second verb is present perfect and indicates an indefinite time. When the orchestra increased in size and quality cannot be pinned down to a particular time, so the present perfect is used. The use of the present perfect to indicate an indefinite time is frequent in newspapers and broadcasting. Here is a lead on a *Washington Post* story that never gave a definite time for the action.

> The Virginia highway department *has approved* a contract for the construction of a $25-million, six-lane elevated highway alongside Arlington County's Crystal City high-rise development to connect Shirley Highway with National Airport.

If approval had come yesterday—or some other definite time—the tense would have been simple past.

> The Virginia highway department *yesterday approved* a . . .

In the interest of tight writing or when the time element isn't important, journalists use the present perfect in leads, which eliminates the need for the time element until, usually, the second paragraph.

> New York City's banks *have received* a new proposal from municipal officials on how the city would repay nearly $1 billion in short-term notes. The proposal calls for an immediate offering of $300 million in Municipal Assistance Corporation bonds and a subsequent issue of some kind of new city bond.
>
> The plan, the details of which *were disclosed yesterday,* combines elements from the city's original plan on how to pay off

the notes and the counterproposal from the banks, which *became known a week ago.*

Whenever a time element appears in the second paragraph the writer used past tense. But the lead, which has no time element, has a present perfect verb. Also note the use of the present tense every time the proposal is cited.

A different tense creates a different meaning, as shown in this sentence taken from a story about a 1-year-old unsolved crime:

That arson case *has* never been solved.

The sentence suggests the police are still investigating. But the simple past would close the books.

That arson case *was* never solved.

Instead of present perfect, a journalist might also use the present tense.

That arson case *remains* unsolved.

If a definite time is given or suggested, scrap the present perfect in favor of simple past.

Each state representative, this year for the first time, will have a full-time secretary (representatives *have shared* secretaries *in the past*).

Correctly tensed the sentence in parentheses would read:

. . . (representatives *shared* secretaries in the past).

Another example:

Jonathan Culler *has recently received* the Modern Language Association's James Russell Lowell Prize, a $1,000 cash award given for an outstanding literary or linguistic study.

Because *recently* (like *in the past* in the other example) suggests a definite time, write:

Jonathan Culler recently *received* the . . .

The past perfect tense denotes an action completed in the past prior to a subsequent completed past action. It is identified by *had* plus the past participle.

The Steelers' defense *had* not *permitted* a touchdown in 22 quarters until the Houston Oilers *scored* on Sunday.

The first verb is past perfect tense because it indicates action completed before the second verb, which is past tense. Here is another example:

> City Council *had agreed* to bring legal action against the contractor if he did not fix the problem. But by the time council *met* again, the contractor *had fixed* the problem.

What you have are three past actions, with the most recent one (*met*) rating past tense treatment and all other actions rating past perfect. But the past perfect has its flaws when adhered to blindly.

> Police said the rifle used by Williams in last Wednesday's shooting *had been* legally *owned* by Black.

The writer of that sentence used past tense attribution (*said*), which left an earlier action. What is not clear is whether the earlier action is a past action—Does Black still own the gun? The sentence suggests he does not. The tense, thus, hinges on that question and not one of past action and prior past action. The problem relates to an earlier discussion on tenses in paraphrased or indirect quotations. And the solution is the same: Don't use the past tense when the situation still exists, that is, is not past.

> Police said the rifle used by Williams in last Wednesday's shooting *is* legally *owned* by Black.

The past perfect can result in much confusion. Here is a one-paragraph newspaper story in which the past perfect implies someone has changed his mind, although the story does not make that clear.

> Members of the Cadbury Volunteer Fire Company did not plan a petition drive against a rumored adult bookstore in Cadbury, a fireman said today. Owners of the building *had insisted* an auto parts store, not a bookstore, would occupy the building next to the fire hall.

Because I believe the owners of the building did not change their position, I would convert the verb in the second sentence to present perfect.

> Owners of the building *have insisted* an . . .

Another situation of two or more subsequent past actions that seems to call for past perfect is the sports event. There you have action every minute (or so we are supposed to believe). Does that then require using past perfect to describe the action in the first inning after using past for the eighth inning? No. Here, though, is an excerpt from a story that did that:

> For just eight innings, New York *had been* almost helpless against the left-handed deliveries of Frank Tanana. The Yankees *had managed* only two hits and a walk while the Angels—who swept three games from New York—*had clobbered* Catfish Hunter for six runs on nine hits in six innings. The first two California runs came on homers by Dave Collins and Tony Solaita, a former Yankee.
>
> The Angels *had added* two runs against Ron Guidry in the eighth, so the Yankees found themselves down by eight as they came to bat in the ninth. Thurman Munson grounded out and a stream of fans started for the exit.

Apparently the writer was trying to develop the action in such a way that when he shifted to the simple past, the reader would then be up to date and at the critical juncture of the game. But simple past would have worked effectively. Below is the excerpt in simple past; decide if there is a difference.

> For just eight innings, New York was almost helpless against the left-handed deliveries of Frank Tanana. The Yankees managed only two hits and a walk while the Angels—who swept three games from New York—clobbered Catfish Hunter for six runs on nine hits in six innings. The first two California runs came on homers by Dave Collins and Tony Solaita, a former Yankee.
>
> The Angels added two runs against Ron Guidry in the eighth, so the Yankees found themselves down by eight as they came to bat in the ninth. Thurman Munson grounded out and a stream of fans started for the exit.

The error of using the perfect form of the verb with a time element occurs in the past perfect, as it did in the present perfect.

> Earlier *last weekend,* the Coast Guard *had estimated* that up to 500,000 gallons of oil had leaked from the barge.

The past perfect would be correct if the next paragraph said the Coast Guard changed its estimate.

> But later the Coast Guard estimated the total leakage at twice that.

But if the Coast Guard did not later change its estimate, the simple past suffices.

> Earlier last weekend, the Coast Guard *estimated* that up to 500,000 gallons of oil had leaked from the barge.

By changing to past tense, one past perfect (*had leaked*) remains, which is correct. Here is another sentence with the past perfect unnecessarily used because there is a time element with the verb.

> Jackson said negotiations *had started* about *three months ago*.

Put into the past tense:

> Jackson said the negotiations *started* about three months ago.

Unlike future tense, which indicates an action that will occur at some time coming up, the future perfect combines the future and the past by indicating the completion of a present, on-going action at a specified time in the future. It is formed by *will have* plus the past participle.

> The president *will have been* in office two years when Congress convenes next month.

> By the time the secretary of state returns from Africa, he *will have made* 15 trips to foreign countries.

> When this book is completed, I *will have used* thousands of sheets of paper.

Simple future conveys a different meaning; it conveys the idea that something is going to happen.

> When this book is completed, I will use thousands of sheets of paper for another book.

Another verb form that sometimes appears in news stories is the *progressive*. It indicates an ongoing condition or a condition continuing over an unspecified time.

> PRESENT PROGRESSIVE
> A small group of professors *is resorting* to full-page advertisements in leading newspapers to defend academic freedom.

> PAST PROGRESSIVE
> Jones *was running* for president until he heard Smith wanted the job.

FUTURE PROGRESSIVE

The new senator *will be representing* our district during a critical time.

PRESENT PERFECT PROGRESSIVE

Kellner, who *has been recovering* from an arm operation, said she was not aware of the most recent proposal until asked about it today.

PAST PERFECT PROGRESSIVE

He *had been writing* poor stories—until someone showed him the mistakes he was making.

FUTURE PERFECT PROGRESSIVE

When the new Congress convenes, he *will have been running* affairs around here for 35 years.

REVIEW

Here is the conjugation of the verb *talk* in all tenses. Note that only in the third person singular of the present and the present perfect tenses is the verb form inconsistent with all other persons and numbers. Knowing that makes the entire process much easier to learn.

PRESENT	PAST	FUTURE	PRESENT PERFECT	PAST PERFECT	FUTURE PERFECT
1 I talk	talked	will talk	have talked	had talked	will have talked
2 you talk	talked	will talk	have talked	had talked	will have talked
3 he *talks*	talked	will talk	*has* talked	had talked	will have talked
1 we talk	talked	will talk	have talked	had talked	will have talked
2 you talk	talked	will talk	have talked	had talked	will have talked
3 they talk	talked	will talk	have talked	had talked	will have talked

VERBS—MOOD

Verbs come in three moods—indicative, imperative and subjunctive. Most verbs are indicative, which is more easily defined by telling you what imperative and subjunctive are.

The *imperative* expresses a command or an entreaty.

Come here.

Leave the room.

Take this with you, please.

It is the language of cookbooks ("Mix well for 10 minutes") and textbooks, not of most news writing.

The *subjunctive* expresses, among other things, improbability and condition contrary to fact.

If I *were* you, I'd take the money.

Obviously, I'm not you, so it is a condition contrary to fact.

If this sea *were* empty, we could walk to Europe on dry land.

Obviously, such a condition is improbable.

Rudolf Flesch sees little use for the subjunctive. Flesch says:

> Another grammatical distinction that's dying out is the use of the subjunctive. In fact, for most practical purposes, the English subjunctive has been dead and buried for centuries; but the old-guard grammarians pretend it's still alive in "condition contrary to fact."

Flesch dismisses any distinction between *shall, will* and *should, would.* There I draw the line, not because I'm an old-guard grammarian but because I see a distinction worth preserving. First, let us examine condition contrary to fact:

If I *were* a door, I would be closed all the time.

If I *was* a door, I would be closed all the time.

Except for the verb, no difference exists between those sentences; the meaning remains the same. It doesn't matter whether I use *were* or *was;* I still can't become a door. The statement still remains a condition contrary to fact, obvious on its face regardless of the verb's mood. But here is an instance where the conditional seems best to preserve a meaning or a status:

> The president proposed a plan that *would* reduce taxes for all but the very wealthy.

The mistake often made is the substitution of *will* for *would,* which changes the conditional to the indicative. To use *will* in that sentence would give the president authority beyond the Constitution. He needs a willing Congress and his own signature to change the *would* to *will*.

Similarly, bills are introduced in Congress, debated, and then approved (or rejected). In the following instance, the Senate has approved a bill and sent it on to the House. Telling what the bill is supposed to do (on the condition it is approved) a *New York Times* reporter wrote:

> Another provision of the bill *would* require for the first time personal financial reports from the president, vice president, other high federal officials and members of Congress. These *would* be filed with the controller general The reports *would* include the source of any income of more than $100 as well as any gifts, including transportation or entertainment, aggregating $500 from a single source [italics added].

Perhaps one way of avoiding the "old-guard grammarian" label is to use the phrase *if passed* somewhere in the story and then use *will* where *would* would normally appear. But I still believe it makes positive something indefinite. That would also happen in the following sentence if *would* were changed to *will:*

> Georgia *would* be called "The Peanut State"—a tribute to president-elect Jimmy Carter's crop—under a resolution introduced in the state Senate Wednesday [italics added].

VERBS—VOICE

Verbs have two voices, active and passive. The active is preferred in all writing and broadcasting because it puts the doer of the action out in front. Here is an active verb:

> The Senate *defeated,* 61–30, an amendment that would have required coal-mine operators to meet the final safety standards a year sooner than the bill required.

The doer of the action, *The Senate,* precedes the action, *defeated.* Here is that sentence again, only in the passive voice. Notice how the sentence limps along and hides the doer of the action and the action.

> An amendment that would have required coal-mine operators to meet the final safety standards a year sooner than the bill required *was defeated by the Senate,* 61–30.

The journalist's penchant to get the news out front in any one sentence sometimes forces the use of the passive voice and sometimes results in an absurd sentence, such as this:

> Ra Tech teaching assistant Penny Chaucer, 28, was discovered pinned beneath a desk by firemen.

The firemen really ought to be fighting a fire or inspecting the damage caused by the explosion, not pinning female teaching assistants beneath desks—which is what the sentence says. The passive voice forces the doer of the action into a prepositional phrase that is difficult to fit harmoniously into the sentence. The sentence is short enough that the active voice will not bury the news.

> Firemen discovered Ra Tech teaching assistant Penny Chaucer, 28, pinned beneath a desk.

Sheridan Baker's criticism of the passive voice tells what's confusing about the preceding examples.

> The passive voice puts the cart before the horse: the object of the action first, then the harnessing verb, running backwards, then the driver forgotten, and the whole contraption at a standstill.

If Baker's sentence makes you ill at ease, fine; it's supposed to. You're not supposed to feel comfortable with the passive voice.

Here are two writers writing about the same thing. The first used passive voice while the second chose active.

> Corporate control of newspapers and networks, pressures for all newspapers to cut back and use cheap syndicated news, no focus on intense local issues, "constitutional numbness in the post-Watergate news" *were* all *cited* by Bagdikian as contributing to the paralysis, apathy, and paranoia felt by society in relationship to the news media.

> Bagdikian *cited* examples of the Nixon administration's open attacks on the press, the first court-ordered censoring in the Pentagon Papers case, attempts to reduce public broadcasting funds, and FBI activities later lied about under oath.

While neither sentence is a paragon of beauty, the second one is easier to grasp because it is written in the active voice. The advice to any writer is to write in the active voice. It is forceful and direct. Besides, active voice verbs are shorter, which makes for tighter sentences. Here are three paragraphs from a student's paper; they are followed by a rewrite—in the active voice.

> Two teachers were hired at the Corl Street Elementary School.
> One will teach fifth and sixth grades, making the class size

26 students per class, 10 less than the previous size of 72 students between two teachers. A teacher was also hired for the first and second grades. Before, there were three teachers for 92 children, a class size of 30.67 students a class. The new teacher will bring the size of each class to 23 students, the average elementary class size in Cadbury.

At Park Forest Elementary School a teacher was added to teach the third and fourth grades, where previously four teachers were divided among 165 students. The new teacher will bring the class size to 27.

The rewrite shifts to the active voice and cuts out 12 words. In addition, another fact was added, which took 12 words.

The board hired two teachers at the Corl Street Elementary School—one for the first and second grades and one for fifth and sixth grades. The additional fifth-sixth grade teacher will reduce class size from 36 to 26 students, which is one under the ideal set by the board last month.

The additional first-second grade teacher will reduce class size from 30.67 to 23, which, according to board member Barbara Dillon, is the average for those grades throughout the district.

The third teacher, who will work at Park Forest Elementary School, will reduce the size of the third and fourth grades from 41 to 33.

Then there is this additional advice: Don't switch voices, especially in the middle of a sentence. Doing so is similar to violating parallel construction.

The president approved the bills, but the resolutions were ignored.

In that sentence our focus has been shifted from *president* to *resolutions,* yet we are concerned with the actions of the president, not the inaction and passivity of the resolutions.

The president approved the bills but ignored the resolutions.

That maintains the focus the sentence started with. Here is one that doesn't:

Alaska scored the national high of $10,178 and the national low of $4,575 was registered by Mississippi.

See how disconcerting it is to begin a sentence with one focus only to be jarred when the focus changes. Correctly written:

Alaska scored the national high of $10,178 and Mississippi reg-
istered the national low of $4,575.

Passive voice is acceptable when we want to focus on the object of the
action, not the doer. It appears most often in leads when the doer is not
as important as what has been done.

A prominent Arizona contractor and a plumber *were arrested*
today and charged with first-degree murder and conspiracy in
the death of Don Bolles, the investigative reporter whose car
was bombed last June 2 [italics added].

Here is an active voice lead to consider:

Cadbury City Council last night approved an ordinance that
bans dogs from all sidewalks during daylight hours.

There is nothing wrong with that lead; it is short enough that the reader
will not be lost among the imponderables. But what if we are more concerned with the ordinance than the approval?

An ordinance banning dogs from all Cadbury sidewalks during
daylight hours was approved by City Council last night.

The passive voice gets the ordinance up front. Regardless of which lead
we use, the headline writer will use the historical present tense for immediacy.

COUNCIL APPROVES DAYLIGHT BAN ON DOGS

Headlines being short and to the point, the problem of focus seldom
arises. But in a lead it can. Which of the following provides the correct
focus?

An automobile struck and killed a 10-year-old Cadbury boy last
night.

A 10-year-old Cadbury boy was struck and killed by an automobile last night.

Journalists don't care about automobiles; they care about people. The
focus of the story is the boy, not the automobile, so the passive voice is
justified. To continue the focus, however, does not mean you have to
continue using the passive voice. The second paragraph:

Johnny Johnson, the son of William and Mary Johnson, ran in
front of a car driven by Harry Collins, Schuylkill, in the 500
block of Sunset Road, police said.

Usually a writer will shift to the active voice in the second paragraph. Take note, also, that the first name given in the second paragraph is the name of the victim. Some reporters writing accident stories put the name of the driver first while the focus of the story (as established in the lead) is the victim.

Here is a paragraph in which the passive voice puts the focus or stress where the writer wants it:

> In 1976 nearly 36,400 seats were used on a seasonal basis by non-students. An additional 18,260 seats were sold to students for each game.

The stress is on the number, then the buyer. Sometimes there is no practical subject to head up an active verb.

> Thomas F. Williams of Madera was admitted to Cadbury Hospital Tuesday.

You don't want to say

> The Cadbury Hospital admitted Thomas F. Williams of Madera Tuesday.

or

> Cadbury Hospital officials admitted Thomas F. Williams of Madera Tuesday.

Here is a story's lead with its opening sentence in the passive voice:

> The battle lines are clearly drawn. Bill Koll makes no effort to conceal what his Penn State wrestlers have to do to beat Clarion. Bob Bubb, his counterpart, is equally open.

To require the active voice would rob the opening sentence of its simplicity.

> Bill Koll of Penn State and Bob Bubb of Clarion have clearly drawn the battle lines.

Not all passive verbs have to remain passive; they can be changed without any recasting of the sentence. The solution: Find an active verb to substitute for the passive.

> The Shamokin Area School Board last night *was given* a budget.

Retaining the same subject, you can still write that sentence in the active voice:

The Shamokin Area School Board last night *received* a budget.

Be cautious of the false passive. If you remember that a passive verb acts on the subject, you will not write:

John Rucker was awarded the Golden Gloves Trophy last night.

Rucker received the trophy; it is the trophy that *was awarded.*

Passive voice, incidentally, is formed by adding the correct tense form of *be* to the past participle of the verb, giving you: *is grown, was killed, were injured, will be approved, has been postponed.*

EXERCISE

Convert the following news story into the active voice.

Americans were told last night by President Monahan that the United States is confronted with a crisis as serious as war and can be met only by inconvenient and painful sacrifice.

A doubtful audience was told by Monahan that the unbridled consumption of past years cannot continue, that the crisis is real and that Americans are to support a program he will detail to Congress tomorrow night.

A week-long blitz intended to sell Congress and the people on a series of stringent steps to reduce gasoline consumption 10 percent by 1985, slash total energy growth by more than half to less than 2 percent a year and cut in half the use of imported oil was launched by the president's talk.

His speech was laced with strong language—terms like "national catastrophe," "a problem unprecedented in our history," "the moral equivalent of war."

Less than half the nation was shown in a recent Gallup poll considering the energy shortages "very serious." The skepticism Monahan faces was acknowledged by him.

The people have no stomach for higher gas taxes was stated by members of Congress, just back from their Easter recess.

Here is the rewrite:

President Monahan told Americans last night a crisis as serious as war confronts the United States—a crisis that can be met only by inconvenient and painful sacrifice.

Monahan told a doubtful audience that the unbridled consumption of past years cannot continue, that the crisis is real, and that he will detail to Congress tomorrow night a program Americans must support.

The president's talk launched a week-long blitz intended to sell Congress and the people on a series of stringent steps to reduce gasoline consumption 10 percent in 1985, slash total energy growth by more than half to less than 2 percent a year and cut in half the use of imported oil.

Monahan laced his speech with strong language, using terms like "national catastrophe," "a problem unprecedented in our history," "the moral equivalent of war."

Less than half the nation considers the energy shortages "very serious," according to a recent Gallup poll. Monahan acknowledged the skepticism he faces.

The people have no stomach for higher gas taxes, said members of Congress, just back from their Easter recess.

STRONG VERBS

Journalists should also use strong verbs. Any form of *be* is considered taboo, except where it links a subject and its modifier (a *complement*). So while *be* has its place, it is not in this clumsy sentence:

> Morocco *is to add* six missile boats to its navy, doubling the size of its combat fleet.

You have at least two choices: You can change the italicized part to *will add,* or if that's too definite for what might be a proposition rather than a fact, try *plans* in place of *is*. Here is another example:

> Reasons given for moving *were,* for the home owners, health, and for the renters, security.

It is a terrible sentence all around. The fact that the writer inverted normal order got him into the mess. Rewritten:

Home owners said they would move for health reasons and renters said they would move for security reasons.

Do not be deluded into using some form of *be* just because it tightens a sentence. A student converted this strong verb

Boyer *posted* a 6–3 record last season.

into this limp one

Boyer *was* 6–3 last season.

There is a virtue in economy, but there is also a virtue in strong verbs.

VERB CLASSES

Be is a linking verb; when one of its forms is used alone, it connects the subject and whatever follows.

The sky is blue, the fields are green.

There is no action in that sentence, just the description of a condition.

The other verb classes are transitive and intransitive. *Transitive* verbs are followed by an object.

The senator sought *assurances* the bill would not be voted on unless he was present.

Assurances is the object of the verb *sought*.

Intransitive verbs do not have objects; there is no noun to receive the action started by the subject because one isn't needed.

The horse neighs.

That sentence is complete; it needs nothing more to fill it out, unlike the sentence with the transitive verb. You could not write:

The senator sought.

Anyone reading that would ask: What did the senator seek?

Dictionaries tell which verbs are transitive and intransitive and which can go either way. If a sentence sounds wrong, it could be because you misused an intransitive or transitive verb.

IRREGULAR VERBS

All principal parts of regular verbs are formed the way you were shown earlier in this chapter. But we also have irregular verbs, irregular because they do not follow the normal pattern. Children just learning the language are the most common culprits in not recognizing irregular verbs. ("I falled down" is a phrase parents hear often from young children.) The children are imitating what appears to be a logical language pattern that really shifts helter-skelter; thus, there is nothing intuitive to guide them through the irregularities. Eventually, though, they learn them—or change them. The approximate 200 irregular verbs in our language may disappear someday. But because they haven't yet, you have to know them or be able to recognize them. Here are some of the more common ones; any good dictionary gives them all.

PRESENT	PAST	PAST PARTICIPLE
arise	arose	arisen
awake	awoke	awakened
be (am, is, are)	was, were	been
bite	bit	bitten
catch	caught	caught
do	did	done
drink	drank	drunk
drove	drove	driven
eat	ate	eaten
find	found	found
get	got	got (gotten)
go	went	gone
hit	hit	hit
know	knew	known
lead	led	led
leave	left	left
lie	lay	lain
mean	meant	meant
put	put	put
ring	rang	rung
say	said	said
tear	tore	torn
write	wrote	written

FIVE

Modification

POSITIONING
MODIFIERS CORRECTLY

Modification problems arise when modifiers are misplaced. By now you should have a clear idea what modification is. You have already seen in Chapter 2 how ideas can be expanded through modification from a basic pattern (subject-verb) into the most complex structure. The place of modification, which can be done with a word, phrase or clause, is crucial. Consider this:

> They maintain that the highway would create a barrier separating Crystal City from the adjoining residential area.

That sentence tells little. Why would the highway create a barrier? And what is so significant about Crystal City that it can't be separated from adjoining residences?

What is lacking is modification at the right place, an explanation of the significance of the highway and Crystal City. The significance cannot be explained two paragraphs later, for you have no guarantee the reader will continue reading past the unexplained information. Nor can you explain the significance two paragraphs earlier in the story because the explanation will lack a context. What must be done is not only modifying but modifying at the right place and time. Here is the sentence as it appeared in *The Washington Post:*

> They maintain that the highway, *sections of which are to be elevated on walls 30 feet high,* would create a barrier separating Crystal City, *with its shops and offices,* from the adjoining residential area [italics added].

Even before we read that the highway would become a barrier, we get a description of the highway, a description telling why the highway would become a barrier. And, even before we read what Crystal City would be separated from, we read what Crystal City contains. When we finish the sentence, we know that the people who live in the adjoining residential area will be separated from Crystal City where they shop and work.

It cannot be stressed enough that modifiers, be they single words, phrases or clauses, must be placed as close as possible—if not next to—to the word or phrase they modify. If they can't be closely placed, rewrite the sentence. Here is a headline, its modification improperly placed:

3 PEOPLE SEIZED
WITH A PIPE BOMB

No, police aren't using pipe bombs instead of revolvers, although that's what the headline says. Actually, the people had the pipe bomb—or so the police say. Correctly modified, the headline would have said:

3 PEOPLE WITH A
PIPE BOMB SEIZED

Some editors, however, would forbid that headline because the prepositional phrase (*with . . . bomb*) is split over two lines—a taboo at some newspapers.

Similarly, the following sign on an interstate highway approaching Baltimore contains misplaced modification:

NO TRUCKS ON EDMONDSON AVE.
IN BALTIMORE CITY OVER ¾ TON

It should say:

NO TRUCKS OVER ¾ TON ON
EDMONDSON AVE. IN BALTIMORE CITY

An editor once argued that the important proximity in any sentence is between the subject and its verb, not the noun or verb and its modifiers. That results in sentences like this:

> Opposition was expressed *to this plan* when it was learned the water level of the dam might go up.

Actually, two clauses are out of place. The italicized one modifies *opposition;* the adverb clause (*when . . . up*) modifies the verb *expressed.* Putting all modification in its place results in:

> Opposition to this plan was expressed when it was learned the water level of the dam might go up.

Following the "rule" of keeping the subject and its verb as close as possible results in sentences that are more awkward than the preceding.

> A *bill* was introduced in February in the state House of Representatives *that stated the methane should belong to the state.*

The italicized clause modified *bill*—yet we must read 10 words before we find out what the bill is about. Here is a rewrite:

> In February, a bill stating that the methane should belong to the state was introduced in the state House of Representatives.

Now everything is in its place.

Sometimes it is not a simple matter of moving a modifying clause next to the word it modifies. Sometimes only a full rewrite can save a sentence.

> Generally, the *requirement* in cases in which the family chooses not to have the body embalmed is *that the final disposition of the corpse must occur within 12 to 72 hours of the time of death.*

There is too much modification in that sentence and it is made worse by the weak verb *is.* The solution is subordination—a complex sentence.

> Generally, when the family chooses not to have the body embalmed, the law requires that the corpse be disposed of within 12 to 72 hours of the time of death.

Now everything is where it belongs; the sentence has a strong verb (*requires*) and is six words shorter than the original. Usually, though, modification misplacement is not as far off base as the preceding. Here is a more typical error:

The idea occurred to Dr. Thomas to *alleviate this obsession with the self* one day at a zoo in Tucson, Ariz.

The italicized clause in the preceding modifies *Thomas* but it should modify *idea*. Therefore, the clause belongs next to *idea*.

The idea to alleviate this obsession with the self occurred to Dr. Thomas one day at a zoo in Tucson, Ariz.

As in an earlier example, another benefit in moving one modifying clause is that it gets another (*one day . . . Arizona*) near to what it modifies—*occurred*.

In improving the placement of modification, you will find that some sentence structures sound better than others. Here is a misplacement:

I couldn't let the *opportunity* pass *to work for any newspaper*.

One ragged rewrite would be:

I couldn't let pass the opportunity to work for any newspaper.

But even though the modifying infinitive clause is next to the word it modifies, the cluster of verbs (*let pass*) is awkward, primarily because the object of *let* is not close to that verb.

I couldn't let the opportunity to work for any newspaper pass.

Sometimes all the moving around in the world won't save a sentence. Try more precise words.

I couldn't pass up the opportunity to work for any newspaper.

It is important, then, to view the whole sentence and not just parts of it as you restructure it. The proximity of objects to their verbs is as important as the proximity of modifiers to the words or clauses they modify.

Sometimes a misplaced adverb creates illiterate sentences.

Turn *on* it.

Put *down* it.

Daddy's always knocking *down* me.

I'm going to close *up* that.

Those examples come from the mouth of a 3½-year-old child. But a college student produced the following:

Let me look the book through.

The student's error was converting a preposition into an adverb. Her request should have been:

Let me look through the book.

The 3½-year-old will someday correctly say:

Turn it on.

Put it down.

Daddy's always knocking me down.

I'm going to close that up. (I'm going to close that.)

Another misplacement put a high school teacher out of work when all he did was quit coaching. A student referred to him as:

former coach and biology teacher

To get the teacher back in the classroom but keep him out of coaching, the structure should be:

biology teacher and former coach

DANGLING MODIFIERS

All modifiers have that mischievous habit of appearing in the wrong place. When they do, they are dangling—just hanging there not clearly attached to what they modify. For the most part, their misplacement is more humorous than damaging. If they damage anything, it is the writer's credibility with readers. The readers may pause, chuckle, and then continue. But they will also question the writer's attention to the writing before them. If the readers sense a sloppy writer, they may stop reading.

The problem of dangling modifiers often arises because writers want to say too much in one breath and forget how they've started a sentence. They get into a jam because they don't like to write simple and direct sentences or because they are too lazy to rewrite poor sentences. To them every sentence must not, as a matter of policy, follow the normal subject-verb-object pattern. Sentence variety is desirable, as long as it is not achieved at the expense of clarity. Here are some examples of dangling modifiers.

Running through the woods, the low branches were not seen by the boy. (That says the low branches were running when it was really the boy.)

As a former university student returned to Cadbury, his local memory extends beyond the period of his 12½ years with the business. (That produces a memory with a college degree.)

As a Unitarian, I want to ask you about your church. (The speaker is not a Unitarian; he is asking a question of a Unitarian. This is a common speech error.)

Entranced, the fire was watched by the arsonist. (Fires don't do that.)

To win a football game, the ball must cross the goal line. (Actually, it's the team that must get the ball across the goal line.)

A free-lance writer and editor, the author's work on Anderson's illustrations has been supported by a grant from the American Council of Learned Societies. (The phrase modifies *work,* not *author's.* This, too, is a common error. The same magazine that produced that example also had this one, which is correct: "A reporter for *The Washington Post,* Michael Kernan often writes on American life-styles.")

As a large corporation, the goal is to maximize profits. (The writer was so slipshod, she never used the word the clause is supposed to modify.)

Not all dangling modifiers appear at the beginning of sentences.

Such a case caused a typical example of strained police-press relations earlier in the day, he said, *involving two suspects wanted for robbery and murder.*

The modifying clause goes with *case* and should follow it immediately.

Such a case, involving two suspects wanted for robbery and murder, caused a typical example of strained police-press relations earlier in the day, he said.

The absent-minded use of a pronoun can create a dangling modifier. In an early draft of this book, I wrote:

In its infancy, the telegraph rate for news stories was $5 a word.

Was I writing about the infancy of telegraph rates? No; I was writing about the infancy of the telegraph. But that isn't what I wrote. This is what I meant; this is what I ultimately wrote:

> In the telegraph's infancy more than a century ago, the rate for news stories was $5 a word.

You should understand that while the error is labeled *dangling modifier,* the word being modified can also be considered out of place. To fix the error, you can move the word modified or the modifier. In the first example of this section, correcting the error would have been a matter of moving the modified word.

> Running through the woods, the boy did not see the low branches.

Technically, the modified word is misplaced in this case.

The second way of correcting a dangling modifier is moving the modifier. The Unitarian sentence suffices.

> As a Unitarian, I want to ask you about your church.

To fix that, move the modifier.

> I want to ask you, a Unitarian, about your church.

Now the modifier is properly placed. Think as you modify and danglers won't hang your credibility.

OTHER FAULTS

Some writers pile a long list of modifiers in front of a noun. The result is a monster.

> *Majority-supported university residence hall* rules that prohibit door-to-door canvassing do not abridge freedoms guaranteed by the First Amendment.

The student who wrote that could have dropped some of the modifiers and brought in the information in later paragraphs. Thus:

> University rules that prohibit door-to-door canvassing in residence halls do not abridge First Amendment freedoms.

Another problem is using a modifier in a first reference without first introducing information to provide a context. In a court case a student, in a first reference to a custody agreement that was being disputed, wrote:

A 1973 custody agreement . . .

Besides suggesting that 1973 was a vintage year for custody agreements, it also suggests there were other agreements, say, in 1970, 1975, and so on. The proper phrasing:

A custody agreement reached in 1973 . . .

There is a difference in meaning and it was the latter meaning the student was after. A few extra words are better if they create a more precise meaning.

A similar fault is using a possessive form in first references, resulting in phrases such as "last night's meeting" before informing the reader or listener there was a meeting last night.

Sometimes the close-as-possible guideline is not followed for idiomatic reasons. We begin our mornings with a *hot cup of coffee* instead of a *cup of hot coffee*. Some people would rather wear an *old pair of glasses* than a *pair of old glasses*. And few speakers say they are going shopping for a *pair of new shoes;* they say a *new pair of shoes*. Acceptable or not, idioms should usually be ignored in writing. To my ear an idiom sounds all right when spoken, but to my eye an idiom looks strange when written.

WORDS AND PHRASES

ARTICLES

The difference between *a(an)* and *the* is the difference between a general reference and a definite one. *A(an)* is an indefinite article usually used in the first reference to something.

A violent storm caused millions of dollars in damage as it plowed through Watkins Island late yesterday afternoon.

The, on the other hand, is a definite article and whatever *the* refers to should have been previously mentioned or be generally familiar to most readers. Thus, the next paragraph in the violent storm story:

The storm started with soft winds that quickly built up to hurricane force, ripping up trees and blowing roofs off houses.

Here is an example of *the* incorrectly used (the report referred to has already been explained in a preceding paragraph):

> The report recommended that local government not develop an elderly housing project because *the* survey indicated no need for such an undertaking.

The writer was on firm footing when he used *an* before *elderly housing project;* there was no specific project. But he slipped on *the survey* because it was the first reference. Seeing such a construction, the reader is likely to return to the preceding sentence or paragraph to find out what survey the writer is talking about. Imagine if the error is made in the lead! Here are two leads where that happens:

> *The* decline of daily newspapers in Pennsylvania is due to family problems, a changing economy and too many dailies to begin with, a journalism professor said yesterday.

> *The* breakdown of small-town identity has caused *the* decline in the number of daily newspapers across Pennsylvania, a journalism professor said yesterday.

All italicized *the's* should be replaced with *a.* The writers of those leads assumed the reader was familiar with newspaper decline and identity breakdown. The reader was not; he or she had to be introduced to the subjects.

Introduce an issue or topic with *a(an).* Once done you can refer to it with *the* in all other references in that story. *A(an)* is usually correct in leads. It is the lead that introduces a subject to a reader, as in the first example of this section—the storm story. Here is a lead with two *the's* that could be dropped (dropping one also gets rid of a preposition):

> The Cadbury School Board last night approved *the* hiring *of* three teachers to relieve *the* overcrowded conditions at two elementary schools.

The *the* that begins the lead is correct because *the* is often used in first references to subjects or issues very familiar to readers. Cadbury taxpayers don't have to be told about the Cadbury School Board. There is only one. With all omissions:

> The Cadbury School Board last night approved hiring three teachers to relieve overcrowded conditions at two elementary schools.

Similarly, *the* can be used in first reference to long-standing organizations:

The Federal Bureau of Investigation

The Congress

The AFL-CIO

The University of Maryland

The president of the United States

To use *a(an)* would suggest there is more than one of each of the preceding, which isn't so.

Issues that have been in the public domain or are continuing news stories don't usually need *a(an)* because of the assumption the public is reading right along.

The on-going controversy between Cadbury City Council and the Cadbury Planning Commission took a new turn last night.

Likewise:

The war in Vietnam . . .

The Watergate scandal . . .

And people who are well known and in the public view a lot are usually *the* references.

"I don't think a vice president will ever be given a serious job by a president," said Arthur Schlesinger Jr., *the* historian [italics added].

What you must remember is what you are referring to.

The death of a Kansas man

A death in the family

The is used in first references when the noun it modifies is specifically identified immediately.

Rightist artillery bombarded leftist positions in *the* mountains *east of Fez* today.

The Fittleton was sailing to Hamburg, West Germany, on a goodwill visit after participating with other allied nations in *the* NATO exercise, "Teamwork '76," off *the* coast *of Norway*.

> The spokesman gave no indication how quickly indictments could be presented to *the* grand jury *that has taken evidence in the case.*

Here are four paragraphs modeled after a newspaper story. Only one *the* is misused. Identify it.

> Jack Monahan, describing himself as a participant in a "family affair" to win the presidency, had some harsh words for his father's opponent Friday.
>
> Monahan, in a press conference preceding the rally on his father's behalf, said President Williams is running "an absolutely filthy campaign."
>
> Monahan, at the rally, said he expected personal attacks on his father because he is the candidate.
>
> "But I take offense when President Williams cuts down my mother and my brother Ed," he said.

The misused *the* is in the second paragraph. Because the writer was making a first reference to *rally,* the correct article is *a.*

Some writers drop *the,* much to the consternation of some editors. I am a *the*-dropper, meaning I *usually* write:

> Council agreed . . .
>
> Congress approved . . .

However, I wouldn't drop *the* before *House of Representatives* or *General Assembly.* It rubs my ear the wrong way.

Whether to use *a* or *an* gives some writers trouble. Generally, *a* precedes words that begin with a consonant sound while *an* is used before words beginning with a vowel sound. Sound is the key. The most confusion results with words that begin with *h.* If *h* is pronounced, use *a;* unpronounced, use *an.*

> A *h*ouse is not a *h*ome but it is an *h*onor to own one.

The italicized letters are the first sounds pronounced and determine whether you use *a* or *an.*

ADJECTIVES

Adjectives are not common to news stories because they can interfere with a reporter's "objective" account of an event or an issue. Describing a school board meeting, a reporter once wrote:

> In a stormy session last night . . .

The entire phrase (*in a stormy*) was removed because it is opinionated. Later, someone who was at the meeting said that for that particular school board, the meeting was relatively calm. The reporter who covered the meeting had never attended any of that board's previous meetings.

If not opinionated, adjectives are unnecessary or vague. They add words to a sentence without enhancing meaning. Some of the adjectives (italicized) in the following sentences are examples of opinion, waste or vagueness.

The previous day had been one of those *cool, crystal* times.

Zonal disputes impair global solutions.

Thousands of *beautiful* coeds attend the university.

On this day, however, haze dulled everything to a *fuzzy* pastel.

These are *critical* times.

Political investigations are always interesting.

Stars gleamed like *spikey* chips of ice.

The *frail* man walked across the street.

Notwithstanding the *widespread* reliance on the tractor, systems involving the *extensive* cultivation of the land do have *certain* disadvantages.

A *faithful* dog is better than no dog at all.

A buffalo hide covered the *wiry* corpse.

The sun filtered through *drab* curtains.

A *heavy* snowfall was recorded last night.

It is difficult to latch on to those adjectives with a firm sense of what they mean. A heavy snowfall in Miami, Fla., may not measure the same as a heavy snowfall in Laramie, Wyo. Miami natives, no doubt, would consider two inches heavy; Laramie residents probably wouldn't notice a snowfall until it measured a foot.

Adjectives of color (*red* barn, *green* grass) and number (*11* council members, *three* senators) provide concrete descriptions and are more acceptable. Also acceptable are those adjectives whose descriptive powers are neutral enough not to interfere with a story, such as *presidential* race, *North American* diplomats, *Midwestern* politicians, *downtown* businessmen, *congressional* sources, *governmental* (or *government*) agencies, *martial* law, *automatic* lights.

Any adjective is probably acceptable if it's backed up with an explanation.

> The president may resign and the vice president is gravely ill.
> There are *critical* times such as the nation has not seen since the Civil War.

Such a sentence probably would appear in an editorial rather than a news story. But whether you're writing a news story, an editorial or a feature story, use few—if any—adjectives.

Adjectives (and adverbs) come in three degrees—*positive, comparative* and *superlative*.

POSITIVE	COMPARATIVE	SUPERLATIVE
wise	wiser	wisest
smart	smarter	smartest
weak	weaker	weakest

As you can see, the ending of each is different, depending on the degree. Adjectives in the comparative degree add *er* to the positive form; in the superlative, *est*. There are irregularities, such as:

POSITIVE	COMPARATIVE	SUPERLATIVE
good	better	best

Adjectives of more than one syllable do not usually show their degree by ending. Instead, we put *more* and *most* before the positive form to indicate, respectively, comparative and superlative.

POSITIVE	COMPARATIVE	SUPERLATIVE
astonishing	more astonishing	most astonishing

Treated that way, multisyllabic adjectives don't become tongue-twisters.

> Your teacher is *astonishinger* than mine.

That doesn't mean *more* and *most* don't work with one-syllable adjectives. However, their use is primarily for emphasis.

> Who is wiser? She is *more wise* than I.

Likewise, short two-syllable adjectives don't require *more* and *most*.

POSITIVE	COMPARATIVE	SUPERLATIVE
pretty	prettier	prettiest
funny	funnier	funniest

Comparative degree is used when comparing two persons or things; superlative is used with three or more.

She is *wiser* than I.

Of the five, she is the *wisest*.

Remember: When you use the superlative, you are placing someone or something in a category by itself. The person or thing has no equal.

ADVERBS

Adverbs share some of the characteristics of adjectives: They can be stated in degrees (*wisely, more wisely, most wisely*); their use steals strength from verbs (the way adjectives obscure nouns); they are not common to news stories, and they are easily identified by function. While adjectives modify nouns and other adjectives, adverbs modify verbs, verb forms and adjectives.

WITH A VERB
He *ran quickly* down the field for a touchdown.

WITH A VERB FORM (VERBAL)
The *easily constructed* building can be used as a second home.

The secretary of state's quest for peace in the *racially troubled* country has been upstaged by a surprise summit of rebel leaders.

WITH AN ADJECTIVE
My dog is *adequately faithful*.

The *ly* adverb form is not often used in news stories. The sentence about the secretary of state is a good example of when to use it. However, like some adjectives, the *ly* form can be more vague than concrete, more interpretive than descriptive, which could raise the issue of unobjective, unbalanced or unfair reporting.

The candidate's forces scrambled *grimly* today along the slopes of the Allegheny Mountains.

The president *exuberantly* predicted victory.

In both instances the adverbs are open to debate. In the first example the candidate's forces could argue that what appeared to be grim to the reporter was seriousness on their part. In the second some observers could argue that the exuberance was conduct typical of a candidate in a tight race.

Journalists, who are supposed to be as fair as is humanly possible, are also constrained to keep value judgments out of their stories. A television newscaster once said:

Unfortunately, there were more deaths today . . .

Let readers or listeners make that decision; give them the information on which to base their own decisions. This journalist did not need to use the adverb.

> Unfortunately, only an inch to an inch and a half of rain fell on the parched Southeast, according to Mr. Wagner, bringing little relief to the drought there.

Still another adverb that expresses opinion:

> Fire extinguishers were of no use, but *luckily* everyone managed to flee the building.

Adverbs are sometimes used for emphasis, although no real need exists in the following:

> Monahan was asked *specifically* by Frank Perry of the Herald-Times if he would reduce the number of government employees as he has promised.

Dropping the adverb would do no harm to that sentence. And the mistake would be removed from the following sentence if the adverb was dropped:

> But during the 1974–75 academic year, 21 incidents of cheating were reported; last year the figure dropped *slightly* to 13.

(The drop from 21 to 13 is not slight.)

Nothing is gained by using an adverb in the following sentence, especially since the direct quotation shows what the adverb is saying.

> To critics who suggested Linder's version may not have been Adley's, the AP newsman replied *briefly:* "Sour grapes!"

Perhaps the writer didn't trust readers to make their own judgments. In some instances, though, reporters make a judgment because they cannot reveal their sources.

> The candidate's strategists were *reliably* reported to be considering two other approaches.

At other times, reporters interpret information for readers, as in these sentences:

> The economic news was certain to cheer the administration, which has been *deeply* worried over price reports in previous

months that showed inflation increasing at a worrisome 10 percent annual rate since Jan. 1.

Prices were reported *sharply* lower for grains, eggs, green coffee, cocoa, tea, soybeans and live poultry. But the decreases were *partially* offset by higher prices for livestock.

The problem is, you have to take the reporter's word for all three adverbs; the reporter never provided concrete information to support them. The reader does not know what *deeply, sharply* and *partially* mean. All three adverbs are vague.

You also have to take the reporter's word on the following adverb:

During the 10-day ordeal, officials *repeatedly* requested the release of the elderly woman, saying she was in need of prompt medical care.

Perhaps the reporter did not know how many times the request was made.

The type of word an adverb modifies determines where it is placed. If it modifies a verb or verbal, an adverb usually immediately precedes or follows the verb or verbal.

He *swiftly* ran to the finish line.

He ran *swiftly* to the finish line.

Despite that, some students still produce sentences like this:

Clifford emphasized his desire *to open* the Legislature's proceedings and records *completely* to the public.

The adverb is too far away from the verbal it modifies. This is better:

Clifford emphasized his desire *to completely open* the Legislature's proceedings and records to the public.

Sometimes an adverb modifying a verb can begin a sentence.

Swiftly he ran to the finish line.

That can create awkwardness and is usually done only for emphasis and only when the verb is near the beginning of the sentence.

When an adverb modifies an adjective, it precedes the adjective.

The *very* beautiful painting was stolen.

The same guideline applies to adverbs modifying other adverbs.

He ran *very* swiftly to the finish line.

Most adverbs are formed by adding *ly* to a root form, which is usually an adjective.

ADJECTIVE	ADVERB
quick	quickly
smart	smartly
virtual	virtually
grim	grimly
exuberant	exuberantly
medical	medically
political	politically

Note that the *ly* ending does not affect the spelling of the root form.

When forming the comparative and superlative degrees, use *more* and *most*. To use *er-est* endings would create tongue-twisters beyond comparison.

quicklier   quickliest

If when using adverbs, you follow the more-than-one-syllable rule of adjectives, you won't have any problems. Many adverbs, by virtue of the *ly* ending, contain two or more syllables.

Adverbs are classified according to the meaning they express—place, manner (how something is done), and time. Adverbs of place (such as *where, in, off, by down, under*) are often redundant.

How did he get *down?* He jumped *off.*

In the first sentence *down* is necessary to complete the sentence. But *off* in the second sentence adds nothing; in fact, it weakens *jump.*

Adverbs of manner usually have the *ly* endings. Adverbs of time, on the other hand, include *later, often, sometimes, then, earlier.* Roberts says that when all three occur after the same verb, the order is place, manner, time.

He gives *in quickly often.*

However, many writers change the order of a sentence either to stress one adverb or to avoid a clumsy pile-up, as in the previous example.

Often he gives *in quickly.*

He *often* gives *in quickly.*

He *quickly* gives *in often.*

One sticky division among editors and teachers of writing is where to place the adverb in a two-verb form (an auxiliary verb and a main verb)—in the middle or at the beginning or end.

He is *quickly* doing his homework.

He is doing *quickly* his homework.

He *quickly* is doing his homework.

The same debate covers the placement of adverbs with infinitives. Borrowing a split infinitive from the television series "Star Trek," I offer:

The crew of the Enterprise was ordered *to boldly go* where no man had ever gone before.

The crew of the Enterprise was ordered *to go boldly* where no man had ever gone before.

The crew of the Enterprise was ordered *boldly to go* where no man had ever gone before.

In the third sentence *boldly* might be read as modifying *ordered*. Were that the case, I would write:

The crew of the Enterprise *was boldly ordered* to go where no man had ever gone before.

Here is another example in which the meaning changes with the placement of the adverb:

He suggested hiring a design professional to plan *further pedestrian nodes*. (That suggests more nodes.)

He suggested hiring a design professional *to further plan* pedestrian nodes. (That suggests more planning.)

Likewise, the title of a magazine article about photography was:

TO SIMPLY SEE

Someone wanted to unsplit the infinitive so it would read:

TO SEE SIMPLY

The split infinitive prevailed, which preserved the author's meaning.

The easy solution is to play the placement of the adverb by ear, which may cause problems for anyone with a tin ear. If you look at the matter as a case of truth in writing, discussed in Chapter 2, the solution should be easier: Let the reader know immediately of any qualifications, in which case the adverb should more often than not split the verb or the infinitive.

You must also make a distinction between an adverb and an adjective when using certain verbs like *smell, taste, speak, feel, hear,* and *look.* Are you modifying the verb's action or the verb's condition?

I smell good.

The adjective means my body gives off a good-smelling odor.

I smell *well.*

The adverb means my nose is superior in sniffing odors.

If the modifier is working on the subject of the sentence or some other noun—that is, describing the condition of the verb rather than modifying it—use an adjective. The following advice concerns the comments you make, not how you make them:

Speak good of the dead.

But to advise on how to make such comments, a person would use an adverb to modify the verb.

Speak well of the dead.

APPOSITION

Appositives do a lot of work in newspapers. In fact, no journalist could do without them. Their function of giving identity or authority to a noun is crucial to any news story. They are coupled with nouns and are usually noun phrases. Rarely are they not used.

American Motors Corp., *the noncomformist in an industry where sameness is a virtue,* once again is financially out of step with its larger Big Three auto competitors [italics added].

Without the phrase in apposition (italicized), the importance of the rest of the sentence would be lost on most readers. The reader must first be told what American Motors is before he or she can be told what the company is doing. Naturally, the phrase in apposition changes to suit the meaning.

American Motors Corp., *long a manufacturer of low- and medium-priced cars,* announced today it was going to build a luxury car similar to the Cadillac and Lincoln Continental.

Appositives appear in many forms but serve only one purpose—providing identity peculiar to a particular story. Here are two appositives stacked one after the other:

> Prince Stanislaus Radziwill, 61, *Polish-born former husband of Lee Radziwill, sister of Mrs. Jacqueline Onassis,* died Sunday in London after a brief illness.

First there is the phrase in apposition to the subject of the sentence (*Radziwill*). Then you are assaulted with a phrase in apposition to the first phrase in apposition. Such writing crams too much into one sentence, which makes clarity impossible to attain. Two sentences and some careful thought on the clearest way to describe the prince's relationship to Mrs. Onassis are needed.

> Prince Stanislaus Radziwill, 61, former brother-in-law to Mrs. Jacqueline Onassis, died Sunday in London after a brief illness. The Polish-born Radziwill was once married to Mrs. Onassis' sister, Lee Radziwill.

Titles, when following names, are in apposition to names.

> John Monahan, president of the United States, said today . . .

Sometimes names are put in apposition to titles: this is common in news stories about people not well known to the general public.

> The superintendent of instruction, Susan Avon, announced plans today for three new courses.

The same thinking can be applied to clauses.

> The person who knows more about this subject than anyone else, Sam Goodman, won't be at tonight's meeting.

Some editors feel uncomfortable (note adjective use) making such a long phrase the subject of a sentence. They routinely exchange the phrase and its appositive so the name becomes the subject.

Finally (and you'll be told this again), phrases in apposition are set off by commas. Students have a bad habit of not using the second comma.

> Timothy Crouse, author of "The Boys on the Bus" wrote for Rolling Stone.

That is incorrectly punctuated; a comma is missing.

> Timothy Crouse, author of "The Boys on the Bus," wrote for Rolling Stone.

PREPOSITIONAL PHRASES

Prepositional phrases should appear immediately after the word they modify. When they don't, they make no sense at all or they create humor where none is intended.

> The board turned down a *request* from the director of the Delaware County Campus in Media *for $12,000* for the improvement of the Library-Learning Center.

The italicized prepositional phrase modifies the italicized noun, yet 10 words separate them. The writer of that sentence, when he wrote the word *request,* should have asked himself: Request for what? Had he done that, he would have written:

> The board turned down a *request for $12,000* from the . . .

The same problem occurs in the following example:

> The university is spending less *money* now than in 1968 *for each student,* Williams said.

Putting the prepositional phrase where it belongs, you will get:

> The university is spending less *money for each student* now than in 1968, Williams said.

Here is an example of unintended humor:

> All board *members* approved a decision to post signs and let the contract *except Dillon.*

To get Dillon out of the contract and onto the board:

> All board *members except Dillon* approved a decision to post signs and let the contract.

The misplacement of a prepositional phrase can sometimes be libelous.

> Harry Sneer, head coach of the Cadbury Tigers, discusses his personal and professional *life with producer-hostess Mary Rubin* on a PBS interview series.

The prepositional phrase was meant to modify *discusses,* but instead it modifies *life*—Sneer's life with Rubin. Correctly put:

> Harry Sneer, head coach of the Cadbury Tigers, *discusses with producer-hostess Mary Rubin* on a PBS interview series his personal and professional life.

But that is awkward, so make two sentences, saving the information on the PBS interview series for the second sentence.

Another misplacement caused some laughs among the readers of an advice columnist who had discussed the problem of a nurse who was "ashamed to take her child to a *doctor with recurring pinworms."* However, the child, not the physician, had recurring pinworms. Placing the prepositional phrase immediately after the noun it modifies would clearly connect the patient with the ailment. To the columnist's credit, she announced the error, which a newspaper editor had pointed out, in her column.

Here is another example, this one based on the style of a sloppy reporter:

> T.T. Smith was arraigned for committing sodomy *before District Magistrate Harry Jones* yesterday.

The italicized prepositional phrase modifies the prepositional phrase immediately preceding it. How can Smith avoid conviction if the district magistrate witnessed the crime? Better written, the sentence would say:

> T.T. Smith was arraigned yesterday before District Magistrate Harry Jones on a charge of sodomy.

From a student newspaper comes this headline, later condemned by a reader because of its double meaning.

> MONAHAN CONDEMNS TORTURE AT U.N. MEETING

A wire service writer unintentionally put secret payments into a book.

> The CIA several years ago went to court to block former intelligence officials Victor Marchetti and John D. Marks from revealing the names of foreign leaders who have *received secret payments in their book* "The CIA and the Cult of Intelligence."

Correctly structured, the sentence would read:

> The CIA several years ago went to court to block former intelligence officials Victor Marchetti and John D. Marks from revealing in their book "The CIA and the Cult of Intelligence" the names of foreign leaders who have received secret payments.

The preceding is an example of back-to-back prepositional phrases creating an unintended meaning because the second one modifies the first.

When that happens, you must find the structure that gives the intended meaning.

Some prepositional phrases can be moved around in a sentence to change the meaning.

> The children *by the public fountain* pointed to the heap *of stones, boards, tin and broken glass* as if it were a national monument.

The second phrase cannot be moved; it modifies *heap.* Moving it would be confusing, even illiterate. But the first phrase can be moved to the beginning of the sentence *if a different meaning is wanted.*

> *By the public fountain,* the children pointed to the heap of stones, boards, tin and broken glass as if it were a national monument.

The first example indicates the women and children were standing next to the public fountain. The second indicates that the women and children were walking and when they reached the fountain, they pointed.

Prepositional phrases indicating time rather than place can be moved around more safely.

> We'll leave here *in the morning.*

> *In the morning* we'll leave here.

As with other modifiers, the stress you want determines where some prepositional phrases are placed.

> *At the outset of the war,* there were few volunteers. But as the war dragged on, more and more people joined the army.

Prepositional phrases should not be broken up; the noun in the phrase should not be separated from the preposition.

> I am neither in favor *of* nor opposed to *the tax-reform bill.*

In addition to the separated prepositional phrase, the sentence is horrendous for its lack of parallel construction. What's wrong with:

> I neither favor nor oppose the tax-reform bill.

It is shorter, not at all pretentious, and it is to the point.

Another fault made with prepositional phrases is trying to make the noun in the phrase the subject of a verb. In the following the subject and the verb are italicized:

The *fad* of job-oriented training will not *open* students to the broader experiences of life.

Fads don't open anything. The writer of the sentence had *job-oriented training* in mind for a subject, but that is the object of the preposition. Objects don't function as subjects. Had the writer forgotten about *fad* altogether and not tried to pile so many thoughts into the sentence, the blunder wouldn't have occurred.

Job-oriented training will not open students to the broader experiences of life.

If *fad* had been essential to that sentence, the word could have been fitted in like this:

Job-oriented training, which is a fad, will not open students to the broader experiences of life.

Prepositional phrases are often overused to the detriment of tight writing. There is no reason to write *in the week just passed* when *last week* will do nicely.

NOUNS

Nouns function as modifiers more often than some purists would prefer to admit. We speak of *journalism schools* without one thought that we might really mean *journalistic schools*. *Governmental agencies* is not as comfortable as *government agencies*. And who will call to the defense the dictionary that lists *news* as a noun with the next entry being *news agency?* After that comes *newsboy* and *newscast*. What newspaper doesn't have its *news editor?* And have you ever watched the news on a *television set?*

You are already familiar with Nounspeak, which is caused in part by the patterning of nouns as adjectives with another noun. And, as noted in Chapter 4, make sure a word does not have an adjectival form or that one can't be created before you go the all-noun route. That advice still stands. But it doesn't mean nouns cannot be used as adjectives in stories and in headlines. Here are some nouns functioning as adjectives:

Grade deflation is slowly replacing *grade* inflation.

"Some of your ideas may find their way into the classroom," the *college* professor told the *alumni* gathering.

A simple *telephone* system is the best.

Present this card at *registration* headquarters.

Police anticipate a *street* confrontation.

As far as the *justice* system is concerned, the worst political scandal in American history will be over. (There is an adjective—*judicial*.)

The *police* officer, while looking for the youth, opened the *closet* door and heard the cry: "Shut the door, the cops are chasing me."

The *surprise* decision to release the pair followed six hours of meetings Saturday.

The campus is so large the university needs a *campus police* force.

The *mine* shaft is 500 feet from here.

I do not like *egg* sandwiches.

A *speech* defect can be very traumatic to a child.

Some *price* increases are easier to understand than others.

All students look forward to *graduation* ceremonies.

Apartment rental costs may increase more frequently in coming years. (However, the writer unnecessarily wrote apartment*al*.)

In headlines a noun modifier can be awkward. But the curse of not enough space to correctly say something forces headline writers to improvise by compacting phrases into single words. Prepositional phrases are almost always converted into grouped nouns in headlines. Because this headline wouldn't fit

UTILITIES DROP COAL
PLANT FOR IOWA

the writer chose

UTILITIES DROP
IOWA COAL PLANT

Sometimes a prepositional phrase fits.

PRESENCE
OF PAROLEE
IRKS JONES

But if it hadn't, that headline would have been best modified with a possessive form

PAROLEE'S
PRESENCE
IRKS JONES

and not a noun

PAROLEE
PRESENCE
IRKS JONES

Sometimes a noun as a modifier is not offensive

DEMOCRATS TAKE REGISTRATION LEAD

but other times it's overdone as a mouthful of modifiers

SOVIET GRAIN IMPORTS DROP UNLIKELY

UNIVERSITY PROPOSES TUITION BENEFIT CUT DELAY

Stumbling on those should make you more aware of the problem. Journalists who are aware don't make stupid mistakes.

VERBALS

Because they are derived from verbs and thus denote action, verbals are ideal modifiers. And, as noted in Chapter 4, entire clauses can be turned into strong verbal modifiers that increase the power of a sentence. *A stalking foe* conjures up a stronger image than *a foe who stalks.*

Reviewing Chapter 4, verbal forms are: the *infinitive* (to stalk), the *gerund* (stalking) and the *past participle* (stalked). Gerunds and past participles precede the word they modify while infinitives follow.

The *stalking* soldier hid in the bushes.

The *wounded* soldier awaited help.

The soldier went on patrol *to stalk* the enemy.

Infinitives modify verbs while gerunds and past participles modify nouns.

The error most frequently made with verbals as modifiers is in the past participle. Some writers forget the *ed,* which results in incorrect constructions like this one from a restaurant's menu:

mash potatoes

You get alcohol from mash, but if you mash potatoes, thay are mash*ed*. Likewise, a *toss salad* sounds like something made from *toss* the way a tuna fish salad is made from tuna fish. The correct word is *tossed*, to describe—like *mashed* in *mashed potatoes*—something that was done—some action—to the salad.

CLAUSES

VERB CLAUSES

Verb clauses are clauses whose initial word is a verbal. Verb clauses can appear after the word they modify

> The congressmen made available letters *received* from the Moroccan ambassador in Paris.

> The press release *announcing the councilman's candidacy* was filled with attacks on the mayor.

. . . or before

> *Weakened by the long hike,* the soldier staggered into camp.

> *Taking his cue from his brother,* Bill helped pick up the debris.

Along with other forms of modification, verb clauses cause the most problems when they dangle (see pages 145–147).

RELATIVE CLAUSES

Relative clauses are clauses introduced by relative pronouns: *who, which, that, what*. Because they show a relationship, they should be as close as possible to the word they modify in order to avoid confusion.

> Monahan is a president *who likes to wear sweaters.*

> The hospital, *which was built outside the town,* can be reached by taking Mountain Avenue.

> The plan *that pleases Sen. Williams the most* is the one on comprehensive tax reform.

> Do you know *what he wants?* (In this sentence the clause functions as the object of the verb *know*.)

Misplacing any of the preceding clauses would be illiterate or confusing, which is what happens in the following:

> Dillon said, however, that to soften water, *salt* must be added to it, *which is a health hazard.*

Once again, get the clause as close as possible to the word or phrase it modifies.

> Dillon said, however, that to soften water, salt, which is a health hazard, must be added to it.

Sometimes the problem isn't the placement of the clause, but of something else. A student wrote:

> The United States, *according to Walsh,* which represents 5 percent of the world's population, must curtail its consumption.

The attribution tag (italicized), because it comes between the clause and the word it modifies, fouls that sentence. Put the attribution tag at the beginning or end of the sentence so the clause immediately follows *United States.*

> According to Walsh, the United States, which represents 5 percent of the world's population, must curtail its consumption.

> The United States, which represents 5 percent of the world's population, must curtail its consumption, according to Walsh.

ADVERB CLAUSES

Adverb clauses function the same way adverbs do—they modify verbs, verbals and adjectives. There is no absolute rule on where they should appear in a sentence. Ususally, though, an adverb clause makes the important modifications or qualifications in a sentence so it should be placed in such a way as to tip the reader. (See "Positioning for clarity," pages 46–50.)

> *When the president enters a room,* the press corps always *rises.*

The italicized clause modifies *rises.*

In elliptic writing the adverb clause is often written without the similar words of the main clause. Hence, the adverb clause, to be clear, must appear after the main clause.

> The president left Washington *earlier than the press* [left Washington].

RESTRICTIVE AND NON-RESTRICTIVE
CLAUSES

All clauses are either restrictive or non-restrictive. They are recognized not by the word that introduces them but by the way they function. A *restrictive clause* is one that is needed to complete the meaning of a sentence.

> The plan *that pleases Sen. Williams the most* is the one on comprehensive tax reform.

If you drop the clause (in italics), the meaning of the sentence will change, if it will have any meaning at all. ("The plan is the one on comprehensive tax reform.") Thus, the clause restricts the rest of the sentence and cannot be discarded without doing violence to meaning. A *non-restrictive clause,* on the other hand, can modify a noun or the main clause, but it is not needed to complete the meaning of the sentence.

> The bookshelves, *which are gray,* take up five feet of valuable space in my office.

Dropping the non-restrictive clause would not make the main clause incomplete.

> The bookshelves take up five feet of valuable space in my office.

Here are two more examples:

> The columnists agree he would win the most votes in the Northeast, *where he is strongest.* (non-restrictive)

> When I retire I want to live *where nobody has lived before.* (restrictive)

Following are two statements made by a person who works most weekends and who is planning to move on a weekend when she doesn't have to work:

> I am moving the first weekend in February, *which I have off.* (non-restrictive)

> I am moving the first weekend in February *that I have off.* (restrictive)

In the first statement, the woman has said she is not working on the first weekend of February and that is when she will move. (The sentence also says she has February off.) But in the second statement she does not say which weekend she has off, only that when she gets a weekend off, she will move. It could be the last weekend of February, which could make a big difference to the person hearing the statement, especially if that person is going to help the woman move.

As you can see, non-restrictive clauses are set off by commas (or one comma when the clause comes at the beginning or the end of a sentence) while no punctuation separates a restrictive clause from the word it modifies. However, punctuation is secondary to the function and intent. Adding commas does not always make a non-restrictive clause.

Two pronouns frequently appearing at the beginning of restrictive and non-restrictive clauses are *that* and *which.* Some editors and professors make a distinction between the two pronouns, depending on the type of clause they begin. Others, however, view *that* and *which* as interchangeable when opening a restrictive clause.

> The plan *which* pleases Sen. Williams the most is the one on comprehensive tax reform.

> The plan *that* pleases Sen. Williams the most is the one on comprehensive tax reform.

In those examples there is no difference between the two. However, when the choice is between *that* and *which,* some editors very strictly follow the convention of using *that* to begin restrictive clauses and *which* to begin non-restrictive clauses. Usually you should use *that* to introduce a restrictive clause, although there are times when *which* sounds better— then use *which.* A good time to use *which* for *that* is when there are too many *that*'s in a sentence.

> Some rules exist despite inconsistencies *that* seem to indicate *that* similar looking words shouldn't be spelled similarly.

The repetition of *that* disappears by replacing the first *that* with *which.*

> Some rules exist despite inconsistencies *which* seem to indicate that similar looking words shouldn't be spelled similarly.

When replacing *that* with *which* make sure it is not followed by a noun lest *which* function as a modifier instead of a pronoun. When *which* is a pronoun, it must clearly refer back to a noun. If that doesn't happen (as would be the case if *which* replaced the second *that* instead of the first), do not substitute.

Some rules exist despite inconsistencies that seem to indicate *which* similar looking words shouldn't be spelled similarly.

In that case *which* functions as a modifier, not a pronoun.

That is never used to introduce a non-restrictive clause. In the next chapter, under the discussion on the comma, you will find a debate that centers on punctuation but could have been avoided had a presidential nominee distinguished between *that* for restrictive clauses and *which* for non-restrictive clauses (see pages 184–185).

For a review, go back through the sections on verb clauses and relative clauses and identify which are restrictive and which are non-restrictive. The first paragraph in this section also contains clauses you can identify for practice.

EXERCISES

A. *Identify the modifiers by circling single words and short phrases and by underlining clauses and prepositional phrases.*

1. Government officials said they had been unable to decide whether Israel's reprocessing move was in contravention of a triangular agreement between the United States, Israel and the World Atomic Energy Administration.

2. Morocco's heavily guarded borders are more relaxed and open now than at any time since the end of the two-month war with Algeria.

3. Her street clothes ragged and rumpled, her unshined shoes bursting at the seams, a social worker masqueraded as a welfare recipient and helped document what her superiors say is massive waste and mismanagement in San Francisco's huge welfare program.

4. Returning to the famous redwoods in the national park where he worked as a park attendant 20 years ago, the governor outlined a park acquisition and development plan that he called an environmental gift to future park lovers.

5. The number of demonstrators engaged in protests has not been large anywhere.

6. The Security Council resolution on the Middle East gave small victories to each side.

7. Iowa State's star runner, who earlier in the game had appeared hobbled by a slight leg injury, burst off tackle, eluded two safety men, then moved swiftly into the endzone for the winning touchdown.

8. Using a radial arm saw and a variable speed drill, she fashioned a bookcase that all agreed was superb in craftsmanship, excellent in design and functional in use.

9. The angry fans stormed the referees' dressing room intent on finding out why the touchdown that would have won the game for their team was nullified by a penalty nobody saw.

10. Defensively, the young professor explained why he had given the student's paper a D grade.

11. The pink, red, green and yellow bookcases that line the walls of her den contain many of the books she acquired as a college student.

12. The mayor heatedly responded, then quickly sat down amid a firm round of applause from the small audience in the council chambers.

ANSWERS

The single word and short-phrase modifiers are italicized. All clauses and most prepositional phrases are underscored. Prepositional phrases within clauses are not underscored.

1. *Government* officials said they had been *unable* to decide whether *Israel's* *reprocessing* move was in contravention of *a triangular* agreement between *the* United States, Israel and *the* World Atomic Energy Administration.
2. *Morocco's heavily guarded* borders are *more relaxed* and *open now* than at *any* time since *the* end of *the two-month* war with Algeria.

3. Her street clothes *ragged* and *rumpled,* her *unshined* shoes bursting at *the* seams, a *social* worker masqueraded as *a welfare* recipient and helped document what her superiors say is *massive* waste and mismanagement in *San Francisco's huge welfare program.*

4. Returning to *the famous* redwoods in *the national* park where he worked as *a park* attendant *20* years *ago, the* governor outlined *a park acquisition* and *development* plan that he called *an environmental* gift to *future park* lovers.

5. *The* number of demonstrators engaged in protests has not been *large* anywhere.

6. *The Security Council* resolution on the Middle East gave *small* victories to *each* side.

7. *Iowa State's star* runner, who *earlier* in *the* game had appeared *hobbled* by *a slight leg* injury, burst *off tackle,* eluded *two safety* men, then moved *swiftly* into *the* endzone for *the winning* touchdown.

8. Using *a radial arm* saw and *a variable speed* drill, she fashioned a bookcase that all agreed was *superb* in craftsmanship, *excellent* in design and *functional* in use.

9. *The angry* fans stormed *the referees'* dressing room intent on finding out why *the* touchdown that would have won *the* game for their team was nullified by *a* penalty nobody saw.

10. *Defensively, the young* professor explained why he had given *the student's* paper *a D* grade.

11. The *pink, red, green* and *yellow* bookcases that line *the* walls of her den contain many of *the* books she acquired as *a college* student.

12. *The* mayor *heatedly* responded, then *quickly* sat *down* amid *a firm* round of applause from *the small* audience in *the council* chambers.

B. *Some of the modifiers in the following sentences are misplaced or misused. Correct them.*

1. The fact that there were children in the audience born since "Star Trek" stopped filming illustrated Nimoy's idea that the show's reruns appeal to all generations.

2. Tied to a tree, the police found the kidnapped woman two days after she had been forced from her home by two men.

3. The senator said he, turned off by politics, would not seek re-election.

4. Five persons with a rifle were shot by a policeman.

5. Bugliosi has a signed statement from one of two Los Angeles policemen who were shown pointing to a bullet lodged in a hotel door jamb in a photo taken the day after the murder.

6. A president of the United States said today relations with China and Russia are improving.

7. The emotional charged statement was a further indication of how wide the gap has grown between the mayor and the council.

8. Sen. Williams is the exuberantist senator I know.

9. The inmate surrendered when the guards fired tear gas quickly.

10. Harry T. Williams, the new superintendent of Cadbury Schools, was introduced to the public for the first time today.

ANSWERS

The misplaced or misused elements are italicized and in the correct place.

1. The fact that there were *in the audience* children born since "Star Trek" stopped filming illustrated Nimoy's idea that the show's reruns appeal to all generations.
2. The police found the kidnapped woman *tied to a tree* two days after she had been forced from her home by two men.
3. The senator, *turned off by politics,* said he would not seek re-election.
4. Five persons were shot by a policeman *with a rifle.*
5. Bugliosi has a signed statement from one of two Los Angeles policemen who were shown *in a photo taken the day after the murder* pointing to a bullet lodged in a hotel door jamb.
6. *The* president of the United States said today relations with China and Russia are improving.
7. The *emotionally* charged statement was a further indication of how wide the gap *between the mayor and the council* has grown.
8. Sen. Williams is the *most exuberant* senator I know.
9. The inmate surrendered when the guards *quickly* fired tear gas.
10. *The new superintendent of Cadbury Schools,* Harry T. Williams, was introduced to the public for the first time today.

SIX

Punctuation

We use fewer internal marks of punctuation today than writers did more than 250 years ago, probably because we don't write sentences of the length acceptable then. Daniel Defoe, considered the first journalist, wrote sentences of 70 and 80 words, sentences that contained anywhere from 4 to 10 internal punctuation marks (such as commas, semicolons, colons and dashes). My sentences average around 20 words and contain usually no more than two internal punctuation marks (usually commas), if any at all.

Because of the length of his sentences, Defoe had to punctuate more than we do today. But his punctuation is also interesting because of how he punctuated. While I might write

> You may have cake or ice cream but not both.

Defoe did write (in "Vindication of the Press")

> Tis easy to imagine, that without the New Testament every person of excellency in literature, and complete in hypocrisy, either out of *interest, or other worldly views,* would have taken the liberty to deny the most sacred traditions. . . {italics added}.

I chose that sentence primarily to show how Defoe punctuated the *or* phrase compared with how I punctuated it.

Defoe set off restrictive clauses with commas, which we don't do.

> Tis owing to writing, that we enjoy the purest religion in the world . . .

He set off non-restrictive clauses with semicolons (we use commas today), and he was not at all bashful about separating subjects and verbs with commas, a habit wrongly imitated by some students.

> The regularity and heavenly decorum of the latter, give an awe and transport to the audience . . .

Ben Franklin also wrote long sentences and punctuated heavily. Like Defoe, Franklin set off modifiers with commas, as the beginning of an essay in Franklin's *Pennsylvania Gazette* shows.

> There are few men, of capacity for making any considerable figure in life, who have not . . .

Despite their long sentences and heavy use of punctuation, Defoe and Franklin were admired for their clarity. Once you become accustomed to their styles, you can read them without any problem. But today's style demands briefer sentences and little punctuation. The following, then, is about today's punctuation.

END PUNCTUATION

THE PERIOD

The period indicates the end of a declarative sentence.

> Officials are baffled about the cause and nature of the disease.

It also indicates the end of an imperative sentence.

> Give me your notes.

The period also appears at the end of a polite request that sounds like a question.

> Would you give me your notes.

Sometimes called a *point* by printers, the period is used in abbreviations.

The Middlemen Inc.

J.C. Penney Co.

U.S. government

Harrisburg, Pa.

Los Angeles, Calif.

It also serves as a decimal point.

1.3 percent

$2.5 million

The period ending a sentence usually appears in front of an ending quotation mark. Some editors make one exception—when the quotation marks are around only the final word. Then some editors put the period outside the quotation mark.

He called the mayor a "redneck".

It is a rare newspaper usage, although *Editor & Publisher,* a newspaper trade magazine, follows that style.

The sentence-ending period appears outside a closing parenthesis when parentheses enclose only a word or fragment.

It is a rare newspaper usage (although *Editor & Publisher* follows that style).

A period appears inside when parentheses enclose a complete sentence.

He called the mayor a "redneck." (*Redneck* is a derogatory term.)

When the period is used in a series of three (. . .), it indicates the omission of some words in a direct quotation. The series of three periods is called an *ellipsis*.

To be, or not to be . . .
Whether 'tis nobler in the mind to suffer
The slings and arrows of outrageous fortune,
Or to take arms against a sea of troubles . . .

Journalists, of course, don't usually quote Hamlet. Often they quote people whose statements were spoken only to them or to a small group, and the public has no idea if something is omitted from a direct quotation. In those circumstances journalists don't usually indicate omissions because the reader won't know what the ellipsis signifies. Here is a direct quotation from a news story:

> We expect the IRA to hit back at any moment. . . . The terrorists have already publicly stated they plan a bombing campaign far worse than anything they have done before.

There is no reason for the ellipsis. What reader would know what was missing? Furthermore, the reader probably wouldn't care. If you do use an ellipsis, remember that it is three periods and is in addition to the final punctuation of the sentence. See the IRA quotation, above, for an example.

Headline writers sometimes use the ellipsis in two headlines to indicate that two stories, one below the other, are related.

> YOUNGSTOWN STEEL UNION ASKS
> FOR PRESIDENT'S ASSISTANCE . . .
> . . . WHILE STEELHAULERS BROOD

Note that the ellipses are used at the end of the first headline and at the beginning of the second.

Some broadcasters use the ellipsis to indicate where the news reader should pause or change pace.

> The president signed into law today a bill that will lower everyone's income tax bite next year. . . . In Madison, Wisconsin, 10 people died when an early morning fire leveled an apartment building. . . . And in London the prime minister devalued the pound. . . . Details after these messages.

THE QUESTION MARK ?

This mark appears at the end of a question. Not using it when it is needed can alter the meaning of a sentence.

> Know what's happening.

That is a command telling you to know what is happening. The question mark makes it a question.

> Know what's happening?

That means, do you know what is happening?

Whether or not the question mark appears inside or outside the quotation mark depends on whether the question mark belongs to the quoted matter or the entire statement.

"Is the mayor going to run for re-election?" Councilman Williams asked.

Did you see the movie "All the President's Men"? When Bill asked me that, I replied: "No, did you?"

Putting the question mark inside the quotation mark in the first sentence of the above example would change the title of the movie to

"All the President's Men?"

EXCLAMATION MARK !

The exclamation mark is an indication of intensity or excitation.

Watch out!

Had that been a calmly made statement, such as a piece of advice, a period would have been used.

Watch out.

The exclamation mark is used cautiously in newspapers. Used too much it is weakened, its intensity made meaningless through numerous appearances. In stories the exclamation mark does not appear outside direct quotations because it could be taken as a reporter's opinion.

Jones was charged with murder!

And even within quotation marks it is seldom used. People do not go through life exclaiming many things (unless they have children). My comments do not preclude the exclamation mark's use in a direct quotation, an editorial or a column of opinion.

PUNCTUATION
WITHIN A SENTENCE

THE COMMA ,

The comma is the most widely used punctuation mark, yet some of its uses are hardly absolute. The comma avoids confusion, although misused it can create confusion as Defoe often did when he put one between a subject and its verb. Here are several sentences whose meanings depend on the comma.

> Robert Williams, junior chairman of the English Department, spoke about Chaucer.
> Robert Williams, junior, chairman of the English Department, spoke about Chaucer.

> On the platform were Victor L. Marchetti, a former CIA officer and six students.
> On the platform were Victor L. Marchetti, a former CIA officer, and six students.

> My wife, Karen, makes many of the children's clothing
> My wife Karen makes many of the children's clothing.

> The highway project list for discretionary funds, approved by the Transportation Commission yesterday, gave link-to-link resuscitation to the Cadbury bypass.
> The highway project list for discretionary funds approved by the Transportation Commission yesterday gave link-to-link resuscitation to the Cadbury bypass.

> The Democrats who run Congress gave him a standing ovation.
> The Democrats, who run Congress, gave him a standing ovation.

> The day was, well, up in the air.
> The day was well up in the air.

> He was first governor of Ohio.
> He was, first, governor of Ohio.

> Most of her story is clear and honest, but before she's done it gets a bit fuzzy.
> Most of her story is clear and honest, but before she's done, it gets a bit fuzzy.

The differences between the sentences in each set or the problems with them are discussed throughout this section.

The comma separates items in a series.

> The students studying football games asked *fans, coaches, players, league officials* and *any other persons who were at the games* to answer 15 questions.

> He can, when necessary, be serious or funny, believing or cynical, even believing and cynical.

More formal punctuation conventions call for the comma to be used before *and* in a series. When the comma there would eliminate confusion, by all means use it. Here is such a sentence.

> Some of the students are majoring in journalism, *history and health* and physical education.

A comma after *history* would make it clear that the italicized portion of that sentence does not belong together.

> Some of the students are majoring in journalism, history, and health and physical education.

The comma sets off titles or suffixes after names.

> TITLE
> James R. Williams, *the mayor,* celebrated his third year in office by holding open house.

> SUFFIX AFTER NAME
> Robert Williams, *junior,* chairman of the English Department, spoke about Chaucer.

The comma in the last sentence changes both Robert Williams' name and his authority in the English Department. Without the second comma, Williams becomes *junior chairman.* Newspapers do not use junior and senior in those forms, but instead abbreviate to Jr. and Sr. (or, jr. and sr.). Furthermore, most newspapers do not set off suffixes with commas. A reporter following the stylebook of the wire services would write:

> Robert Williams Jr., chairman of the English Department, spoke about Chaucer.

The comma also sets off titles preceding names when the title, not the name, is the subject of the sentence.

> The mayor, James R. Williams, celebrated his third year in office by holding open house.

Short titles are placed before names without any punctuation.

> Mayor James R. Williams celebrated his third year in office by holding open house.

> Secretary of State Joseph Shaw appeared before a congressional committee today.

The comma sets off modifying words or phrases in apposition to a noun.

> The ceremony, *a contrast to the policies of the past,* had special meaning for Josephine M. Williams, *the college's 32-year-old sociology professor.*

> The second photograph, *a sweeping panorama shot of Viking 2's new neighborhood,* showed an uneven horizon.

> Some Johns Hopkins University scientists are studying the geometry of human arteries, *the way they bend and branch out to various portions of the body,* to see whether arterial patterns can contribute to the disease.

> Ariel Durant, Los Angeles, *winner of the 1968 Pulitzer Prize,* spoke last night.

> Barnhart, *questioned about the possible breach of ethics,* said there was none that he knew of.

If the first comma were dropped in the last example, people might begin the sentence as though the noun and the verb go together.

> *Barnhart questioned* about the possible breach of ethics, said there was none that he knew of.

A second reading would obviously clarify the meaning, but you do not write with second chances in mind.

Similar confusion or lack of clarity results in the Marchetti sentence at the beginning of this section. The comma can decide how many people are on the platform.

> On the platform were Victor L. Marchetti, a former CIA officer and six students. (There are eight people—Marchetti, a former CIA officer and six students.)

> On the platform were Victor L. Marchetti, a former CIA officer, and six students. (There could be seven people, which is what I would count, or eight, which is another possible count. By my count there is Marchetti, who is a former CIA officer, and six students.)

The following could lead the reader to believe there are three speakers.

> In a speech at Kansas State, Fran Lee, a former consumer editor and a broadcaster said she warned the president against a nationwide vaccination program.

A comma after *broadcaster* makes it clear that *editor* and *broadcaster* modify *Lee*. Likewise, from a non-fiction book the numbers problem appears:

> He, in turn, communicated it to two more people, the Governor General, Lord Mountbatten and Field Marshal Auchinleck.

That reads like three people unless you know that Lord Mountbatten was also the governor general.

A modifying phrase is often a restatement or further explanation, only from a different perspective. It is still set off with commas.

> The meeting will be held Wednesday, *Nov. 10,* in City Hall.

The italicized portion of that sentence defines Wednesday further.

Don't be fooled into believing that just because a sentence has a connective it doesn't need a comma. Again, the restatement guideline applies.

> The Cadbury Tigers, who have not scored a touchdown in 33 straight quarters, *or since the first period at Clive nine weeks ago,* could not make a 3-0 lead stand up despite holding Bakersfield without a touchdown.

Without the comma after *quarters,* the sentence would lose its clarity because it would read as though there are two different times.

> The Cadbury Tigers, who have not scored a touchdown in 33 straight quarters or since the first period at Clive nine weeks ago, could not make a 3-0 lead stand up despite holding Bakersfield without a touchdown.

The reader might wonder which is correct—33 straight quarters or since the first period nine weeks ago. They are the same thing: the second being a restatement of the first from a different perspective. Only commas make that perfectly clear.

And only commas make clear how many wives I have. In the following I have one.

> My wife, Karen, makes many of the children's clothing.

All the word between the commas does is further identify the subject of the sentence. Karen can be discarded in the sentence but she will still be my wife.

> My wife makes many of the children's clothing.

In that sentence my wife is still Karen. But in the following, with no commas, the word *Karen* restricts the word *wife*.

My wife Karen makes many of the children's clothing.

Without commas, that sentence suggests my wife Mary, my wife Sue, my wife Anne, and so on.

The comma sets off *non-restrictive clauses* (clauses that can be dropped without damaging the meaning of the main clause).

> The house, *which was built in 1857,* was sold twice to family members before someone outside the family bought it.

The comma is not used to set off a *restrictive clause* (clauses that cannot be dropped without changing the meaning of the main clause).

> The man *who served as our first president* will also be remembered for his military ability.

> This is the house *that Jack built.*

Here are two sentences that are identical except for two commas. The commas change the meaning.

> The highway project list for discretionary funds, approved by the Transportation Commission yesterday, gave link-to-link resuscitation to the Cadbury bypass.

> The highway project list for discretionary funds approved by the Transportation Commission yesterday gave link-to-link resuscitation to the Cadbury bypass.

The first sentence says a list for discretionary funds exists and that it was approved yesterday. The second suggests more than one list exists and one of them was approved yesterday.

Similarly, the Democrats are the majority party in Congress; they control Congress.

> The Democrats, who control Congress, gave him a standing ovation.

But if only some of the Democrats in the majority control Congress, then the clause is restrictive and goes unpunctuated.

> The Democrats who control Congress gave him a standing ovation.

That suggests that not every Democrat stood and applauded—just the ones in power.

The misuse of a comma has caused debate in the U.S. Senate. In

1977, when Paul C. Warnke was before the Senate as President Carter's nominee to be the country's chief arms control negotiator, a dropped comma became headline news. From the floor of the Senate, Sen. Henry M. Jackson of Washington pointed to a statement Warnke had made in 1972.

> Under those circumstances, it seems to me, Mr. Chairman and Senator Cooper, that the continuation of the missile numbers game is in fact a mindless exercise, that there is no purpose in either side's achieving a numerical *superiority, which is not translatable into either any sort of military capability or any sort of political potential* [italics added].

As punctuated, what follows *superiority* is a non-restrictive clause and it can be dropped without doing damage to the meaning of the sentence. Jackson told his colleagues there was a contradiction in the 1972 statement and he asked Warnke for a clarification. Warnke replied, in writing,

> I specifically stated that "numerical superiority *which is not translatable into either any sort of military capability or any sort of political potential* has no purpose" [Warnke's emphasis].

As punctuated, the italicized portion of the preceding is a restrictive clause and cannot be dropped without changing the meaning of the sentence. Warnke blamed the comma problem on a sloppy typist; Jackson said it was an intentional distortion, magnified by the alteration of the original sentence. The comma aside, the statement could have been clear from the start had Warnke used *that* to lead off a restrictive clause (if that's what he intended) or *which* to lead off a non-restrictive clause (if that's what he intended). But because *which* is sometimes used for *that*, the solution for this case lies in correct punctuation.

The comma distinguishes parenthetical expressions.

> The day was, *well,* up in the air.

Without the commas, the condition of the day changes.

> The day was well up in the air.

Commas also make the difference in these sentences.

> "This is a good budget for our investigation," the congresswoman said; "any cut, *in my opinion,* will weaken what we are trying to do."

> "This is a good budget for our investigation," the congress-woman said; "any cut *in my opinion* will weaken what we are try-ing to do."

Another way of not cutting the congresswoman's opinion is to use parentheses, although it is a second-rate approach.

> "This is a good budget for our investigation," the congress-woman said; "any cut (in my opinion) will weaken what we are trying to do."

The comma sets off the year in a complete date.

> July 4, 1776, is the birthday of the United States.

However, a comma is not needed in month-year combinations, such as *July 1776*.

The comma sets off standard transition words at the beginning of sentences and in the middle of sentences.

> *Nevertheless,* the ousting of the liberal editors is equivalent to the silencing of independent opinion in Mexico.

> The ousting of the liberal editors, *nevertheless,* is equivalent to the silencing of independent opinion in Mexico.

However is also set off by a comma when its meaning indicates that a contradiction or contrary information is to follow.

> This car is just the right size for our family. *However,* I don't like the color.

But when *however* means *no matter how,* it is not set off by a comma.

> *However* great he may have been, historians will never rank him with the greatest.

> *No matter how* great he may have been, historians will never rank him with the greatest.

Here is one final example of setting off transitional markers with commas. In this case—as in many other examples—the absence of commas changes the meaning.

> He was, first, governor of Ohio.

The story goes on to explain that *he* was later a senator and then a newspaper publisher—all within recent history. But the absence of commas sends the time back approximately two centuries.

He was first governor of Ohio.

A comma sets off long introductory phrases at the beginning of a sentence.

> *In an attempt to learn more about the crowds at football games,* the students conducting the study asked fans, coaches, players, league officials and any other persons who were at the games to answer 15 questions.

The same principle applies to introductory modifiers, such as a verbal, verb clause or prepositional phrase (which begins the preceding example).

> *Running through the woods,* Jack tripped over a rock in the middle of the path. (verb clause)

> *With much less fear than we had expected,* Tracey bravely entered the hospital for an ear operation. (prepositional phrase)

> *Blindfolded,* the kidnap victim could not tell where his abductors drove him. (verbal)

> *By using three steps,* we can get to the room before they do. (prepositional phrase)

Here are four more sentences whose italicized portions are misleading or unclear because of a missing comma. Correct versions follow in parentheses.

> *To eat the survivors* of the plane crash had to dig up roots. (To eat, the survivors of the plane crash had to dig up roots.)

> After the large coal mines *closed the economies* of the towns died. (After the large coal mines closed, the economies of the towns died.)

> If *I published my mask* would disappear. (If I published, my mask would disappear.)

> Most of her story is clear and honest, but before *she's done it* gets a bit fuzzy. (Most of her story is clear and honest, but before she's done, it gets a bit fuzzy.)

In all four examples a verb or verbal is involved. Because the reader might read the word after the verb or verbal as the object of the verb or verbal, the comma is necessary.

Sometimes clauses not appearing in their normal place in a complex sentence are set off by a comma, although the decision to use them should depend on clarity, not convention.

If I were you, I'd take the job.
If I were you I'd take the job.

When we were young, we played stickball.
When we were young we played stickball.

Modifiers in a series take a comma if you can substitute *and* without changing the meaning. In such cases, the modifiers have equal rank.

The long, drawn-out meeting ended when the chairman collapsed.

That sentence could also be written:

The long *and* drawn-out meeting ended when the chairman collapsed.

In the following a comma is not needed between modifiers because they are not equal.

The boys wanted to spend a *five-week summer* vacation with their father.

When you have doubt, insert *and* and see if the sentence still makes sense.

The boys wanted to spend a *five-week and summer* vacation with their father.

That sentence makes no sense so the modifiers of *vacation* need no punctuation.
Commas also substitute for *and* in other places.

Go, *and* see it.
Go, see it.

Try more *and* shorter stories.
Try more, shorter stories.

The last sentence would be non-standard usage without the comma. The comma-for-and convention also applies to headlines.

TROJANS, RAMS FACE TOUGH TEAMS

Contrasting ideas are set off with a comma or commas.

Sometimes, clauses not appearing in their normal place in a complex sentence are set off by a comma, although the decision to use them should depend on *clarity, not convention.*

The mayor, not the vice president of the council, will preside at tonight's meeting.

The student wants to study *literature, not grammar.*

Natural gas, not oil, may provide the richest payoff in the billion-dollar gamble that began last week when American companies put down their bids for the first offshore leases in the Atlantic Ocean.

Commas generally are not used in newspapers before a connective in a short compound sentence.

The president eats breakfast alone and his wife eats with the children.

The congressman would like to visit our town but his schedule for that day is full.

However, as in the case of items in a series, the comma should always be used for clarity, especially when you are connecting sentences with *and,* or for reader convenience when you are connecting long sentences.

At all evening meals, the mayor *serves the wine and his wife* serves the meat.

The reader may have to read that sentence twice to understand that the mayor does not serve *the wine and his wife.* The description of a movie on television provides another example.

Chicago underworld boss Al Capone plots *to kill Bugs Moran and the famous St. Valentine's Day Massacre* in which seven of Moran's men are gunned down in a warehouse is recreated [italics added].

As you can see, the problem develops because of a verb followed by its object, then a connective, and then a noun that could be read as another object of the verb. It reads as a compound object. These don't.

At all evening meals, the mayor serves the wine, and his wife serves the meat.

Chicago underworld boss Al Capone plots to kill Bugs Moran, and the famous St. Valentine's Day Massacre in which seven of Moran's men are gunned down in a warehouse is recreated.

Usually the comma is not used in a simple sentence with a compound predicate, as is shown in the following misuse.

The judge found that the husband has assumed parental responsibility, and has shown an interest in his children.

There is no need for a comma in compound modifiers joined by *and*.

The home of the husband and his girlfriend is normal, and morally satisfactory in every respect except for the absence of a marriage certificate.

The comma is used in place of a verb to show the verb is being repeated.

Williams had 35 marbles; Smith *had* 10, Jones *had* 5, and Wentzel *had* 2.

Williams had 35 marbles; Smith, 10; Jones, 5, and Wentzel, 2.

Direct address is set off from the rest of the sentence by a comma. Try the first example without.

It's time to eat, Amy.

Amy, it's time to eat.

A comma gets a lot of use in direct and indirect quotations by setting them off from the speech or attribution tag.

Williams said, "We need a vote on this proposal tonight or it will be too late."

"We need a vote on this proposal tonight," Williams said, "or it will be too late."

"We need a vote on this proposal tonight or it will be too late," Williams said.

"City Council must vote on this proposal tonight," Williams said.

According to Williams, City Council must vote on this proposal tonight.

City Council must vote on this proposal tonight, according to Williams.

City Council, according to Williams, must vote on this proposal tonight. (Attribution tags are not normally placed between a subject and its verb.)

A comma is not needed, though, in an indirect quotation when the attribution tag is the beginning and (really) the main clause in a complex sentence.

Williams said City Council must vote on this proposal tonight.

If you remember that the preceding is a complex sentence—a main clause and a subordinate clause—you won't put in a comma. Reporters often discard the pronoun that would begin the clause in more formal writing.

In a similar vein, a comma is not used to separate a partial quotation from the rest of a sentence.

According to Lee, dogs give humans, "a present they'll never be able to get rid of."

That sentence does not need the comma after humans.

According to Lee, dogs give humans "a present they'll never be able to get rid of."

The partial quotation is the object of the verb. Unless you are Daniel Defoe or Ben Franklin, you do not put a comma between a verb and its subject or object. The quotation marks don't change anything.

If the direct quotation is a question or (perish the thought) an exclamatory sentence, the appropriate mark is used *without a comma.*

"Do you honestly believe we need this bypass?" Council member Williams asked the mayor.
"Yes!" the mayor screamed.

The unnecessary comma would appear as such:

"Do you honestly believe we need this bypass?", Council member Williams asked the mayor.
"Yes!", the mayor screamed.

If the order of the sentence quoting Council member Williams is reversed, a comma or a colon could be used.

Council member Williams asked the mayor: "Do you honestly believe we need this bypass?"

Council member Williams asked the mayor, "Do you honestly believe we need this bypass?"

Sometimes the comma masquerades as a punctuation mark in a series when it is really setting off a phrase in apposition. How many people were arrested in the following?

Scotland Yard today announced the arrest of 10 alleged slayers, seven Irish terrorists and three Palestinians.

If you said 20, you are wrong. Try 10. Also try a dash or a colon.

Scotland Yard today announced the arrest of 10 alleged slayers—seven Irish terrorists and three Palestinians.

A similar example:

Bulgaria has already concluded friendship treaties with at least two other Western countries, the United States and Canada. (That's four countries.)

Bulgaria has already concluded friendship treaties with at least two other Western countries: the United States and Canada. (That's two.)

There are countless examples of how a dropped comma can change or fuzz the meaning of a sentence. I misread the following sign in my oral surgeon's office.

Because of the nature of *oral surgery appointments* are for the approximate time only.

Because of the nature of oral surgery, appointments are for the approximate time only.

The place of a person's death can hinge on a comma.

The American Legion Auxiliary of Mapleville Post 261 will hold a memorial service for Mrs. Mary C. Linn, *who died Sunday at the T. F. Williams Funeral Home* in Mapleville today at 7:30 p.m.

The American Legion Auxiliary of Mapleville Post 261 will hold a memorial service for Mrs. Mary C. Linn, who died Sunday, at the T. F. Williams Funeral Home in Mapleville today at 7:30 p.m.

A comma can make a difference to a vote-counter.

The tally shows Monahan with *1,526 delegates more than the 1,505 needed to win the nomination.* (That gives Mohahan 3,031 delegates, but he really has 1,526—or 21 more than needed to win the nomination.)

The tally shows Monahan with 1,526 delegates, more than the 1,505 needed to win the nomination.

Sometimes reporters write such involved sentences they forget to punctuate non-restrictive clauses at both ends.

TMSA's decision apparently ends more than three years of hot-and-cold negotiations among several parties, including TMSA, the county commissioners and the hospital authority (which owns Sunbank) aimed at finding an answer of how best to use Sunbank.

A comma is needed after the parenthetical phrase. But because that is such a long sentence, it should be made into two.

TMSA's decision apparently ends more than three years of on-again off-again negotiations among several parties, including TMSA, the county commissioners and the hospital authority (which owns Sunbank). The negotiations were aimed at finding an answer to the problem of how best to use Sunbank.

Usually a semicolon is used in a compound sentence when a connective is not used. But when both sentences are very short and their forms are similar, a comma suffices.

The people lost, the bureaucracy won.

If the door is closed, don't knock, don't bother me.

THE SEMICOLON ;

The semicolon's primary function is to separate complete but coordinating sentences (called *compound*) not joined by a connective.

The house is big enough; I think there's room for everyone.

It wasn't the subfreezing playing conditions or a matter of being outplayed; the game was decided by puck luck.

Among unanswered questions, Foege said, are: "How did it get to the people; why didn't it spread among individuals; were other factors needed for it to spread?"

The press was lucky with Watergate; only a small fraction of the press was actually involved, Bagdikian said.

Emerson Boozer, the halfback, is a football analyst on national television; Dave Herman, an offensive guard, analyzes the Jets' games on radio in New York; Earl Christy, the return specialist, is a sports broadcaster in Wilmington, Del.; Johnny Sample, the defensive back who had an interception against Baltimore, is involved in a sporting goods store in Philadelphia.

Some writers—newspaper and otherwise—will put in a period where a semicolon could be used and go on to a new sentence. That doesn't make the preceding examples wrong or uncommon. In fact, they are very good examples of when the period might jar the reader because it would disjoint tightly related ideas.

One place in newspapers where the semicolon is called for is after an attribution tag that separates two coordinating sentences. Often a reporter will make an attribution tag do double work, letting it refer to a statement just made and a statement to follow. Misuse occurs when a comma appears in the place of a semicolon.

"It was an even game," Jones said, "I felt both defenses were strong."

Correctly punctuated, that sentence would read

"It was an even game," Jones said; "I felt both defenses were strong."

"It was an even game," Jones said. "I felt both defenses were strong."

Conditioned as they are to attributing, some journalists are afraid to allow a direct quotation stand by itself because they fear the reader will not tag it correctly. In stories with only one speaker, the fear is unfounded. The quotation marks make the attribution clear.

A second necessary use of the semicolon is with items in a series in which some items have apposition. Count the number of people in this sentence.

Present at the party were John Jones, the butler; Mary Smith, a private secretary; two attorneys; Bill Jackson, a former judge; Karen Harpster, a maid and a horse trader.

Now in this one.

> Present at the party were John Jones; the butler; Mary Smith; a
> private secretary; two attorneys; Bill Jackson; a former judge;
> Karen Harpster; a maid; and a horse trader.

By using semicolons to clarify the ambiguities of possible apposition, I
correctly show 11 people at the party, not 6.

In the following examples note how the semicolons neatly keep related items separate from other sets of related items.

> In addition to the congressional pay hikes, other pay raises
> include: vice president, chief justice, House speaker, from
> $65,000 to $75,000; associate Supreme Court justices, $63,000
> to $72,000; cabinet members, $63,000 to $66,000; majority
> and minority leaders in Congress, $52,000 to $65,000; district
> judges, $42,000 to $54,000.

> Their roles on the paper were typical of their relationship: Apte
> the fast-dealing businessman, Godse the outraged editorialist;
> Apte the chairman of the meeting, controlling its flow, Godse
> the fiery orator; Apte the formulator of their political schemes,
> Godse their vocal proponent.

> And there were Michael Howlett, the Irish machine politician
> whom Daley had forced to run for governor last year but who
> lost to Republican James Thompson by an unprecedented
> margin of 1.39 million votes; Congressman Daniel Ros-
> tenkowski, the Polish machine politician and a powerful man in
> the U.S. House of Representatives; Cecil Partee, the black ma-
> chine politician who gave up his post as president *pro tempore* of
> the Illinois Senate to be Daley's sacrificial lamb in the most
> unwinnable election against Republican state Attorney General
> William Scott (the boast was that Partee was the first black can-
> didate for statewide office; the reality was that he was being
> pushed aside in an attempt to create a spot in the legislative
> leadership for the mayor's son, state Senator Richard M. Daley);
> William Singer, the Jewish antimachine politician who
> mounted the first meaningful reform-Democratic challenge to
> Daley in 1975 but went down to ignominious defeat in that
> year's mayoral primary; labor leaders, patronage workers, civil
> rights protagonists, university people, churchmen.

> He gave them "evidence" of a secret alliance between Ei-
> senhower and McCarthy; of tantalizing rivalries between the

staffs of the Internal Security Committee and the McCarthy Committee; of imminent plans to enter into forbidden communication with Igor Gouzenko, *the Soviet defector in Canada;* of marital problems developing between Senator and Mrs. McCarthy; of a clandestine White House conference at which a smear campaign against the Democratic Party was programmed; of McCarthy's informers *in the White House, in the Louisville Courier-Journal, in the New York Post (the cooking editor)*; excruciating teasers about informants whose identity had not been disclosed and (my very favorite), news that Senator McCarthy had amassed an arsenal of pistols, Lugers and sub-machine guns in the basement of the Senate office building {italics added].

Only the first example comes from a news story. The others are from a book (*Freedom at Midnight*), a magazine article (in *The Atlantic*) and a syndicated newspaper column (by William F. Buckley Jr.). Such sentences are not normal in newspapers. But it is the punctuation you should pay attention to. Note that in the final example semicolons appear where commas are normally slotted. That happens because later on commas are needed to set off a phrase in apposition and items in a series (both italicized). Thus, Buckley started with semicolons in place of commas.

THE COLON :

The colon is used to show a relationship. Think of it as an equals sign— whatever follows it is equivalent or similar to what precedes it or is an explanation of what precedes it.

> With the outbreak of war, another dress is common on campus: green army fatigues.

> Students' grades in writing courses reflect a dramatic change: The basics are being taught again in high schools, which shows up in better written term papers.

Note the difference in capitalization. The initial letter that follows the colon in the first example is not capitalized while it is in the second example. When what follows a colon is a complete sentence (subject-verb construction), the initial letter is capitalized. When what follows a colon is a series or list, do not capitalize.

> You have three choices: the Army, college or work.

The colon is also used to separate long introductions from a following direct quotation.

> The president did not speak during the applause. After the crowd had quieted, he resumed: "I stand here today to explain my energy plan in full."

> He said he was confronted by Mrs. Jones, who told him: "I did it. I hope he doesn't die."

THE HYPHEN -

The difference between the hyphen and the dash is a difference in function: a hyphen connects, a dash separates. The two create problems because some people use them interchangeably. The two not only function differently but they are also not the same length. The hyphen, which every typewriter has, is - while the dash—on a typewriter—is two hyphens --. Printers convert double hyphens to dashes so that they appear correctly in print. But printers aren't mind readers, so you must make the distinction in usage on your copy.

The hyphen is used in a compound modifier that precedes a noun.

> Three of the area's best known fashion stores have offered $5.2 million to settle seven *class-action* suits brought on by *price-fixing* allegations by their credit customers.

> But in Yugoslavia, where there is now at least one car for every four families compared with one car for every 100 persons 10 years ago, the *end-of-August* crush is worse than elsewhere.

The hyphen is extremely crucial when a noun and a verb function as a compound modifier. Without the hyphen a person might read the noun as the subject of the verb.

> U.S. RUN TRUCE
> QUIETS LEBANESE
> AND ISRAELI GUNS

Granted the verb *run* does not agree with *U.S.* in number, but the addition of the hyphen would clear all doubt.

> U.S.-RUN TRUCE
> QUIETS LEBANESE
> AND ISRAELI GUNS

You do not hyphenate when the compound modifier is an adverb and a participle. The first example in this section appeared in a newspaper punctuated like this:

Three of the area's *best-known* fashion stores have . . .

Also, no hyphen is needed (although it often appears) in constructions like this:

the heavily guarded road

the well built fort

the happily married couple

the well known composer

Readers understand the function of adverbs; it is unlikely they will get confused without the hyphen. That is why the hyphen should be used only when necessary for clarity. In football, some players are *running backs* and play in the *running-back position.* That is not the same as the *running back position,* which sounds like somebody running backward. Likewise, there is a difference between a *child teaching expert,* which suggests a child teaching an expert, and a *child-teaching expert,* an expert who teaches children.

The hyphen is also used to attach a prefix to a proper noun. It is *anti-American,* not *antiamerican* or *antiAmerican.* Similarly, you should use the hyphen when the prefixed word might be misread. A favorite example of one editor is *anticrime,* which he says could be mispronounced as *an-TICK-re-mi.*

When a vowel is repeated in the prefixing process, use a hyphen, as in *re-election.* That convention, however, isn't absolute, as *cooperation* shows. (But you need the hyphen in *co-op* lest you write *coop.*) Sometimes a writer uses the hyphen when adding an ending to a word to create a new word.

The latter hookup, according to one listener, was "echo-ey."

The reader might have difficulty with the hyphenless word *echoey.* Similarly, the reader would have difficulty realizing you meant *co-inmates* if you wrote *coinmates.* The hyphen distinguishes between two words that look the same. Hence, you *recover* from an illness but you *re-cover* a book; you *recount* a story but *re-count* the results of an election. And to duplicate a painting is a *re-creation,* which you might do for *recreation* if contact sports aren't for you. Likewise, you might *resent* it when your grades are missent, but you'll be happy when they're found and *re-sent*.

Imagine if one of those words was hyphenated at the end of a typewritten line of copy, with *re-* on one line and the rest of the word on the following line. What does the person setting type do if the word fits on one line? Will the person know the difference? Rather than hope so, you should not hyphenate any word at the end of a line of news copy. If anyone or anything is going to make a mistake, such as *the-rapist* for *therapist,* let it be the computer. Then shoot it.

Self is followed by a hyphen when it begins a word. Likewise, the hyphen is used in some *paired nouns* (my label), such as *chess-player* and *well-being* and a host of others that are in any dictionary. Some paired nouns also function as verbs; then the hyphen is not used. The noun *fade-in,* to mention one of many, is *fade in* as a verb. (Some paired nouns, following the traditional process of many of our words, are written solid—*breakout, shutdown*—but the verbs remain two words—*break out, shut down.*)

Most prefixes (which precede a word) and suffixes (which follow) are not hyphenated when attached to words (except proper nouns). *All* as in *all-star, ex* as in *ex-governor* and *non* as in *non-restrictive* seem to be the only hyphenated ones. As a prefix, *in* is not hyphenated (*insatiable*) when it means *not.* But it is hyphenated in such constructions as *in-service,* where it does not mean *not.* As a suffix, it is *sit-in* and *break-in.* Most other prefixes and suffixes are not hyphenated.

The hyphen can make a difference in a headline or sentence that begins with the article *a.*

A-BOMB EXPLODES	A BOMB EXPLODES
IN CITY SUBWAY	IN CITY SUBWAY

And it can make a difference in those words that function as nouns when hyphenated but function as verbs when written as separate words.

BREAK-IN WEATHER	BREAK IN WEATHER
WON'T EASE CRISIS	WON'T EASE CRISIS
GALLUP REPORTS	GALLUP REPORTS
CHURCH-GOING UP	CHURCH GOING UP

In the following example the lack of a hyphen creates confusion, but not until you've read about half of the sentence, at which time you must start again to get the meaning.

> After tax earnings last year were reduced by about $2.3 million because of interest not recorded on some loans.

Read the sentence again with a hyphen in the compound modifier *after tax* and you'll get the message.

> After-tax earnings last year were reduced by about $2.3 million because of interest not recorded on some loans.

In the following a hyphen would make the sentence clearer by creating a paired noun.

> Still pictures were allowed only before the president went on television.

> Still-pictures were allowed only before the president went on television.

Without the hyphen the first sentence appears to need a comma.

> Still, pictures were allowed only before the president went on television.

But what is meant is *still-pictures,* the kind you see in newspapers or have in the family album.

The hyphen is also usually used in constructions like this:

> The people paid the 50-cent fares.

Without the hyphen the sentence could mean the people paid *50 one-cent fares.* Likewise, don't hyphenate *50 dollar bills* if you mean *50 one-dollar bills.* The hyphen would mean *$50 bills.*

The hyphen is also used to show a person with two jobs or identities.

> Harry Sneer, head coach of the Cadbury Tigers, discusses with *producer-hostess* Mary Rubin . . .

And:

> When the two-hour show began in February 1969, *actress-interviewer* Mary Todd was co-host.

The 1970 stylebook jointly prepared by *The Associated Press* and *United Press International* contains a good example of how a hyphen can change a meaning.

> The 6-foot man eating shark was killed. (the man was)

> The 6-foot man-eating shark was killed. (the shark was)

Suspensive hyphenation is the tying of two prefixes to one word by using hyphens.

> The 20- and 30-degree temperatures common to this area do not suit me.

Theodore M. Bernstein suggests, however, that you avoid the opposite construction.

> University-owned and -operated airplanes are always an issue at budget hearings.

There's nothing wrong with repeating university; it makes the sentence clear.

> University-owned and university-operated airplanes are always an issue at budget hearings.

The hyphen is used in ages functioning as compound modifiers and nouns.

> Tracey, an 8-year-old girl, won the prize for 8-year-olds.

The hyphen is used in fractions (four-tenths, eight-tenths) and in numbers when the first word ends in *y* (seventy-five, sixty-eight).

In broadcast copy the hyphen appears between letters of abbreviations when the letters should be read individually. A broadcast newswriter would use the hyphen like this:

> Y-W-C-A
>
> C-I-A
>
> F-B-I
>
> U-C-L-A
>
> U-S Information Agency
>
> U-S Supreme Court

Where there are hyphens each letter is pronounced. The newspaper equivalent is the period, although the period is not used as much in abbreviations as it once was.

THE DASH --

The dash is used for emphasis, usually to set off material you want stressed. Journalists tend to overuse the dash, sometimes making it do

the work of the colon or parentheses. In pairs, the dash sets off something you want stressed.

> With the routine business out of the way, the chairman in-
> troduced the two candidates—T. F. Stein of Clive and Leonard
> E. Tressler of Cadbury—and began the interview by asking the
> first question.

The dash is used in lengthy lists in apposition to a noun.

> Members of the trustee advisory committee—Michael Baker Jr.,
> chairman; Harry R. Ulrich, Ralph Hetzel, Walter J. Conti,
> Helen Wise, Samuel F. Hinkle and J. Lewis Williams—will
> screen persons for the provost position. (Note the use of the
> semicolon.)

> A number of oil company executives said they expect the 101
> tracts—more than 800,000 acres—lying off the coasts of New
> Jersey and Delaware to be more valuable for producing natural
> gas than oil.

The dash is also used to stress a word or phrase at the end of a sentence.

> A 25-year-old Vasilia man was charged yesterday with posses-
> sion of cocaine and attempting to conceal it—in his stomach.

The dash also completes or sums up an involved sentence.

> The Sachs team said the dam collapse resulted from internal
> erosion—water seeped inside the dam and ate away at it until it
> was so weakened that it burst.

Journalists also use the dash where a colon could work as well.

> The contributing factors fall in three groups—natural condi-
> tions, the type of materials used and the design elements of the
> day.

or where parentheses might also fit.

> But he added that the problems of recovery are always greater in
> deep water where divers risk nitrogen narcosis—the "rapture of
> the deeps."

> Under apartheid the "coloreds"—people of mixed race con-
> sidered neither black nor white—live apart from the other races
> and have more advantages than blacks but fewer than whites.

Occasionally dashes are used where commas are better.

> Proving assault will be difficult—T. L. Holt, the chief of po-
> lice, said—because the alleged victim had no marks on him
> when he made the charge.

Dashes are used by some journalists to indicate a continued subject
and verb throughout a list.

> The Council also:
>   —Voted not to meet next week.
>   —Postponed action on May Day plans.
>   —Set June 21 as the date for a public hearing on the pro-
>   posed sidewalk ordinance.
>   —Told James H. Andrews he could proceed with his plans to
>   clean up Walnut Spring Park as part of a Boy Scout project.

> The Council voted to:
>   —Keep meeting the first Monday of the month.
>   —Call special meetings when necessary.
>   —Ban smoking in the meeting room.

Because continuity from line to line is desired, some editors punctuate
all but the last line of such a list with semicolons. Others prefer periods.
Whichever, it is a matter of newspaper style, not some convention of
punctuation.

PARENTHESES ( )

Information enclosed within these marks is usually an explanation, qualification or an example. Such information is not usually crucial to the
main thought of the sentence. Journalists use parentheses to enclose information that could almost as clearly be handled in a subsequent sentence. Doing that, however, does not make the information as readily
available to the reader. A similar situation would be:

> T. R. Williams died today. Williams was the mayor of Cad-
> bury.

Most journalists would write:

> T. R. Williams, the mayor of Cadbury, died today.

The idea is the same for parenthetical information.

> If the icebreak drift begins in 1977 it will contribute to the first
> worldwide experiment of GARP (the Global Atmospheric Re-

search Program). GARP includes Soviet and American POLEX (Polar Experiment) projects seeking factors responsible for climate changes and ice ages.

Most ethologists (students of animal behavior) hold that the activities of almost all living creatures except humans are usually automatic responses to external stimuli, responses that are the result of genetic patterning.

When that matter was settled in late August (through a government promise to indemnify the manufacturers) the Center for Disease Control in Atlanta once again asked for an advertising campaign.

A journalist will use a parenthetical insert to call attention to something the journalist wants stressed, as John Sherwood of the *Washington Star* did in an interview with Theodore A. Wertime, a Smithsonian research associate.

The affluent American way of life as we knew it (he uses the past tense) is already over.

Sometimes information is inserted parenthetically into a direct quotation to explain the quotation.

"They are joined by tsotsis (gangs of thugs) and loafers and then it becomes not so peaceful," the spokesman said.

Quoting the coach of the Cincinnati Bengals, a sportswriter wrote:

"We had a tough game with them in Cleveland early in the season (the Bengals won 45–24) and we were fortunate to win."

(You may also read the preceding insert as an attempt to balance for the reader what the coach said. After all, 45–24 doesn't sound like a tough game.) Again from the sports pages, this time quoting a football player:

"I think the secret to this team's success (Baltimore is 6–1) is that we don't have any one guy we rely on."

A sports story also provided this example:

Other winners included Dwayne Evans of Phoenix, Ariz., in one of eight sections of the 200-meter dash (20.6 seconds); Miruts Yifter of Ethiopia in the 5,000-meter run (13:22.6); Cindy Poor of San Jose, Calif., in the women's 800 (2:01.5); a patchwork United States team in the men's 1,600-meter relay (3:01.7);

(another American team ran 3:02.7), and the United States in the women's 1,600-meter relay (3:29.8).

And from a front page story:

Six men were in the pumping room when the explosion occurred at 3:45 p.m. Alaska daylight time (8:45 p.m. Eastern daylight time).

Parentheses also set off information that is not part of an official name but is necessary for complete identification.

Warren (Pa.) Times Observer
Tamaqua (Pa.) Historical Society

Sometimes editors will insert two or three paragraphs of local information into a wire story. The information is set off by parentheses in the following manner.

Todd accused Hill of choosing this weekend to call a strike because Hill knew 35 percent of the drivers would have pulled off the highway for the holiday weekend.

(No protesting or striking truckers were reported at the Bald Eagle Truck and Auto Plaza at the Milesburg interchange of the Keystone Shortway this morning.

(Milesburg state police said truck traffic on the Shortway appeared to be normal today.

(They said it generally tapered off a bit over long holiday weekends.)

Early reports on truck traffic were mixed.

The convention is the same one used for direct quotations continued uninterrupted over two or more paragraphs—a parenthesis at the beginning of each new paragraph and a parenthesis also at the end of the last paragraph.

One place a parenthetical insert does not belong is in a lead. If information is worth the lead, then it is worth showing off, not hiding within parentheses—a structure that disrupts the lead's flow.

The present New Mexico Power Company line could be improved without any sizable expansion (which would considerably lower the cost), a Taos Planning Commission member said last night.

The parenthetical information rates its own sentence, perhaps leading off the second paragraph.

Holding down on expansion would also lower the cost, William
Kitchen said last night.

Broadcast newswriters use parentheses to insert a phonetic spelling
behind a word or name.

W. Somerset Maugham (mom)

When a name is uncommon, the phonetic spelling is repeated every
time the name appears.

BRACKETS [ ]

Many newspapers do not use brackets because of mechanical limitations.
Instead, they use parentheses. Regardless, the function is important.

Brackets indicate to the reader that a reporter or editor has inserted
something into quoted matter. The reporter or editor may do it to substitute a name for a pronoun where the antecedent is unclear or to give
additional information to the reader.

> Harry Williams, Wentzel's nomination convention director,
> said that the Democratic party platform, the nomination of
> Tracy, and Monahan's statement that he and his running mate
> are compatible on the issues "all move [Monahan] considerably
> leftward."

No doubt Williams said "all move *him* considerably leftward." But the
antecedent of *him* could be *running mate,* which is incorrect. Here is a
similar example; only parentheses are used.

> "The nation is looking at Georgia," said Sen. Frank Sutton, one
> of the measure's sponsors, "and a great part of his (Monahan's)
> publicity is built around the fact that he is a peanut farmer."

The difference between the two that is worth noting is that the first one,
based on a sentence from *The New York Times,* does not use the pronoun
from the original quotation while the second, based on a sentence from a
United Press International story, does. There is no absolute rule on the
usage.

The following quotes a speaker who quotes a newspaper, leaving gaps
for a *New York Times* reporter to fill in.

> "I think it was The Milwaukee Sentinel the next day that spoke
> for America when they said: 'Senator Mondale's decision has
> shocked this nation as it has not been shocked since [Senator]
> Vance Hartke [of Indiana] withdrew in 1972.' "

Here are two similar examples of bracketed matter providing immediate explanation.

"We are against it, absolutely, completely opposed to it even if Eddie Monahan [the governor's brother] wanted it," said the head of the teachers' federation.

"We have two helicopters on stand-by [to help with the drying]. The field is covered, but there has been some flooding from the tunnels."

Sometimes bracketed information functions as transition.

Harold Ockenga announced last week that the magazine would move to a suburb of Wheaton, Ill., a liquor-free, overwhelmingly white residential area 25 miles west of Chicago.
"Deleterious things happen to attitudes if a person lives here [in Washington]," Ockenga said.

Besides getting the reader from Wheaton to Washington, the bracketed information also makes clear that *here* is not Wheaton.

When reporters quote a grammatical error or misuse of the language, they tell the reader by doing the following.

"You can speculate all you want," the coach told reporters. "That seems to be the tempo [sic] of this group anyway."

The coach apparently meant *temperament.*

Brackets are sometimes used to set off *refers*—a phrase at the end of a paragraph indicating where a story giving more detail on the paragraph appears.

Meanwhile, the White House announced that the president would take a vacation next week. [Story on Page 6.]

Here is a *New York Times* story that shows the use of parentheses and brackets. Imagine how confusing this story would be in a newspaper that uses parentheses only.

The Federal Aviation Administration took a gentle swat at the "human fly," George Willig, who recently scaled the outside of the World Trade Center, for using the agency's weather service to determine what the winds were like at the 110-story building's upper reaches. The F.A.A. weekly newsletter Intercom said Mr. Willig had a friend call the F.A.A. weather service at Teterboro Airport, in New Jersey, for details about wind speed and direction. "It was on the basis of [this]," said Intercom, "that the human fly (not certificated by the F.A.A.) went ahead with his escapade. The stunt was a success, but [we want] to emphasize that aviation weather is strictly for aviators and not for human flies."

The apostrophe, which is a sign that a letter has been omitted, is used to indicate possession. At one time in our language, possessive forms were made like this:

the presidentes spokesman

the kinges English

the boyses tent

Today we use the apostrophe.

the president's spokesman

the king's English

the boys' tent

Generally, it is not necessary to add *'s* to show possession when the singular noun ends in *s*. *Charles'* or *Charles's* is acceptable, although the trend is toward the apostrophe alone.

The apostrophe also shows omitted letters in contractions.

wouldn't for would not

don't for do not

can't for cannot

she's for she is

he's for he is (avoid he's/she's for he has/she has)

The apostrophe also indicates the omission of the current century in a date.

Spirit of '76 (Spirit of 1776—an understandable exception—in the United States)

a child of the '50s (a child of the 1950s)

The plural of letters and symbols is usually formed by adding *'s*.

mind your p's and q's

dot all the i's, cross all the t's

learn the abc's

he wears size 13's

a list of do's and don'ts (not don't's)

Some editors don't use the apostrophe to form plurals of capital letter abbreviations and acronyms or numbers. They favor POWs over POW's, GIs over GI's, and '50s over '50's. Regardless, it is pros and cons, not pro's and con's.

QUOTATION MARKS " and '

When journalists quote someone, that is, report the person's words exactly (or almost as exactly as it is humanly possible to transcribe), the person's words are enclosed in quotation marks.

> "A woman can never become a great mathematician," a math professor said recently.

It is the misuse of quotation marks that makes editors scream. The misuse is called *orphan* or *fragmentary quotations*. To understand the misuse, you must first appreciate the convention of using quotation marks around single words to signal an ironic or sarcastic use, a misuse, a shading of meaning or a slang use of a word.

Here is a sarcastic use:

> "When you remove all the fancy words from my opponent's campaign 'promises,' you'll see he really hasn't committed himself to do anything," Sen. Smith said.

Promises is not what Sen. Smith meant. He was denigrating his opponent's campaign statements by suggesting they weren't what his opponent said they were.

A misuse:

> The editor told the cub reporter to get a lot of "quotes" for his story.

What the editor meant was *quotations; quote* is a verb used as a noun only in newsrooms.

A shading:

> Back in 1970 there were four men on the Supreme Court who
> took the "absolute" view of the First Amendment.

Relative to the other justices, the four were absolutists. But there has
never been a pure absolutist on the Supreme Court, at least in First
Amendment decisions.

Slang:

> As a consumer advocate, Lee is constantly on guard against
> being "taken" and is now in court with 14 cases.

A professor who believed a political campaign received too much coverage in the news media made up a word to describe the situation. A reporter wrote:

> The campaign has been "overmediated," he asserted.

Labor problems can be overmediated, perhaps, which has nothing to do
with intensive news coverage. Hence, the quotation marks. Two more
examples of coined words:

> The latter hookup, according to one listener, was "echo-ey."

> They had friends who reacted to the social pressure to "devirgin-
> ize" themselves, as one of them put it.

Usually, the quotation marks around slang and coined words are
dropped in subsequent references.

There are times when a writer wants to make clear that a certain usage
belongs to someone else. Writing in *Newsweek,* columnist George F.
Will punctuated a paragraph this way:

> And only extremely dogmatic majoritarians think democracy
> would be "subverted" (Bayh's word) if the electoral college gave
> the presidency to a candidate who lost the popular vote by a
> wafer-thin margin. It is odd to say the "nation's will" could be
> "frustrated" in a standoff.

You know from the way Will set up his punctuation that all phrases in
quotation marks belong to Bayh, not Will. You also know in the following example that the word in quotation marks is President Monahan's.

> Monahan also defended the "superb" performance of his U.N.
> ambassador, Gary Nelson.

Now for the orphan quotes:

> The student, a major prosecution witness, testified that he lost all fear of his abductors "one block" after they commandeered his van.

Perhaps the student indicated that when he said *one block* he wasn't being literal. But the story doesn't support that interpretation and the reporter shouldn't have placed his interpretation into the story without supporting evidence. There is nothing special about *one block;* the quotation marks are unnecessary. They are also unnecessary in the following:

> That action had a "prejudicial" effect on the jury, the judge ruled.

On the other hand, if the preceding two examples were literal and didn't need quotation marks, the following isn't literal and does need them:

> Richard Rosenthal, head of the arbitrage department at Salomon Brothers, recalls how he got "murdered" recently in a situation similar to the United Technologies-Babcock & Wilcox deal.

This example is made up.

> The mayor said he is "angry" with Councilman Williams.

If the mayor is angry, drop the quotation marks so the reader doesn't believe you're misusing the word. If the mayor is being facetious, make the context clear and use the quotation marks.

It's puzzling to read news stories of someone's retirement or resignation that include this phrase:

> The resignation was accepted with "regret."

The reader might read between the lines, although the person who wrote the story wasn't aiming for that.

Phrases can also be placed in quotation marks for no apparent reason. The following example is a good one, although the over-all sentence is terrible. Regardless, it raises the question: Why the quotation marks?

> He said "the end of summer" should see the first phase of a proposed highway signing program completed.

In the same story quotation marks were used correctly to indicate a non-standard or slang phrase.

However, the supervisors said at a recent meeting that the whole plan was "shot down" by the Federal Highway Administration.

There are times when you must use quotation marks around a single word or short phrase to make clear that you are using someone else's words, not your own.

An "astoundingly large number of children" are mistreated by their parents and a new study on child abuse says mothers are more likely to do the mistreating.

A bank lawyer said the suit was a "preventive measure" to insure the debt will be paid in light of Williams' arrest in connection with the Jamison kidnaping case.

He said that will depend on the "revenue picture" and the need for increased subsidies to public schools.

In a significant departure from most of his campaign speeches on the economy, Mr. Carter said he would attempt to "target" government spending and federal programs to create jobs.

Target received the quotation marks because in 1976 it was a noun used as a verb. It became popular very fast and the use of quotation marks stopped.

Sometimes quotation marks are used around a word or phrase because there is no clear meaning for that word or phrase and the reporter must indicate to the reader that he is offering what he can. Congress once passed a bill that gave the president a reason for doing something but it never defined the reason. When reporting on the measure, a *New York Times* reporter signaled readers this way:

Once in office, the prosecutor could be removed by the president only for "extraordinary improprieties" and his removal could be challenged in the courts.

What will happen in this case is that some federal judge, perhaps even the nine justices of the Supreme Court, will define "extraordinary improprieties" someday.

There are times when people understate situations and use euphemisms. They, too, should be in quotation marks.

One son, a 27-year-old dope addict, was killed by a shotgun blast, and another died at the age of 23 when he "ran into a knife," his mother said.

Where a scholarly publication would use italics, newspapers often use quotation marks, such as around foreign words.

The proposal, two years in the making, stems from a joint effort by the commission and a neighborhood group, the Little Italy Restoration Association, to bring about a "resorgimento"—a resurgence—of a historic section of Manhattan that has lately suffered from urban decay and a decline of its ethnic population.

Single quotation marks are used in place of double quotation marks in newspaper headlines. They are also used to indicate a quotation within a quotation in a story.

The speaker said: "It was Hamlet, I believe, who said, 'To be or not to be.' Well, that is the question facing us tonight."

Quotations continued from one paragraph to the next are used thusly:

"We're not necessarily looking for a direct tie," Williams said.
"Those cases may be another disease that we have to thoroughly investigate. [No closing quotation marks.]
"They wanted to call it a sort of virus or flu."

The joint stylebook of the wire services calls for quotation marks around titles of books, operas, plays, television programs, works of art, songs, movies, lectures and speeches. Newspapers, however, seem to be very selective in applying that guideline, enclosing the titles of books but not the titles of movies, or the names of newspapers but not the names of magazines. The trend seems to be away from using quotation marks when the meaning is clear.

The story first appeared in the November edition of More magazine.

Finally, there is this warning on something quotation marks don't do—they don't get a newspaper off the hook in a libel case.

"She's a no-good whore," Williams said of his daughter-in-law, the former Mary T. Meade.

While it is true that the speaker can be held libelous, so can the newspaper. Quotation marks don't change that fact.

Punctuate these sentences according to standard newspaper usage.

1. Public property losses in New Mexico included initial estimates of up to $7 million

2. "Maybe we could dance to Frosty the Snowman."

3. For breakfast I had toast bacon and eggs fried potatoes grapefruit and a glass of milk

4. Mary Sue Nelson the movie star will appear here next week

5. "It was assumed that I got the piece of mail a statement of fitness to serve and there was no way for me to prove I did not get it I find the conviction in your own words inherently incredible."

6. The superintendent of education Lawrence Johnson said the new program will begin in the middle of the school year

7. The spokesman said the workers had won a cost of living increase a new issue in bargaining talks this year.

8. Requiring everyone to pay taxes which was not part of the measure will increase the Treasurys revenues by $10 billion a year.

9. The touchdown that won the game came on a quarterback option a new play in Clive's playbook.

10. People, who live in glass houses, shouldn't throw stones.

11. The highway department expects to complete the bypass by April 1, 1994 a spokesman said

12. The proposal however does not consider what the department will be doing 15 years from now

13. In answer to a question today Dr. Eugene Kellner director of the bureaus research division said the serum will be available in four weeks.

14. When the bank shut down the town died too.

15. Since the vaccination program began there have been no flu outbreaks.

16. They said they intend to live together arguing that a marriage certificate does not make a marriage

17. The big fast football player also likes dancing

18. In a long editorial the new leaders of Excelsior said they "would continue the newspapers policy of informing the people.

19. Both facilities officials said are crowded.

20. The conservative dissidents, who last night ousted the editor of the newspaper cooperative Julio Schere Garcia and 200 of his top staff were apparently encouraged and assisted in their move by the government.

21. On stage at Harrisons Williams told joke after joke after joke

22. "John when are we going to get off dead center and do something" the mayor asked.

23. The president likes the bill he will sign it into law.

24. Here are my suggestions give the map to Jim, the shovel to Amy and the pick to Tracey.

25. The network's proposed schedule thereby looks like a corporate giant surrounded by business as usual fillers.

26. Recounting the votes from the last election will take about three weeks the county commissioners said.

27. But some middle class area residents have challenged these figures saying that a number of low income welfare receiving families are living in apartments that the city counts in its middle income and moderate income totals.

28.   The recently-elected congressmen are not familiar with all of the procedures of Congress.

29.   The news editor Thomas L Jones will rewrite the stylebook.

30.   There are five mile relay teams entered in the mile relay competition.

31.   There is only one man who can lead this country out of the depths of despair Thomas F. Williams

32.   City Council will vote tonight on a proposal to ban dogs from public streets the first such proposal on the issue.

33.   The president called for removing some of the burdens the public must bear in reporting taxes Story on Page 8

34.   I said, Isnt it enough that Jims idea was discussed

ANSWERS

1.   Public property losses in New Mexico included initial estimates of up to $7 million.
2.   "Maybe we could dance to 'Frosty the Snowman.' "
3.   For breakfast I had toast, bacon and eggs, fried potatoes, grapefruit and a glass of milk.
4.   Mary Sue Nelson, the movie star, will appear here next week.
5.   "It was assumed that I got the piece of mail [a statement of fitness to serve] and there was no way for me to prove I did not get it. I find the conviction, in your own words, 'inherently incredible.' "
6.   The superintendent of education, Lawrence Johnson, said the new program will begin in the middle of the school year.
7.   The spokesman said the workers had won a cost-of-living increase, a new issue in bargaining talks this year.
8.   Requiring everyone to pay taxes, which was not part of the measure, will increase the Treasury's revenues by $10 billion a year.
9.   The touchdown that won the game came on a quarterback option, a new play in Clive's playbook.
10.   People who live in glass houses shouldn't throw stones.
11.   The highway department expects to complete the bypass by April 15, 1994, a spokesman said.
12.   The proposal, however, does not consider what the department will be doing 15 years from now.

13. In answer to a question today, Dr. Eugene Kellner, director of the bureau's research division, said the serum will be available in four weeks.

14. When the bank shut down, the town died too.

15. Since the vaccination program began, there have been no flu outbreaks.

16. They said they intend to live together, arguing that a marriage certificate does not make a marriage.

17. The big, fast football player also likes dancing.

18. In a long editorial, the new leaders of Excelsior said they "would continue the newspaper's policy of informing the people."

19. Both facilities, officials said, are crowded.

20. The conservative dissidents, who last night ousted the editor of the newspaper cooperative, Julio Schere Garcia, and 200 of his top staff, were apparently encouraged and assisted in their move by the government.

21. On stage at Harrison's, Williams told joke after joke after joke.

22. "John, when are we going to get off dead center and do something?" the mayor asked.

23. The president likes the bill; he will sign it into law.

24. Here are my suggestions: Give the map to Jim, the shovel to Amy and the pick to Tracey.

25. The network's proposed schedule, thereby, looks like a corporate giant surrounded by business-as-usual fillers.

26. Re-counting the votes from the last election will take about three weeks, the county commissioners said.

27. But some middle-class area residents have challenged these figures, saying that a number of low-income welfare-receiving families are living in apartments that the city counts in its middle-income and moderate-income totals.

28. The recently elected congressmen are not familiar with all of the procedures of Congress.

29. The news editor, Thomas L. Jones, will rewrite the stylebook.

30. There are five mile-relay teams entered in the mile-relay competition.

31. There is only one man who can lead this country out of the depths of despair—Thomas F. Williams.

32. City Council will vote tonight on a proposal to ban dogs from public streets—the first such proposal on the issue.

33. The president called for removing some of the burdens the public must bear in reporting taxes. (Story on Page 8.) [Story on Page 8.]

34. I said, "Isn't it enough that Jim's idea was discussed?"

SEVEN

Spelling

Many editors and journalism professors believe that a person who is careless with spelling is probably careless with facts. Writing in *The Gannetteer,* John H. McMillan, executive editor of Gannett's Huntington, W.Va., newspapers, complained:

> Look at a sentence published this fall in a Gannett Group newspaper:
> "Each year the principle payment will be $320,000."
> Almost anyone can figure out from the whole of the sentence that the newspaper really meant "principal."
> But if the newspaper doesn't know the difference between "principle" and "principal," the reader may fairly ask, how can anyone be sure it's right about that $320,000? Perhaps it's $220,000 or $420,000.

Once in the routine of checking spelling, journalists will probably find themselves in the routine of checking facts, a habit that needs no defense.

I use a dictionary a lot; I am never satisfied to say I am positive about the way a word is spelled. I have learned that the more positive I am, the more likely I am to be incorrect. To improve my spelling in the past I made lists of troublesome words, then studied the pattern of those words. I even learned some rules. And there are some rules, despite surface inconsistencies in words that would seem to indicate, for example, that *tough* and *through* shouldn't be spelled so similarly.

Although time consuming for someone writing against a deadline, one way to check spelling is to read a story backward—that is, the last sentence, then next to last and so on. Doing that breaks the continuity of the story and makes you concentrate on spelling alone. Of course, that doesn't remove the obligation of reading the story from beginning to end.

Much of our spelling comes from pronunciation. But pronunciation has changed while spelling hasn't. Pronunciation and spelling are not as closely related today as they were 200 years ago. But where there is a relationship today, you should learn it.

You can devise memory tools to help you learn troublesome words. Don't worry if the tools are silly. "There is *a rat* in separate" has reduced my usage of a dictionary. Sometimes the memory tool is not some silly ditty but an association you give to the word and its spelling. Maybe you learned to spell *easy* the correct (that is, standard) way because you became tired of seeing signs at the interchanges of turnpikes that boasted so-and-so's service station was E-Z Off, E-Z On. If negative re-inforcement is going to make spelling easier for you, so be it. Keep in mind that problems with spelling are usually not with the entire word but with part of it, such as *a rat* in *separate*. You don't have to master the whole word when the solution is merely making one of its syllables your servant.

Before I put you through the rules of spelling, I must qualify them. I found some of them through research for this book, although I could spell decently before I knew the rules. Many of these rules have exceptions, which I shall note. To me an exception disproves a rule. After the rules, a list of commonly misspelled words with borrowed or made-for-the-occasion memory tools follows. I showed some of them to a colleague who responded: "It's easier to learn the spelling than some of the memory tools." I agree. There's no substitute for a dictionary.

PREFIXES AND SUFFIXES

PREFIXES

You won't *misspell* words if you remember that a prefix does not change the spelling of a word. If something is not natural, it is *un* plus *natural,* not *unatural.* Prefixes such as *il* (*illegal*), *im* (*immoral*), *dis* (*dissatisfied*), *un* (*unnecessary*) and *mis* (*misstep*) do not affect spelling.

SUFFIXES

When you change an adjective to an adverb, you add *ly,* which is a suffix. Like a prefix, that suffix does not affect spelling. To convert *accidental* to an adverb, add *ly,* which results in *accidentally.* That word is often misspelled because people convert *accident* (the noun) to an adverb, which results in *accidently.* Other suffixes that don't affect spelling are: *less* (*heartless*), *ness* (*outspokenness*), *al* (*occasional*), *ful* (*spiteful*) and *ment* (*arrangement*).

Er and *est* (as in *bigger* and *biggest*) are not as consistent. When adding either to a word that ends in *e,* just add *r* or *st.* Think of the second *e* as redundant.

Also remember that *y* changes to *i* when adding *er* or *est* (*happy, happier, happiest*).

ADDING *ABLE* AND *IBLE*

For words with the endings *able* and *ible* I check my dictionary or the *Government Printing Office Style Manual,* which contains a list of *ible*-ending words and the rule that "other words in this class end in *able.*" Harry Shaw has compiled a relatively extensive set of rules on these endings, which indicate many more exceptions than the government style guide suggests.

Generally, *able* is the correct ending when it is being added to a complete word. Complete words include those that drop the silent *e* or change *y* to *i* before adding the suffix. Some typical *able* words are: *work, workable; consider, considerable; believe, believable* (drop the *e*); *rely, reliable* (change *y* to *i*). However, forget this "rule" with *discernible.*

Ible is the standard suffix when you are not starting with a complete word, as in *horr*ible, *tang*ible and *plaus*ible. Drop *ible* from the preceding words and you are left with meaningless syllables, not words. One major exception (major because it would seem to follow the *able* rule but doesn't) is a word that ends in *ion*. Dropping the *ion* leaves a complete word (deduction, deduct) which would suggest *deductable*. Not so. Words ending in *ion* are converted to adjectives by adding *ible*, as in *reduction, reducible; contraction, contractible; digestion, digestible; connection, connectible; suggestion, suggestible.*

DOUBLING THE CONSONANT

This rule is based on pronunciation. It is important because the possibilities of getting the wrong word are endless and self-defeating to any writer. There is a difference between a rabbit *hopping* down the trail and *hoping* down the trail. And soldiers can be either *scarred* in battle or *scared*. The duties of a candy *striper* and candy *stripper* (if there is such a thing) are the difference between a hospital and a candy factory. *Taping* telephone calls is not the same as *tapping* them.

One-syllable words that end in a consonant (except *h* and *x*) double the consonant for the suffixes *ed, ing, er, est*. Thus, *hop* becomes ho*pp*ed and *scar* becomes sca*rr*ed. You might remember the rule another way: If the word ends in *e*, don't double, just add the appropriate ending. To turn *slope* into a participle, add *d* (*sloped*). *Slop*, of course, doubles the *p* when adding *ed* (*slopped*). Exceptions exist, such as *row, rowed*.

Multisyllable words double the consonant when the accent falls on the last syllable of the main word. The accent in *excel* is on *cel:* Double up. For years the one-syllable rule was mistakenly applied to *cancel*, which resulted in cance*ll*ed. But the accent is on *can*, not *cel*, so the consonant is not doubled. The wire services once followed that rule for *kidnap, kidnaped*. They have since changed to *kidnap, kidnapped*. If you remember this rule with words like *total* and *travel* (both accented on the first syllable), you'll always produce the preferred spelling, *totaled, traveled*.

NATIVES OF STATES

The following list for the spelling of natives of states is taken from the *Government Printing Office Style Manual*.

Alabamian	Connecticuter	Illinoisan
Alaskan	Delawarean	Indianian
Arizonan	Floridian	Iowan
Arkansan	Georgian	Kansan
Californian	Hawaiian	Kentuckian
Coloradan	Idahoan	Louisianian

Mainer	New Jerseyite	South Dakotan
Marylander	New Mexican	Tennessean
Massachusettsan	New Yorker	Texan
Michiganite	North Carolinian	Utahan
Minnesotan	North Dakotan	Vermonter
Mississippian	Ohioan	Virginian
Missourian	Oklahoman	Washingtonian
Montanan	Oregonian	West Virginian
Nebraskan	Pennsylvanian	Wisconsinite
Nevadan	Rhode Islander	Wyomingite
New Hampshirite	South Carolinian	

PLURALS

CHANGING *Y* TO *I*

When you pluralize a noun ending in *y* or put a verb ending in *y* into third person singular, change the *y* to *i* and add *es*. However, that is true only when a consonant precedes the *y*. Thus, it is ci*ty*, ci*ties*; f*ly*, f*lies*; c*ry*, c*ries*. But if the letter preceding the *y* is a vowel (*a, e, i, o, u*), just add *s,* as in attorn*ey,* attorn*eys;* vall*ey,* vall*eys;* donk*ey,* donk*eys;* chimn*ey,* chimn*eys.*

Some writers have ignored the second part of this rule without undue harm to meaning (as in *monies*), but I recommend that you follow it strictly. Readers no doubt will know what you mean when you write *attornies.* But are you going to be in their living rooms to explain you meant the plural of *alley* when you wrote *allies?*

PROPER NOUNS ENDING IN Y

Proper nouns ending in *y* do not follow the preceding rule. Just add *s.* Thus, when referring to East and West Germany, it is *Germanys,* not *Germanies,* a mistake one headline writer magnified by erring in 36 point type.

TROUBLESOME WORDS

GUIDELINES FOR *IE, EI*

i before e, except after c,
or when sounded like a
as in neighbor and weigh.

Followed blindly that rule wouldn't get you through this sentence:

The knights *seized* the village after a five-day *siege*.

There are exceptions to the rule and there are even exceptions to the exceptions. Try this rule:

When the rules are a fright,
Your dictionary's right.

SEED-SOUNDING WORDS

Only one word ends in *sede* (*supersede*). Only three end in *ceed* (*proceed, exceed, succeed*). All others end in *cede* (*precede, secede,* and so on).

WORDS ENDING IN *EFY* AND *IFY*

Only four commonly used words end in *efy* (*liquefy, putrefy, rarefy, stupefy*). Learn them or consult your dictionary.

SOME MEMORY TOOLS

a*ccomm*odate (*accommodate* accommodates 2 c's and 2 m's)
account*a*nt (think of fis*ca*l)
a*dd*ress (pronounced a*d-d*ress)
advi*c*e (the noun)
advi*s*e (the verb)
all*ege* (not the same thing as a le*d*ge)
all right (think of all wrong; alright is all wrong)
a lot (not *alot,* but the opposite of a little)
altogether (keep it altogether)
ar*c*tic (the *arc* at the top of the world)
ar*gum*ent (don't *gum* it up)
*assass*ination (there are two *ass*es)
be*lie*ve (never believe a *lie*)
benefi*t*ed (get the accen*t* right)
*candi*date (think of sweet talk)
canvas (a piece of material; think of one stitch, one *s*)
canvass (a *s*urvey whose *s* you add to canvas)
capit*o*l (*o*nly a building)
ce*metery* (every cemetery has a meter in the middle)
co*mm*ittee (co*mm*only used to avoid making a decision)

complement (something that completes)

compliment (I *li*ke them)

con*s*ensus (derived from consent)

counc*il* (speak no *il* of it)

coun*s*el (advice for the *self*)

defend*ant* (size not import*ant*)

defin*ite* (f*i*rm)

depend*e*nt (the ending d*e*pends on the beginning)

develop (lop off the *e*)

discrep*ancy* ("F*ancy* that," the accountant said when he found a discrep-
ancy in the books.)

dou*b*t (*b*ut . . . *b*ut . . . *b*ut)

envi*ron*ment (*iron* out the spelling)

*fund*amental (what a *fund* is)

gover*n*ment (think of gover*n*)

gram*mar* (misspelling this will *mar* any paper)

hazard (pronounced *haz-ard*)

hum*o*rous (j*o*y)

indispens*able* (not able to dispense with the *a*)

inte*rr*upt (don't interrupt the *r*'s)

judgment (preferred spelling)

le*i*sure (*I sure* like it)

lightning (two syllables; strikes twice)

*mem*ento (*mem*ory)

*mil*eage, *mill*age (nothing changes with age)

*mort*gage (which *mort*als pay)

municip*al* (loc*al* government)

notic*e*able (notice the *e*)

ord*i*nance (in which every *i* is dotted)

ordnance (short fuse; that is, two syllables)

perso*nn*el (more than one *n*)

Philip*pines* (pines for Philip)

*pie*ce (have a piece of pie)

preventive (preferred spelling)

princip*al* (the principal is your *pal;* also think of m*a*in, which it also
means)

princip*le* (as in ru*le*)

priv*i*lege (I want all I can get)

q (is always followed by *u*)

re*pet*ition (think of *pet*)

station*a*ry (at *a*ttention)
station*e*ry (think of pap*er*)
superinten*dent* (tries to *dent* out ignorance)
there (where?)
utilize (use *use* instead)
vene*real* (from Venus and the *real* thing)
*vi*cinity (think of *vi*rginity)
*vill*ain (lives in a *villa*)
*wo*man, *wo*men ("wo" to the *man* or *men* who misspell these words)
xenophobia (you're going to have to define it anyway; why use it?)
Xerox (not zerox. A trademark, not a verb. Use *photocopy.*)
y*ie*ld (i before e; e yields to i)
zoology (zo-ology, not zoo-ology; learn the correct pronunciation of this
   commonly mispronounced word)

EIGHT

Meaning

TIME AND MEANING

"Words are inexact tools to say the least," retired Supreme Court Justice William O. Douglas said in 1958. As the cause of inexactitude, Douglas cited the different experiences each person brings to a word. He could have also blamed the ever-changing meaning of words. Nothing is as old as yesterday's meaning of a word. Nor is anything as uncertain as what its meaning will be tomorrow. To rely on the past to define a word is not as secure as some believe. S. I. Hayakawa says:

> In choosing our words when we speak or write, we can be *guided* by the historical record afforded us by the dictionary, but we cannot be *bound* by it, because new situations, new experiences, new inventions, new feelings are always compelling us to give new uses to old words. Looking under a "hood," we should ordinarily have found, five hundred years ago, a monk; today we find a motor car engine [italics in original].

And L. M. Myers, a college English teacher, provides an example of a change that occurred within four generations (approximately 120 years).

To my grandfather, who was born in Ireland, the "natural" meaning of the word *car* was a small horsedrawn vehicle; to my father, it was a railroad coach; to me, a street-car. Of course all of us had to recognize new meanings as conditions changed. To my son, the natural meaning is an automobile; and it is quite possible that to his son it may seem the obvious word for what we now call airplanes, especially if our roads get so full of automobiles that they can't move any more.

Hayakawa's interest is that of a *semanticist,* a person who studies the meanings of words. A semanticist will never tell you what a word must mean, only what it means to the people who use it. Edwin Newman, on the other hand, is not willing to accept every change that occurs. Known as the house grammarian at NBC-TV, Newman is both eloquent and witty—and upset with the dilution of words in the English language.

Hayakawa could tell us that at one time *disinterested* and *uninterested* meant two different things but that today the distinction is seldom made. Newman would argue persuasively that we shouldn't let the distinction die because we have no substitute for *disinterested* and we need it.

There is nothing sacred about the meaning of a word. Any word can change, like *hood,* to fit the times. Written 200 years ago the following sentence would have had nothing to do with tennis:

The shot *killed* Jones, and Sweeney served an ace for the coup d'etat.

Thirty years ago a *camper* was a person who camped in the forests; today a *camper* is also a motorized vehicle people can live in. A *capsule* once did nothing more than hold medicine; today space technology has added another definition. If the man who invented the diesel engine had been named Rudolf Schultz instead of Rudolf Diesel, we would have cars powered by schultz engines instead of diesel engines. Nothing in the history of any word preordains its meaning for eternity. There is nothing inherent between a word and its meaning. Langacker calls the relation "a matter of convention," and Rubinstein and Weaver see it as "a social contract whereby persons agree on the meaning occupied by a word."

The social contract is handed down to us in dictionaries, which are put together by people who *record* and *report* the meanings used by people. Dictionary-makers do not determine meanings. The meaning (or definition) given in any dictionary is denotative; it is the objective fact of a word stated as dryly and impartially as possible. From *The American Heritage Dictionary of the English Language:*

> bee: Any of various winged, hairy-bodied, usually stinging insects of the order Hymenoptera, including many solitary species as well as the social members of the family Apidae, and characterized by specialized structures for sucking nectar and gathering pollen from flowers.

Ask anyone who has been stung by a bee or chased by a swarm of bees to tell you what a bee is.

You may have trouble getting someone to define the next word for you, but be assured there's more to it than this:

> copulate: To engage in coitus.

And the definition of *coitus* is no less objective.

Still, we know more about bees and copulation than the dictionary tells. We can speak from our own or someone else's experience about these words, and when we think of the words later, those experiences will mean more to us than the dictionary's definition. The experiences or associations people add to a word are a word's connotative meaning, which is far more crucial in communication than any dictionary definition could hope to be. It is the difference between a house and a home—a physical structure and a state of mind.

An article in *Smithsonian* magazine began:

> Neighborhood: the very word is pleasant. Its syllables flow with deliberation and warmth, connoting a realm of peace, stability and fellowship.

According to the dictionary, a neighborhood is "a district considered in regard to its inhabitants or distinctive characteristics." That doesn't make the *Smithsonian* article incorrect. The author apparently feels this way about *neighborhood*. He did include *connoting* in his second sentence. But not everyone feels that way about the word *neighborhood,* and we would have to know more about any person using the word and the sentence in which he or she uses it to understand better what is meant. Does this use not mean something different?

> The damn neighborhood ruins everyone who lives in it.

You have now seen *neighborhood* in two different contexts. And it is in the context where the meaning of a word can go astray and it is in the context where a precise meaning can be conveyed. You know what the word *light* means. Before you produce 10 definitions from a dictionary, read this sentence from *Scientific American:*

Light can appear dim or bright but not light or dark.

Do you still need a dictionary? You shouldn't. The context says it all. And if you had to define the second light as it related to dark and dim or bright, you were relying on context. Here are similar examples:

As they *tear* down the old hotel, it brings a *tear* to my eye.

Show me a *bear* who can *bear* to be held in captivity and I'll show you one tough *bear.*

Take the words *since* and *because.* Although few make a distinction today, the two words don't always mean the same thing, as shown in this sentence from *More* magazine:

Since—if not because—Hayes left, ad linage has dropped disastrously, to little more than half the 1,280 pages the magazine had in 1973.

Despite the difference, people still use *since* for *because,* which is acceptable if the usage isn't ambiguous.

Since I'm the oldest member, I'll serve as president.

The context makes the preceding clear, but context isn't enough to help in the following:

Since the Bahamas will be holding its first national election this week since independence was granted in 1973, the political opposition . . .

The first *since* should be *because.*

In the following example *doctor* (meaning to treat or tamper with) is misused. But the reporter, Alice S. Kountz of the *Centre Daily Times,* first provided a context to make the misuse clear.

He asked Mr. Branigan to justify the number of specialists recently admitted to Centre Community's medical staff. "At what point will you become *over-doctored* . . . ?" he asked [italics added].

The first sentence gives the context to the second.

The italicized portion of the following example does not mean what it says, yet the context gives it the meaning the writer wanted to convey.

Most are connected with other dailies, and, with the Times'
bureaus around the world, they form a global net through
which *little news* passes unnoticed [italics added].

A memorandum telling faculty members that a maintenance crew was
going to wash their venetian blinds included this humorous phrase:

Please care for papers, books, etc., which might be lost in the
movement of equipment by the *blind crew* [italics added].

Nobody who read the memorandum believed the maintenance crew was
sightless. And who reading a story about housing for senior citizens
would mistake *elderly housing project* for anything but housing for elderly
persons?

Context sometimes deprives us of using words that are otherwise
okay. In a court trial, where charges are made, the following use of
charged for *attacked* is confusing:

Williams also said that one day Jones *charged* the judge.

When Walter Cronkite of CBS News asked the American public "to
declare a honeymoon" with President Gerald R. Ford, Jean Stafford, a
staunch defender of pure usage, asked:

How is a honeymoon declared? Who has vested in Mr. Cronkite
the power to let precision of speech go to hell in a handbasket?

She argued that in the strict sense of the language, you cannot "declare a
honeymoon." But I like the phrase—I like it now; I liked it when I
heard Cronkite use it. It evokes the history of a troubled presidency, of a
constituency turned against the presidency and of a president who re-
signed from office (Richard M. Nixon). We could have declared a truce,
but there was a new man in office; in effect, it was a new marriage. And
because of the embattled condition of the office of the president, Cronkite knew the bitterness of the past might continue. By asking us "to
declare a honeymoon," Cronkite effectively combined the language of
war and the language of domestic joy. It worked because events of the
time provided the context.

Even unfamiliar words or regional usages can be quite clear in the
right context, as the following from *The New York Times* shows:

The work is, as they say here, "seasonable," running from *ice-out*
around mid-May to *ice-in* in late November or December—the
state of the river having once been the most important way to
measure time here [italics added].

The good writer is aware of context and is extremely careful with it. Nothing angers an editor more than to be told someone has been "quoted out of context" by a reporter. People who have been quoted out of context may wonder if the press is completely fair.

Still another problem arises when the context changes, then the thought you want to convey may also change. Yesterday's meaning is dead. *Urchin* on the lips of a social worker may be someone to be helped; to a police officer an *urchin* may be a juvenile delinquent.

Sometimes the meaning of a word can change from page to page. In *The New York Times Book Review,* Margot Hentoff wrote:

> "Barred From School" is an informal study of some of these involuntarily *de-schooled* children and their families [italics added].

Her review made the meaning clear—children denied access to school. On the facing page was another review in which Joseph Featherstone of the Harvard Graduate School of Education wrote:

> He is now a convert to Illich, a true believer in the proposition that the compulsions of formal schooling rule out the possibility of any genuine learning or teaching; he feels nothing can be done until society is *deschooled* [italics added].

As Featherstone's review makes clear, he is using the word to mean a deemphasis in schooling. That meaning, Featherstone says, is the more common. Given the contexts, both meanings are clear.

When you find yourself in a situation where a person is putting great stress on connotation, try getting the person to be specific. You obviously can't say, "Would you be more denotative than connotative, please." But you can ask the person to be more precise by explaining what he or she means. Journalists aim for denotation; they can't afford to give the reader even a slight chance of interpreting any word differently. To guard against misinterpretation, the journalist has to keep context in mind at all times.

TAMPERING WITH MEANING

Many journalists would deny that they unintentionally do harm to the meaning of words. In reality, they are no more or less guilty of tampering than anyone else, but they'd like to believe their purity. Regardless, journalists should be extremely cautious of the way they use their language. Tampering with meaning devalues the language, leaving, for example, *disinterested* and *uninterested* as synonyms when, in fact, we need to preserve the original distinction between the two.

A commonly misquoted phrase from the Bible is the following:

> He that is without sin among you, let him first cast a stone at her. (John 8:7)

That says that after casting a stone the thrower may do something else. But the statement is misquoted to make it sound as though Christ is proposing a stoning. The misquotation:

> He that is without sin among you, cast the first stone.

That says there will be more stones.

Whether or not journalists are responsible for the change in that meaning doesn't matter. But they have been criticized for other changes. Consider, first, the complaint of H. L. Mencken:

> The copy-reader accordingly makes heavy use of very short words . . . and these words tend to be borrowed by the reporters who must submit to his whims and long for his authority and glory. Their way into the common speech thus comes easy.

Those copy-readers are also headline writers who need short words, not only because they fit in a limited space, but also because they can be readily understood during a fast paced scan by the reader. But, as Mencken says, headline writers are not satisfied with existing short words so they extend the meanings of some (just as they change nouns into bastard adjectives) to cover every possible news story. Objects of Mencken's scorn include (all italics are his):

> *Ace.* In the sense of expert or champion it came in during the World War. It has since been extended to mean any person who shows any ponderable proficiency in whatever he undertakes to do. I have encountered *ace* lawyers, *ace* radio-crooners and *ace* gynecologists in headlines.

> *Car.* It is rapidly displacing all the older synonyms for *automobile,* including even *auto.*

> *Chief.* Any headman, whether political, pedagogical, industrial, military or ecclesiastical. I once encountered the headline *Church*

Chiefs Hold Parley over a news item dealing with a meeting of the Sacred College.

Drive. Any concerted and public effort to achieve anything.

Fete. Any celebration.

Head. It means whatever *chief* means.

Plea. It means *request, petition, application, prayer, suit, demand or appeal.*

Slate. Any programme, agenda, or list.

Talk. Any discussion or conference.

Mencken was equally disturbed by clipped forms of words in headlines. He observed that *ad, confab, duo, exam, gas, isle, mart, photo* and *quake* were common. Four decades later, when there was a shortage of natural gas and gasoline, the clipped word *gas* became confusing. Today we have clipped, for example, *airplane* to *plane, memorandum* to *memo, telephone* to *phone, omnibus* to *bus, bicycle* to *bike, smoke* and *fog* to *smog,* and *coeducational* to *coed*—and changed that word's meaning to boot. Headline writers and imitative reporters are still at it. In addition to using many of the words Mencken mentioned, today's headline writers and reporters have added the following:

Air. Takes up less space than *discuss.*

Back. It means *support, endorse,* even *approve.*

Bogus bills. Synonymous with *counterfeit money,* but a lot shorter.

Decry. Often a substitute for *criticize,* the word really means *belittle.*

Eye. As a verb, it replaces *study.*

Feds. For *federal officials,* as in this headline: "FEDS BATTLE MEDS IN AID FRAUD CASE." Obviously, *meds* are doctors.

Grill. A substitute for *quiz* (which is the same length), it means *intense questioning* (which isn't the same length).

Gyn. From a headline, "ROUTINE GYN EXAMS HARD TO GET," it was clipped from *gynecological.* Fortunately, it wasn't used in the story.

Ink. Sports page talk for *sign,* as in "ROOKER INKS CON-TRACT." Despite the fact it's a verb usage going back at least a century, one contemporary dictionary lists it only as a noun. You will also hear the word in newspaper pressrooms when presspeople ink the presses.

Loom. Large storms *loom,* but to headline writers, anything in the future *looms,* including meetings. For reporters, it's inflation, as in: "Inflation has loomed suddenly as an increasingly important administration concern in recent months."

Meet. Short for *meeting;* also more common to headlines than news stories.

Nip. The misfortune of this word is in its misuse, as in this headline: "DODGERS NIP GIANTS, 10–3." The word should be preserved for close scores and short drinks.

OK or *OKs.* It takes in all the meanings of *back* and is often written as *okays* in news stories.

Pen. Perhaps to give a quill-and-ink effect, headline writers use this verb to describe the labor of authors of books and songs. After all, *pen* is shorter than *write.*

Pick. As a noun, it means *choice, selection, nominee.*

Rap. What happens when somebody criticizes your *pick.*

Rip. When you rebut the critic of your *pick.*

Set. A shorter version of *slated,* which is a shorter version of *scheduled.*

Slap. No harm intended; it takes the place of *rip* and *rap.*

Tap. When you select a *pick.* "MONAHAN TAPS BROWN AS STATE PICK."

Unit. Indicates part of a whole—"HOUSE UNIT OKS PLAN." But it can get confusing, especially with the Justice Department, which is both a whole and part of a whole (the federal government). "JUSTICE UNIT PLANS PROBE" could be anything from the entire department to one subdivision of the department.

Vie. Usually seen in political and sports stories, it is a shortened form of the Middle English *envien,* to challenge. "CHAUCER VIES FOR FAVOR."

Mencken has been replaced by Newman, it appears. Newman complains that "American journalism has a way of . . . fastening on words and sucking them dry." Today not an issue that arises goes without the label *controversial*. And problems aren't really problems unless they're *serious*. One of Newman's examples of abuse comes in a news story of an airplane hijacking that was foiled. The story referred to it as a *successful foiling,* a dilution that foils the import of foiling. Had the foiling not been successful, a serious crisis no doubt would have followed. Newman writes:

> Crises that are not serious are not worth the trouble. It's like the true facts politicians so often demand or, conversely, insist that they are giving us. True facts are the only facts worth having. False facts are no use at all . . .

Based on a newspaper column by a school teacher, this sentence makes a point about misused words:

> Cadbury Area's programs in reading, writing and mathematics are *spearheaded* by teachers {italics added}.

The word means to be the leader of a drive or an attack and is more apt in the description of a movie on television that said "a police investigator is assigned to spearhead the search for a mad bomber who has terrorized the city." The word is too long for Mencken's list and perhaps not abused enough for Newman's. But a lot of spearheading goes on, both in searching for mad bombers and the bombastic mad.

Words are misused because of a writer's laziness to think about what he or she is writing. Here are some examples from journalism students and journalists (all italics are mine):

> *Conclusive* evidence has been found of the *possibility* of a second gun in the senator's death.

Perhaps the writer wanted to protect herself from all sides. But if the evidence is conclusive, how can there be any doubt?

> "We understand three bodies have definitely been *visualized* in the debris," Allegheny County Coroner Cyril Wecht said.

The coroner meant *seen*. The obligation of the journalist in such instances is to paraphrase the speaker rather than quote abominable language.

> A Utah State fraternity has been *sanctioned* for an alleged hazing incident.

When something is sanctioned, it is approved. Only in the realm of law, does it mean penalized.

> He *alluded* to a secret charter.

An allusion is a vague or oblique reference. Actually, the person referred to a secret charter by naming it and telling who authorized it.

> Covert action ranges from propaganda to *coups de grace.*

The correct word is *coups d'état,* a foreign word that probably shouldn't appear in newspapers.

> The government pressures journalists not to pursue *exposés* of the CIA.

An *exposé* is something already revealed, not something that can be revealed.

> The CIA *catalyzes* wars.

The word is too technical; it has a very special meaning to scientists. The second sin is that it is an uncommon word; what's wrong with *instigates?*

> Dr. Thomas criticized the scientific *instinct* of reductionism.

Because instinct is innate, it's difficult to imagine people born with scientific instinct. Better words are *approach* or *method.*

Finally, an editing student took the following sentence and changed its meaning by changing one word:

> She went to Buenos Aires alone on their 15th wedding anniversary *early* this month.

> She went to Buenos Aires alone on their 15th wedding anniversary *earlier* this month.

The first sentence appeared in a story published in the last week of the month. It means that during the first week (approximately) the action took place. But when *early* is changed to *earlier* it could mean any time in the first three weeks of the month.

The same student changed the meaning of the following

> The council voted to urge a review by the pope of a recent declaration *against allowing* admission of women to the priesthood.

by substituting

> The council voted to urge a review by the pope of a recent dec-
> laration *prohibiting* admission of women to the priesthood.

The distinction is this: The pope's declaration reaffirmed a centuries-old
ban on the admission of women to the priesthood; it did not, for the
first time, ban women from the priesthood. Unfortunately for good
reporting, the editing student changed history.

The lazy journalist may ask: What's one more *fete,* one more *controversial issue,* one more *successful foiling?* But measured against the many
times they are used, they are meaningless; they say nothing and do
nothing except take up space. As a journalist, you must be alert that one
writer's well turned phrase does not become your cliche. Find your own
phrases and use them precisely. Don't use a word whose meaning you
don't know for sure; look it up. Don't rely on sound and sight; *fortuitous*
does not mean *fruitful* or *fortunate; fulsome* doesn't mean *bountiful; essay*
does not mean *to write an essay* and *mitigate* does not mean *militate.* As
Emily Dickinson wrote:

> A Word that breathes distinctly
> Has not the power to die.

HIGH-SOUNDING
WORDS AND PHRASES

The Washington Post reported one day that a designer had difficulty getting anyone at the U.S. Department of Transportation to listen to his
proposal on taxis. "But when he said 'para-transit vehicles' they were all
ears."

According to The Associated Press, "People in government find that
you can get things done by using the right words." When officials of
one state feared that a needed swimming pool at a state police academy
would not be approved, they scratched the words *swimming pool* in favor
of *water training tank.* The academy got its swimming pool.

The government abounds with examples of language abuse, either in
the name of making something sound better than it is or for the sake of
hiding something. I'm not sure which applies to this statement by a
governor:

> You know, when we were talking about budget, perspectively, it's easier to talk retrospectively with specifics than prospectively.

Another governor:

> And I indicated at that time, that we are talking about just one area of the state, and that in the Pittsburgh area the 50-cent fare was prevalent, and I didn't think it would be fair to the taxpayers of Pennsylvania to step in and help settle the situation in one part of the state where other riders were paying higher prices than were being paid in that area, and I think with the budget restrictions and problems we are having this year, it is quite apparent that trying to pick up the differential would be extremely difficult.

The practice of saying obscurely what could be said plainly dominates this country. Politicians and bureaucrats are infamous for toying with the language. They have discovered that the wrong word at the right time often escapes the notice of a public numb to language abuses. For that matter, bureaucrats are notorious back-scratchers; let one of their own get into difficulty and they'll try to help him or her out of it.

When the Army's role in testing drugs on unsuspecting people became public knowledge in 1976, the U.S. Department of Justice investigated. In one particular case, a drug was given to a patient (to quote *The New York Times*) "in an attempt to create an exaggerated mental state (schizophrenia)." Later in the same story a Department of Justice memorandum on the matter is quoted. The reporter, seeing an effort on someone's part to make something bad look good, wrote:

> Furthermore, the report quoted a Department of Justice memo as saying that "neither the patient nor his family were advised of the proposed therapy [sic] or gave permission" [*Times'* brackets].

Therapy is treatment of an illness; its connotations are so positive they would escape only unschooled children. What nicer way to get a fellow bureaucrat off the hook than to describe his or her misdeeds in positive terms?

J. L. Dillard, a linguist, writes: "Semantic changes take place easily in the domain of politics . . ." Such was the case in the 1976 presidential campaign when Jimmy Carter was seeking the Democratic Party's presidential nomination. *Time* magazine wrote:

Carter also tended to frame his stands on hot issues in ways that had broad appeal. He drew a distinction between amnesty for Viet Nam draft evaders and the "full pardon" that he promised to grant in the first week of his administration. Amnesty, he said, implied that draft evasion was all right, while a pardon merely granted forgiveness. He thus brought audiences around to accept the idea of a pardon. In fact and in law, however, amnesty does not imply approval. Reminded of this by a *Time* correspondent last week, Carter smiled and rather archly said: "I'll define the word any way that suits me."

In *Through the Looking-Glass,* Humpty Dumpty says: "When I use a word, it means just what I choose it to mean—neither more or less." After Carter had gotten the party's nomination he appeared before a national convention of the American Legion. The Associated Press story on his speech included these paragraphs:

> In his speech to the legion convention, Carter said he does not favor "blanket amnesty, but for those who violated Selective Service laws, I intend to grant a blanket pardon.
> "To me, there is a difference," Carter said. Amnesty means that what you did is right. A pardon means that what you did—right or wrong—is forgiven. So, pardon—yes, amnesty—no."

My dictionary says that *amnesty* is "a federal pardon for offenders by a government" and *pardon* is "the act of forgiving." Regardless, Carter's efforts did not go unrewarded. Shortly before Carter was inaugurated, no less a newspaper than *The New York Times* carried a story containing this unattributed sentence:

> But a pardon implies guilt, and many of the men who could be eligible might again feel compelled to turn it down.

Carter granted the pardon-amnesty and within months it was forgotten. It remains to be seen if his definitions will last.

Specialists of every discipline are no less guilty of inflating empty ideas with the air pump of meaningless words. Even educators, alas, are guilty of using as many vague words as possible as often as possible. From *Journalism Educator,* a publication for journalism professors:

> Since students make self-selections in course taking and thus form naturally assembled collectivities, I approached the measurement with a "nonequivalent control group design."

A letter from the New Hampshire Executive Council said a grant would:

> Develop groups of evaluation modules for several types of programs to consist of sophisticated and quantitatively oriented research designs to be used in evaluation programs.
>
> Establish minimal data requirements as required by the evaluation modules and set in place a system through which a continual flow of empirical data will be directed toward the commission's evaluation staff.
>
> Establish through the use of computer analysis modules a highly empirical and quantitative means for policy makers to make decisions about programs.

The Associated Press said: "Approval was unanimous."

The AP also reported about a parent in Houston, Texas, who received the following from his child's high school principal:

> Our schools' cross-graded, multi-ethnic, individualized learning program is designed to enhance the concept of an open-ended learning program with emphasis on a continuum of multi-ethnic, academically enriched learning using the identified intellectually gifted child as the agent or director of his own learning.
>
> Major emphasis is on cross-graded, multi-ethnic learning with the main objective being to learn respect for the uniqueness of a person.

United Press International quoted a communique from the Arms Control and Disarmament Agency:

> Under the previous arrangement, the Verification and Analysis Bureau had theoretical responsibility for all verification questions of interest to the Arms Control Agency. However, its separation from operational activities creates a bureaucratic gap between the area (in ACDA) that handled SALT and MBFR, for example, and the verification experts.

The journalist's job is to restrain from quoting the miscast pomposity of experts and at the same time find out what it means. And so that you will be familiar with such language, here are several other examples. They are a mixture of obscurity, euphemism and ignorance. Ignorance may be an excuse for talking and writing like this, but it is not an excuse for journalists reporting such nonsense.

advance downward adjustments. A reduction in social services.

adjustment centers or mediation rooms. Solitary confinement, which is sometimes also called segregation.

cost effective. Economical.

precipitation protective contrivance. What Archie of the comic strip says is an *umbrella.*

perspiration garment. A *sweatshirt,* Archie says.

mandatory flotation device. Which turns out to be a raft in "B.C.," also a comic strip.

extremely adverse operating environment. Sounds like a serious crisis magnified.

device system benefit. Computer talk to be avoided.

idea sharing and governance input. Not something for computers.

locational preference. Where you choose to live.

interpersonal and academic improvement houses. Coeducational dormitories.

communication feedback loop. A gives his views; B can't give her views until she summarizes A's to A's satisfaction, and vice versa.

circular area possibility. The chance that civilian buildings near military targets might get bombed.

inverted aerial maneuvers. Every skier knows they are *flips.*

adequately or comfortably affluent. Either you are or you aren't affluent.

semi-independent living environment. No, it doesn't mean the college student living away from home; I don't know what it means.

facilitation of professional development. Advance upward adjustment made easy.

coal severance taxation revenue implications. From a list telling faculty members of a university what type of research projects could get support money.

pedestrian-oriented improvements. Sidewalks.

illustrated a tendency. Not something done with illustrations.

spatial mean-wage-salary disparity. Some people make more money than others.

forward-looking aspects of the programs. Futuristic?

crisp memoranda. An admission, finally, that many aren't.

his desires relative to his future residence. Forward-looking locational preference, in case it isn't clear.

the entire coal procurement philosophy and practice. Phrases like that could be used as fuel.

acute grief situation. When final grades are given.

general salary distributional pattern. Has nothing to do with how salaries are disbursed by employers.

sameness is not necessarily equality. Strikes down the separate-but-equal myth.

operational programs or activities. Watch out for inoperational ones.

operational responsibility. A person so designated is really in charge, not a figurehead.

marital experience. Marriage, according to a court decision.

mature woman. Another way of saying *fat.*

queen size pantyhose. For mature women.

power system. Used by one company to describe the batteries it sells.

language contact situation. When two or more languages collide.

injury situation. What football coaches hope to avoid.

fire suppression system. Despite the suggestion that it puts out fires, it can also be a heat or smoke detector that only warns people.

automotive replacement products. Auto parts.

emotional marginality of teenagers. Immaturity.

aesthetic relationism. Any *ism* is abstract.

index of work alienation-indifference-attachment. At least the sociologist who made that up wasn't struck by the noun plague.

internalize a set of moral values. Beware of externalized ones.

periodicity and chronicity in criminal careers. A detective from any television program won't solve it in an hour.

a meteorological prognosis. Weather forecast.

learning process. What college students endure. (To get there they had to pass through a *reading situation.* In elementary school, during recess, they enjoyed a *play situation.* To which Edwin Newman adds: "If children who go through play situations and learning experiences have nothing to look forward to but being in a hostage situation, what will it do to their self-image? What will happen to their potential to develop a potential?")

hostage situation. I found it in a wire service story and called it to Newman's attention, which resulted in the preceding communication situation with the author of this book.

Here are some sentences:

> It is interesting to note that coal prices were quick to follow oil prices on their upward spiral. (coal prices quickly increased after oil prices)

> The concept of a single faculty in geographic dispersion and complementary function is appealing. (as long as it remains a concept, I'm safe)

The income distribution seems to indicate that on a mean/total basis there was a disproportionate distribution of basic manufacturing wage/salaries. (sounds like a case for the National Labor Relations Board)

Health-wise, the region's senior citizens enjoy a high degree of good health. (they're healthy)

. . . a like percentage profess "good" health. (Did they profess a belief in God?)

We recommend that the company consider the current and future feasibility of buying or leasing fleet coal trains. (current and future! also, *feasibility* is jargon and is overused and vague like *input*)

The college wants a history instructor who can combine synchronic and dischronic analyses of events in a transcultural and holistic mode. (who said history is boring?)

It is very often the case, however, that apparent morphological irregularities turn out to be regular phenomena when examined carefully in relation to the entire phonological system. (spelling is related to pronunciation)

It is not apparent to me she is socially inadequate and certainly her educability under the ordinary acoustic environment is not jeopardized. (an ear specialist telling a family doctor one of his young patients can hear)

Because approximately 50 percent by volume of refinery output is now exempt, increased costs allocated to those products on a pro rata volumetric basis but historically recovered through sales of gasoline may no longer be recovered through such sales because the regulations do not afford a means for refiners to reallocate to gasoline amounts of increased costs allocated to a pro rata volumetric basis to exempt products. (Courtesy of the Federal Register)

SYNONYM PROBLEMS

Synonyms are words that have a similar meaning. *Similar* does not mean *identical*. Synonyms cause problems when an editor or writer insists that you never use the same word twice in any one sentence or paragraph. Synonym faddists might write:

The five-mile *bypass* is the best *road* in the state. The *highway* can handle 55,000 cars daily, which is twice the capacity of any other *autobahn* in the immediate area. When the latest *expanse of concrete* is filled to capacity, it can be expanded.

My made-up example borders on the ridiculous. But I was encouraged after seeing a journalist use four different words in seven paragraphs all to mean . . . Well, that's just it; I don't know what the writer meant. He started his story by writing about *missile boats* then shifted to *vessels.* Later he used *craft* and still later, *ships.* I'm confused because, as a former sailor, I know that a boat and a ship aren't the same, and that craft are landing or pleasure, but not missile carrying. And vessels can hold water or ride on top of water. I'm not discounting the use of synonyms. Using them aids you in varying your writing. But don't toss them into sentences just because you don't want to repeat a word. Have a better reason first.

VALUE WORDS

A *Journal of the Plague Year* by Daniel Defoe is an outstanding book. True or false?

Your response to that question should be: "What do you mean by *outstanding?*" The word suffers not only from it vagueness, but also because it is a *value word*—it means different things to people at different times. And while we normally associate the word with excellence, reporters have described disasters as outstanding. Value words are easily identified by their vagueness; there's nothing there for us to set our minds on. Some people also think of value words as relative terms. ("The play was outstanding." "Relative to what? A garbage can?")

Only is a value word (an adverb of opinion, you'll recall) that should be used only when it's necessary to explain a situation or context the reader would not normally understand (such as sports stories for non-sports fans). *Only* can load a sentence with opinion and show reporter partiality where none is intended.

For example, the state House of Representatives approves a pay raise for its members. "Only five legislators voted against the raises," a reporter writes, perhaps signaling that he or she's angry because more didn't oppose the proposal. Let the taxpayers be angry. Remove *only* from that sentence and you remove the onus.

In many cases where *only* is misused it is not necessary anyway. Supposing 5 out of 200 persons survive an airplane crash. "Only five survived" or "Five survived"—which is more objective and less emotional? The second one. If you've told the reader 200 persons were in the crash, adding that 5 survived makes the tragedy clear enough.

A reader of *Harvard Magazine* provided this exercise on how the shift of *only* in a sentence changes the meaning:

> Only he kissed the girl yesterday.
> He only kissed the girl yesterday.
> He kissed only the girl yesterday.
> He kissed the only girl yesterday.
> He kissed the girl only yesterday.
> He kissed the girl yesterday only.

Jack Cappon, the general news editor of The Associated Press, offered a similar sentence:

> Only I hit him in the eye yesterday.
> I only hit him in the eye yesterday.
> I hit only him in the eye yesterday.
> I hit him only in the eye yesterday.
> I hit him in only the eye yesterday.
> I hit him in the only eye yesterday.
> I hit him in the eye only yesterday.
> I hit him in the eye yesterday only.

Hayakawa lists several words that often give both a fact and a judgment at the same time, which makes them value words. A person can express disapproval by use of any of the following words: *prostitute, racketeer, pickpocket, liberal, radical, Holy Roller, heretic, atheist, materialist.* Imagine, then, what happens when the journalist uses them. Who knows how the audience will accept those words? It should also come as no surprise that some of the preceding words plus hundreds more are libelous by themselves, still another reason to avoid them.

Still other value words:

abhorrent	great	easy
able	deserving	dynamic
abominable	cute	beautiful
brave	fantastic	handsome
good	courageous	lovable
outstanding	fearless	long

short	small	terrible
lengthy	magnificent	wonderful
liberal	massive	progressive
conservative	flashy	warm
little	slender	cold
big	terrific	unfortunately

Note that they are adjectives and adverbs, parts of speech not common to good newswriting.

Nouns and verbs, however, can also be value words, depending on the context. The gymnastics coach asking for an addition to the high school gymnasium to be used exclusively by his or her team may call the addition an improvement to the school. But the school board member who has to approve raising taxes to pay for the improvement may see it as a waste and vote against it. Similarly, the negative connotations of *failed* make it a good word to avoid, especially in this usage:

City Council failed last night to approve next year's budget.

Because there are enough neutral words to go around, a good journalist doesn't have to resort to value words.

FRAME OF REFERENCE

Often in writing news stories you are forced to write in abstract or general terms. Such terms cannot stand alone. They must be explained clearly, and part of explaining them clearly is using terms and contexts readers are familiar with. How would you describe a tree to someone who has grown up around cornfields and never seen anything higher than corn stalks? The corn stalks are a possible frame of reference for you and the other person. Describe the rigors of farming in Iowa to a coal miner in Pennsylvania. Before beginning, you need a frame of reference, something the reader can identify with, something you hope is not so rigid it can't ease the reader into your frame. A story on changes in car sizes included this line:

They are noticeably shorter than their 1976 predecessors—9 to 15 inches to be exact.

The 9 to 15 inches phrase serves as a frame of reference, something specific for the reader. But numbers don't always work. I have a hard time visualizing 100 yards without thinking of the length of a football field. Perhaps the writer of the following sentence from *Newsweek* had me in mind:

> One storm after another piled a total of 199 inches of snow on the beleaguered city, and some of the drifts billowed as high as 30 feet—*the level of a third-floor window* [italics added].

I can visualize 30 feet very well with that frame of reference.

Following is a sentence without a frame of reference:

> Mr. Narayanan's vasectomy, which took five minutes and earned him a government bonus of $11, was one more statistic in what officials say is by far their most intensive and successful sterilization campaign yet.

To an American $11 is not a lot of money. Knowing that, *The New York Times* reporter who wrote the preceding gave his American audience a frame of reference:

> Mr. Narayanan's vasectomy, which took five minutes and earned him a government bonus of $11—*as much money as he makes in a month*—was one more statistic in what officials say is by far their most intensive and successful sterilization campaign yet [italics added].

Now you know what $11 means to Mr. Narayanan.

FROM THE
GENERAL TO THE SPECIFIC

When you use general terms, back them up with specific examples, as this student did with parenthetical information:

> Bugliosi said the interest in the trial, one of the longest (9½ months) and most expensive ($962,000) in history, continues because the strange, bizarre murders actually happened.

A *New York Times* story provides another example:

> In September the Federal Reserve began a series of actions designed to let a basic interest rate, the rate on federal funds, decline. (Federal funds are overnight loans between banks.)

It's not always possible to be specific in one parenthetical swoop, as these paragraphs from an AP story show:

> Under certain conditions, a public body, by a majority vote of its total membership, may close the doors to the general public.
>
> If disclosure would imperil the public safety, disclose the identity of a law enforcement agent or informer or imperil the investigation or prosecution of a criminal offense, the governmental body could call an executive session.
>
> The public could also be excluded during discussions of personnel matters, collective bargaining or the acquisition of real property.

Now you know what certain conditions are. The next time they may be different. Even if they aren't, you can't take the liberty of never redefining them. Be specific at all times.

Other Language Tips

In this section, problems encountered by journalism students or problems considered common by a committee of Associated Press managing editors are discussed and help is offered on how to handle them. For greater detail of these problems and their solutions, you are encouraged to read Roy H. Copperud's *Words on Paper* and Theodore M. Bernstein's *The Careful Writer,* both of which any good journalism school has in its library.

above   Too often a journalist will write: "The above example . . ." When the journalist wrote the sentence, the example was *above* on the copy paper or video display terminal. But what if the layout editor puts the example and later reference in separate columns? Better to write: "The preceding example . . ."

abbreviations, acronyms   Acronyms are formed from the beginning letter of each word in a name, such as WAF for *W*omen's *A*ir *F*orce, or by combining initial words and syllables, such as *scuba* for *s*elf-*c*ontained *u*nderwater *b*reathing *a*pparatus.

While many say that abbreviations and acronyms are an aid to better writing I contend they are just the opposite. At two newspapers where I worked some of the popular acronyms and abbreviations were: CATA, COG, CRPC, CA&DRB, SCPC, CHJA, PFJA, UAJA, PIDA, DA, CD, CTIDA, PennDOT, PSU, PUC, CPFA. Imagine a 20-inch story filled with those!

There is no reason why, when referring on second reference to the Cadbury Planning Commission, you can't write *the commission* instead of *CPC*. A shortened title will not make the reader grope back through a story to find a meaning; the meaning is quite clear.

Some editors argue that acronyms and abbreviations make for brevity, a worthwhile objective but a spurious argument when tested against the goal of clarity. Acronyms and abbreviations—except the more common ones like FBI, and so on—are eyesores that clutter the path to understanding. (Some of them, by the way, have unfortunate side effects, such as the acronym for Citizens League of Audience Professionals.)

adage   An adage is old so *old adage* is redundant. Remember that age is part of adage.

affect, effect   A student once quoted a speaker as saying, "I'm talking about this because it effects children." However, the subject was not procreation, which is when *effect* (to bring about) might work. The student meant *affect*.

Affect is usually a verb; *effect* is usually a noun. *Effect* as a verb appears in instances such as: "When trying to effect change in a bureaucracy, start at the bottom."

allege   Inserting this word into a story does not remove the responsibility for libel. Nor, for that matter, does attributing something to the police: "Police said Jones murdered Smith." That sentence convicts Jones before he's been tried. "Police charged Jones with murdering Smith" is a fact.

allude, elude   To *allude* is to make reference to. To *elude* is to escape a pursuer.

among, between   *Among* is used with three or more persons or objects. "The plane fell among the trees." *Between* is for two. "Between you and me, his plan is no good."

Sometimes, however, *between* works with three or more, especially when two of the persons or objects are related or in the same camp. A student familiar with only the first half of the among-between rule wrote:

> The vote was divided among people who were against building codes in general, people who were reluctant to get involved with regional government, and people in favor of the program.

However, only two types of votes could be cast—yes or no. Two of the groups the student delineated were clearly in the "no" column. The sentence needs *between* and some rewriting.

> The vote was divided between those who were against building

codes or were reluctant to get involved with regional government and those in favor of the program.

annual   Once the Super Bowl was played the second time, you could call it *second annual,* and so forth, as the years went by. But for the first one, it was nothing more than the first Super Bowl, not first annual.

as, because   In good usage the two words are not interchangeable. "As I am the oldest person in the group, I'll serve as president" is considered bad form. "Because I am . . ." is considered good form.

attribution   In those cases where it is impossible to check the truth of a person's statement, a journalist should make certain he or she clearly attributes the person's statement. A political candidate once appeared before a class of journalism students and to prove he was not the candidate of the party's machine, he told the class he had been excluded from a meeting of party bigwigs. "But I'd rather be here with you," he said.

The students wrote a story saying the candidate had been excluded from a meeting of party bigwigs, but many of the students failed to attribute the claim. The next day the local newspaper carried a brief story telling how the candidate's brother had appeared for him at the meeting. At the very least, the candidate's interests were represented. Did the candidate lie? Yes. However, had the students been writing their story for a newspaper, the unattributed statement would have made the newspaper the liar, not the candidate.

In addition to attributing, journalists should be suspicious of boasts and investigate them before publishing.

averse, adverse   If you oppose something, you are *averse* to it. If something is bad, it is *adverse.*

believe, think   Thinking is an intellectual exercise, an evolving process. Believing, on the other hand, can be the result of that process; it is a static condition. Hence, the two words are not interchangeable.

bi, semi   *Bi* means two; *semi* means one-half. A bi-monthly magazine is published every two months; a semi-monthly magazine is published twice in one month. If you remember that someone who is bi-lingual speaks two languages, you won't confuse the two prefixes. However, because *bi* means one-half to some, cautious journalists use *every other* instead.

burglary, robbery   Robbery requires a threat of force against a victim; burglary needs a breaking into or entering, such as a house. The victims of a burglary need not be present during the crime. One finer point needs to be made about burglary: The burglar doesn't have to take anything to commit such a crime; he or she need only break in or enter with the intent to remove something.

can, may   Misuse often appears in court stories when a journalist says a court ruled that a person *can* do something. *Can* means the ability to do something; *may* denotes permission. In questions of law, judges decide permission, not ability.

capitalization   Each newspaper has its own style, and does not need to be a slave to someone else's. Government agencies like to capitalize a lot, perhaps because it adds luster to a word that has none to begin with. Such disguising should not be blindly copied by journalists. We don't need Federal Revenue Sharing Fund and Federal Free and Reduced Lunch Policy when lower-casing the phrases does no damage to meaning.

center around   If you think of a bullseye with its attendant outer rings, you'll understand what is entailed in *center around*. The bullseye is the center, so it cannot also be around. Hence, *center around* is a contradiction in fact and in terms. Use *center at, center on, center in*.

coequal   Another unnecessary word from the people who also bring you other misuses of the language—the government. "However, officials said Williams would be more of a coequal to the agriculture secretary than a subordinate." What's wrong with equal?

completely destroy   *Destroy* means completely. Likewise, many editors enforce the rule that something cannot be partially destroyed. Either it is destroyed or it isn't. If you sense something is partially destroyed, say it was damaged. After the front end of a 1961 compact car was damaged by a bomb, a policeman said: "The retail value of the car is about $50, so you could say it was demolished. But actually, the damage was limited to the front end." Even though the entire car was not damaged, it was considered destroyed because the repair bill would have been higher than the value of the car.

compose, comprise   The whole *comprises* the parts; the parts *compose* the whole. Iowa comprises 99 counties; 99 counties compose Iowa.

Comprise is pretentious, which is reason enough to avoid using it. If you must, use it correctly.

convince, persuade While you are trying to change someone's mind, you are *persuading* the person. Once the person's mind is changed, the person is *convinced*.

currently, presently These words are not synonymous. *Currently* means now; *presently* means soon.

damage, damages *Damage* is a dent in the fender of a car; *damages* are awarded by juries in a court of law. The words should not be interchanged.

ecology, environment *Ecology* is the study of the relationship between organisms and their *environment*. We worry about gasoline waste polluting our environment, not our ecology.

either This word does not mean both. "City Council voted to install stop signs at either end of the street." That means there won't be signs at one end of the street. "Do you care at which end of the street the sign goes?" the city manager asked the mayor. "Either end; doesn't matter," the mayor replied.

ex- Bernstein says *ex-* is primarily a headline word and that *former* is better in stories.

farther, further While both are used with distances, the distinction is that *farther* is used when writing or speaking about measurable distances while *further* is used for figurative distances.

"Parliament is *farther* away from Buckingham Palace than Congress is from the White House, but on many political issues Congress and the White House are *further* apart than Parliament and Buckingham Palace."

fewer, less *Fewer* is a matter of number; *less* is a matter of degree or collective quantity. "With fewer contestants participating, there is less excitement this year." An exception is when numbers are considered as a sum: "He earned less than $20,000 last year." When numbers can be enumerated, the word is *fewer*. "There are fewer five-dollar bills in the cash register today than there were yesterday."

former, latter "I read two books this week: *Essays of E. B. White* and *The Decameron*. Both are good books, of course, but the former is more modern while the latter is racier." Now you have to back up to find out what *the former* is and what *the latter* is. Such impediments to clarity should be avoided in good writing and good broadcasting (where the listener has nothing to doublecheck). If you insist on using *former* and *latter,* the words work best with two items only. Referring to the first of three items in a list as *the former* can be very confusing, as can also be the case when referring to the last of three as *the latter.* Better to repeat the word referred to than to cloud meaning.

gas, gasoline   *Gasoline* is a byproduct of oil; *gas* is a product of nature and is often called *natural gas.* Because we face a future with apparent shortages of both, it is safer not to use the words interchangeably. Cars run on *gasoline;* homes are heated by *gas.*

hopefully   This word does not mean "it is hoped." It describes how a person feels—with high hopes or expectations. "He placed his hand on her knee hopefully." That is correct; this isn't: "Hopefully, Congress will approve the tax reform bill."

imply, infer   A speaker *implies,* a listener *infers.* Neither word should be common to straight news reporting because they mean somebody wasn't clear and somebody else made a judgment on what was said. Do not *infer* from a speaker's words; ask the speaker what he or she means.

include   *Include* does not take in everything: *inclusive* does. You cannot say a five-part report *includes* five parts. You cannot *include* everything. "My family includes three females." "My family includes one male." But not, "My family includes four persons."

innocent, not guilty   Technically a jury does not find a defendant *innocent;* it finds him or her *not guilty.* A person is innocent until proven guilty. Therefore, a jury cannot find a person to be in a condition he or she is presumed to be in already. Looked at another way, a trial is a forum where points of evidence and law are debated. Perhaps a person cannot be proved guilty because the evidence was not clear enough to convict. Thus, the defendant would be declared not guilty. Fearful that *not* might be dropped or turned into *now,* many editors require the use of *innocent* for *not guilty.* A possible compromise between legal technicality and the concern for a libel suit is the word *acquitted.*

its, it's   We have all learned that to form the possessive of nouns, we add *'s.* But that rule doesn't apply to *it.* The possessive form of *it* is *its,* not *it's.* Perhaps the best way to remember the correct form is to remember that the apostrophe represents a missing letter in *it's* (it is).

"It's hard to imagine a house with *its* roof missing." If learning a rule on this usage is too difficult, consult a dictionary.

media   Two points must be stressed: 1. *Media* is plural (although for how much longer, I won't predict); the singular is *medium*. 2. It is not a substitute for *news media.* There are many kinds of media, including literary magazines, the theater and advertising billboards, that have nothing to do with news.

new, recent   *New* does not mean recent. Referring to a recently published survey as *new* might cause the reader to infer there must be an old survey or an earlier one. Of course, if that is the case, new is proper.

next   *Next* in expressions of time should be used to indicate there is nothing of similarity in between today and the day you are writing about. It is a word you cannot use on any given day. A story appearing in today's paper (Thursday, for our purposes) about an event in seven days would say the event was scheduled for *next* Thursday. However, if today's paper is Monday's, the reporter would write that the event is scheduled for Thursday (no next). In that context, next is unnecessary and confusing. Some readers might believe you mean a week from Thursday.

odd   Saying there were 30,000-odd people at a convention when you mean *approximately* or *estimated* will not mollify the 30,000 people who might feel they were called *odd.* The hyphen helps, but the phrase, because it is two faced, can still cause some problems, the least of which could be humorous.

over   *Over,* as in "There were over 95 people over 60 years of age at the meeting," is overused. Use *more than. Over* has the sense of above.

percentages   The difference between 5 percent and 10 percent is 5 *percentage* points, not 5 percent. Calculated differently, the difference is 50 percent. The second computation says the most.

reek, wreak   After spending a night in a smoky bar, your clothing will *reek* of smoke, which is not the verb to use in this statement: "A no-tax budget would *wreak* havoc from one end of the state to the other."

refute, rebut   To *refute* someone is to successfully argue your point. If you say a speaker *refuted* another speaker's argument, you are making a judgment. *Rebut,* on the other hand, means respond, and is a neutral word.

reiterate   *Reiterate* is not a substitute for *repeat*. *Iterate* means to repeat. *Reiterate,* thus, means to re-repeat. *Reiterate* best describes the result of a record player's needle stuck in a crack on a record.

their, there   *Their* is the possessive form of the pronoun they; *there* is an adverb (among other functions). *Their* is never used as the subject of a sentence. "There is no doubt their entry was the best."

under way   Except in the U.S. Navy, *under way* is two words. Besides, editors prefer *started* or *began* unless the story is about a ship.

Language Usage Test

The following sentences may have errors in grammar, usage, redundancy, preferred spelling and punctuation. There are no capitalization errors nor are there errors in proper nouns. There is no more than one error to a sentence.

Every sentence could be rewritten to make it better. However, that is not the purpose of this test. If a sentence is correct as written, write *E* beside the sentence. If it is incorrect, mark beside the sentence the letter designating the area of the sentence in error. The designated section may not be in error by itself but might be if considered in the context of the entire sentence.

1. (a) There are cave drawings which prove (b) that, like Atlantis, a large (c) number of wild animals (d) inhabited the area.
2. (a) U.S. and Mexican industries (b) are integrated with autos and parts (c) flowing unhindered (d) across the border.
3. (a) The concensus was (b) that O'Hara stands to gain (c) in the South, (d) where he is weakest.
4. (a) Even as a native of Cadbury who lives in a university residence hall, it is (b) easy to forget that (c) there is more to life than (d) classes, dining halls, concerts, parties and the library.
5. (a) George Washington University, (b) which was named in honor of this (c) country's first president, is (d) situated in the nations capital.
6. (a) The committee said (b) their work was finished (c) although it was not (d) in final form.
7. (a) The article says journalism education (b) inspires idealism in students (c) that gradually fade away (d) after the students work in the real world.

8.   (a) Leaving home for the (b) first time is not really (c) that difficult an ordeal and college students (d) except it as part of growing up.

9.   (a) William Williams has traced the history of the (b) system in detail from 900 B.C. through the 14th century, his book (c) is recommended for anyone (d) who is interested in the history of art.

10. (a) When Wentzel stepped to the plate, (b) he hit the first pitch, (c) lofting it in a high arc (d) that ended in the centerfield bleachers.

11. (a) Nobody in a democracy, (b) regardless of race, creed or religion, (c) can be taxed (d) without their consent.

12. (a) Neither John nor Bill have (b) the good sense (c) to come in (d) out of the rain.

13. (a) When Judy and Sally worked (b) for the Youngs a decade ago, (c) they were well-paid (d) by today's standards.

14. (a) What makes the English so (b) interesting, aside from the rhythm of their writing is the (c) serious intensity with which they (d) absorb concepts.

15. (a) Working journalists who are daily exposed to the intricacies of government (b) have an insider's understanding of the subtle relationships (c) among the rules, institutions and personalities (d) that comprise our legal system.

16. (a) Floor coverings will cost $37351 (b) to replace while (c) finishings and fixtures will cost (d) at least another $43,200 to replace.

17. (a) It wasn't the subfreezing playing (b) conditions or a matter of being (c) outplayed, the game was decided (d) by puck luck.

18. (a) A combination of the aging Walt Jones, (b) a rash of injuries, and a new generation of uncooperative talent (c) are (d) primarily responsible for the poor season.

19. (a) The 15 bears he has shot (b) represent an unusual hunting record, "that's (c) pretty good for Montana," (d) the game warden said.

20. (a) Orange County Judge Ralph E. McFarland (b) ordered the Joneses to keep their farm reasonably clear (c) of manure and (d) the removal of the manure piles near the fence.

21. (a) The further away I walk (b) the better (c) that painting looks (d) to my untrained eye.

22. (a) He is a registered (b) dietition and a (c) member of the Minnesota and American (d) Dietetic Associations.

23. (a) Last seen in the vicinity of Bowe Street, police say (b) the suspect is dangerous (c) and could assault anyone (d) without provocation.

24. (a) Sears, the largest department store (b) in the area, is (c) putting their best (d) merchandise on sale.

25. (a) She implied from what he said (b) that he was (c) ill and would not (d) attend the party.

26. (a) Five persons—Wildavsky, Jones, Phalan, Emerson and me— were (b) chosen to research and write (c) the Herald-Republic's first series of articles (d) on nursing home care.

27. (a) I took it (b) as a complement when (c) he told me I have teeth (d) as white as chalk.

28. (a) If you want to observe (b) Congress, you (c) must go to Washington, D.C. the capital (d) of the United States.

29. (a) The facts of the Watergate (b) scandal (c) will not be learned until each (d) major and minor figure write his own book.

30. (a) The secretary (b) is in charge of (c) ordering the stationery (d) for the office.

31. (a) The woman on the stage (b) is a professor of child teaching; she's (c) considered by many (d) to be a child teaching expert.

32. (a) Plato said Atlantis was situated (b) beyond the Pillars of Hercules, (c) which is 200 miles (d) east of the Strait of Gibraltar.

33. (a) Traditional espionage, such as the penetration (b) of the intelligence agencies of other countries and the covering up (c) of clandestine information is the (d) CIA's function, according to Tressler.

34. (a) Jones noted further (b) that the two city's zoos (c) are comparable, but that Cadbury has nothing (d) equivalent to Clive's public parks.

35. (a) Neither the environmental nor the drug issue hold (b) the promise for controversy (c) the way the food (d) issue does.

36. (a) "This is a good budget (b) for our investigation," the congressman said; (c) "any cut in my opinion will weaken what (d) we are trying to do."

37. (a) Irregardless of what people say, (b) most of them (c) are opposed to restricting (d) industrial pollution.

38. (a) The following afternoon, (b) which was a Wednesday an (c) Air Force transport landed in an (d) abandoned dirt strip that once was the Clive airport.

39. (a) Since—if not because—Hayes (b) left, advertising linage has dropped (c) disasterously, to little more than half (d) the 1,280 pages the magazine had in 1973.

40. (a) It is possible that the widely-publicized (b) and twice-canceled

meeting between the dictator and all Britons in his country (c) was a device to divert (d) world attention from the three deaths.

41. (a) When he saw the fire damage, (b) he exclaimed: (c) "That must have been (d) some fire!

42. (a) Packard suggested closing (b) the loopholes for the rich (c) and rejection of salary increases (d) for government officials.

43. (a) When your nerves are frazzled, (b) there's nothing like a (c) soothing tranquilizer (d) to make everything seem right.

44. (a) The news media is (b) the major source of information (c) in this country (d) and in other democracies.

45. (a) Pamela Rubin, who once (b) worked for a local newspaper, (c) now works for one (d) of the wire services.

46. (a) One of every five (b) of the state's residents (c) live in the sort of poverty (d) that forced Bert Collins to leave the area.

47. (a) The fourth annual conference which (b) was held after the disaster, (c) left the participants as confused and discouraged (d) as before the disaster.

48. (a) A newspaper or magazine without advertising (b) is a phenomena not often seen (c) in a media system (d) that depends so heavily on advertising revenues.

49. (a) All of the animals (b) in the zoo are fed (c) at the same time so that the workers (d) can stay on a regular schedule.

50. (a) The petition (b) alledges (c) that the privately owned road (d) is unfit for use.

51. (a) The psychiatrist (b) wanted to know (c) the affect the drug had (d) on his patients.

52. (a) Budget limitations (b) of a newspaper this size (c) prevents the hiring (d) of a staff for investigative reporting.

53. (a) The project requires cleaning (b) and reconstruction of a water channel, repairing dikes (c) and complying with (d) anti-pollution measures.

54. (a) During that time, (b) a passing motorist saw the (c) fire in the Garber Mansion (d) and called the fire department.

55. (a) The survey conducted by two nationally known testing authorities show (b) that only one of 50 students (c) finds college less demanding (d) than high school.

56. (a) He says he does not (b) like basketball, I doubt (c) that he has seen two games (d) in his life.

57. (a) He saw a dog (b) who's coat he described (c) as being as stiff as (d) a wire brush.

58. (a) Neither Cadbury nor Pilsdon are (b) the kind of city (c) I would like (d) to raise children in.

59. (a) James Stein of Cambridge was (b) promoted by Harvard College, (c) his alma mater, (d) two weeks ago.

60. (a) If you think she's (b) intelligent, you (c) should meet her (d) 5 year old sister.

61. (a) While the likelihood of (b) such an occurence is small, (c) care must still (d) be exercised by everyone.

62. (a) Pressures that result from arguments and mistrust (b) between local conservative and liberal groups—as well as (c) the influence of various local political (d) leaders—brings about this scrutiny.

63. (a) To criticize him however is (b) to hold him accountable to a high standard—indeed (c) one beyond most journalists, most researchers (d) and most college professors.

64. (a) Maybe it's the black (b) jerseys the Oakland Raiders (c) wear that make them appear (d) formidable to their opponents.

65. (a) Its very odd (b) how a person can have (c) so many different feelings about (d) something he plans to do.

66. (a) While in Lexington, (b) the Parnells only saw one house (c) they really liked (d) enough to consider buying.

67. (a) The North Carolina senator, (b) an expert on government relations and services, (c) eluded to the growing gap between what the government receives in taxes (d) and what it provides in services.

68. (a) A proposal to rezone part of Schuylkill Avenue (b) may be voted on by council (c) tonight or the proposal may be (d) remanded back to the planning commission for further discussion.

69. (a) Hopefully, City Council will pass (b) a human relations ordinance (c) before the students (d) return to the Bakersfield College campus in September.

70. (a) Required mandatory (b) conservation measures must be (c) followed if we (d) are to conserve energy.

71. (a) Forty hours of work (b) a week tires anyone (c) who has never worked (d) that much before.

72. (a) The writing of both authors (b) continue to (c) reflect their contrasting (d) basic philosophies on history.

73. (a) Occaisionally children will watch (b) a long program on television, (c) but it has to be a program (d) with special appeal. ·

74. (a) The city's recently formed (b) transit system (c) comprises 35 formerly independent (d) rail and bus lines.

75.   (a) Studies indicate that (b) a word commonly mispelled (c) by college students is (d) occurrence.

76.   (a) Twain's stories are (b) very interesting, (c) they represent several (d) styles of writing.

77.   (a) He took the dead soldier's (b) helmet because (c) he wanted a (d) momento of the war.

78.   (a) The judge ruled (b) that University of Florida students have (c) the legal right to vote in the (d) district where they attend college.

79.   (a) The value of all of Mexico's exports (b) to the United States (c) are given as (d) 183 million pesos.

80.   (a) Timothy R. Klingaman, (b) assistant superintendant of instruction, said (c) he is pleased with (d) the committee's work.

81.   (a) The new faculty member (b) proposed the following changes, (c) discontinue two writing courses, add three theory courses (d) and increase the length of class sessions.

82.   (a) The intelligence unit tried to illicit (b) as much information as possible (c) from the spy who (d) had been captured during the last coup.

83.   (a) The good old (b) days of (c) free enterprise (d) are over.

84.   (a) Studying is (b) one of those chores (c) that makes college life (d) more than just one big party.

85.   (a) Nebraska Attorney General, Joseph Dalton, (b) argued that it doesn't cost (c) the Postal Service 15 cents to deliver (d) a first-class letter.

86.   (a) The organization needs (b) someone who (c) can provide liason (d) with other community groups.

87.   (a) The system did not seem (b) to be working on this day, it kept (c) rejecting the (d) operator's instructions.

88.   (a) William K. Steigerwalt, (b) president of the Missoula National Bank has (c) announced the promotion of two officers from (d) the bank's main office.

89.   (a) He has three sisters; (b) his sister Judy (c) is a registered nurse (d) who just received a college degree.

90.   (a) Sally another one of his sisters (b) is licensed by the (c) state of Indiana as (d) an x-ray technician.

91.   (a) His third sister, Lyn, (b) is a old hand (c) at reporting on intermediate (d) school units.

92.   (a) One of his brothers-in-law covers (b) high school and college (c) sports for a medium-sized (d) newspaper in Alabama.

93. (a) The president of the (b) company puts (c) alot of trust in the old-fashioned (d) common sense of his workers.

94. (a) The principle of our high school (b) has three college degrees, (c) including one (d) from Wayne State University.

95. (a) Although he had followed (b) all of the proper proceedures, (c) the student could not persuade the registrar (d) to change his grade.

96. (a) The jury was convinced to find (b) the man not guilty, (c) although some people had (d) their doubts.

97. (a) He found the (b) book a 950-page volume, (c) very difficult to read (d) to himself or to his children.

98. (a) This sentence may be (b) all right with you, (c) but its not (d) all right with me.

99. (a) A professor of renowned scholarship, the faculty (b) entrusted Wentzel with the chairmanship (c) of the department in an effort to raise (d) the department's standards.

100. (a) On the platform were (b) two people—a former FBI agent, who is a (c) 1941 graduate of Oregon (d) State and the moderator.

101. (a) The reform-minded (b) government's nationalization (c) of some U.S. businesses has strained (d) relations between the United States and Chile.

102. (a) Some social workers prefer (b) to work with young juveniles (c) rather than (d) adults.

103. (a) Numerous researchers have (b) complained about the time and effort (c) that has been wasted trying (d) to replicate shoddy experiments.

104. (a) Only Barnhart considered what (b) the adverse national publicity would do (c) to the players' careers athletically and academically and (d) to the players psychologically.

105. (a) The accomodations (b) were insufficient (c) to house everyone (d) at the conference.

106. (a) In the American system of justice, (b) judges are (c) trained to be (d) uninterested observers during trials.

107. (a) "It's going to be a long time (b) before I learn how to spell," (c) John Streeter, a student (d) told his teacher.

108. (a) Not one of (b) the members of the team (c) were able to explain the loss (d) to the satisfaction of the fans.

109. (a) There were less jellybeans (b) in the jar than (c) we had first (d) imagined.

110.   (a) When we had (b) finished eating (c) John opened the beer (d) we had brought on the picnic.

111.   (a) Because the legislature is concerned (b) with safety, their members (c) approved the new school (d) bus code.

112.   (a) Hussey said the resolution is "unecessary (b) legislation that is (c) designed to force our (d) police department to hire homosexuals."

113.   (a) Staunton police allege (b) that the man, who was not identified broke (c) into the Smiths' house, (d) shortly after midnight.

114.   (a) The candidate told his supporters (b) he is confident he will win the (c) farm bloc and hold (d) his own among urban voters.

115.   (a) Eleven units (b) from the Oklahoma Panhandle (c) is scheduled to appear (d) in the Bicentennial parade.

116.   (a) The Cougars, who in their initial year (b) of conference play handed Texas Tech (c) its first loss, 27–19, (d) needs only to beat Rice to gain the title.

117.   (a) Women having handstand contests and wheelbarrow races is (b) far from the concept of collegiate (c) gymnasts getting ready (d) to go to the Nationals.

118.   (a) Police arrested a total of (b) 15 terrorists, 9 Lebanese, (c) 3 members of the IRA, (d) 2 Algerians and a Brazilian.

119.   (a) Collective nouns take a singular verb (b) when considered as one unit (c) and a plural verb when (d) considered by its individual parts.

120.   (a) The tax collector said that (b) the new tax law, with its many exceptions and qualifications, (c) make the tax forms (d) difficult to understand.

121.   (a) At twelve noon (b) many university employees (c) go downtown (d) to eat lunch.

122.   (a) The student and professional chapters (b) of Sigma Delta Chi is sponsoring (c) the interview with (d) the candidates for the Senate.

123.   (a) Not only are the schools not doing what they should be doing. Higher education is (b) also falling short because some professors are supposed to be training (c) the teachers who go into (d) the elementary and secondary schools.

124.   (a) While the Senate took action in the conspiracy case, (b) discussions were under way (c) to modify the president's (d) proposed secrecy legislation.

125.   (a) Born in Germany in 1922, Jacob Schmidt's literary activities

(b) began after he came (c) to this country with his uncle (d) and settled in California.

126. (a) The administration is seeking to (b) help the farmers of this country (c) by increasing price supports, and (d) stepping up foreign sales.

127. (a) When the candidate completed (b) his speech, the audience was given (c) by his campaign aides (d) copies of his literature.

ANSWERS

1. (a) There are cave drawings which prove (b) that, like Atlantis, a large (c) number of wild animals (d) inhabited the area.
    (b) *like Atlantis* is a misplaced modifier. It fits best in (d) this way: ". . . inhabited the area the way they inhabited Atlantis."

2. (a) U.S. and Mexican industries (b) are integrated with autos and parts (c) flowing unhindered (d) across the border.
    (b) A comma is needed after integrated so the sentence does not say the "industries are integrated with autos and parts . . ."

3. (a) The concensus was (b) that O'Hara stands to gain (c) in the South, (d) where he is weakest.
    (a) *"concensus"* is misspelled; it is *consensus*.

4. (a) Even as a native of Cadbury who lives in a university residence hall, it is (b) easy to forget that (c) there is more to life than (d) classes, dining halls, concerts, parties and the library.
    (a) Technically a dangling modifier, an error compounded by the lack of a subject in a sentence in which the bashful writer didn't use the personal pronoun *I*. Best: "Even as a native of Cadbury who lives in a university residence hall, I find it easy . . ."

5. (a) George Washington University, (b) which was named in honor of this (c) country's first president, is (d) situated in the nations capital.
    (d) *nations* should be *nation's* to signify possessive.

6. (a) The committee said (b) their work was finished (c) although it was not (d) in final form.
    (b) *their* should be *its* so the pronoun agrees with its antecedent, *committee*.

7. (a) The article says journalism education (b) inspires idealism in students (c) that gradually fade away (d) after the students work in the real world.
    (c) The verb should be *fades* to agree with the pronoun *that*

which agrees with its antecedent, *idealism.* Singular antecedent, singular verb.

8.   (a) Leaving home for the (b) first time is not really (c) that difficult an ordeal and college students (d) except it as part of growing up.

(d) *except* is misspelled; it is *accept.*

9.   (a) William Williams has traced the history of the (b) system in detail from 900 B.C. through the 14th century, his book (c) is recommended for anyone (d) who is interested in the history of art.

(b) A compound sentence, this needs a semicolon, not a comma, between *century* and *his.*

10. (a) When Wentzel stepped to the plate, (b) he hit the first pitch, (c) lofting it in a high arc (d) that ended in the centerfield bleachers.

(c) *in a high arc* is redundant; that's what *lofting* means.

11. (a) Nobody in a democracy, (b) regardless of race, creed or religion, (c) can be taxed (d) without their consent.

(d) *their* should be *his;* a pronoun agrees in number with its antecedent.

12. (a) Neither John nor Bill have (b) the good sense (c) to come in (d) out of the rain.

(a) *have* should be *has.* In *neither . . . nor* constructions, the verb agrees with the noun following *nor,* not both nouns. In this sentence, that noun, *Bill,* is singular.

13. (a) When Judy and Sally worked (b) for the Youngs a decade ago, (c) they were well-paid (d) by today's standards.

(c) Drop the hyphen in *well-paid. Well* is an adverb modifying a verbal, *paid.*

14. (a) What makes the English so (b) interesting, aside from the rhythm of their writing is the (c) serious intensity with which they (d) absorb concepts.

(b) A comma is needed after *writing.* The phrase *aside . . . writing* is non-restrictive modification, which is set off by commas—front and back.

15. (a) Working journalists who are daily exposed to the intricacies of government (b) have an insider's understanding of the subtle relationships (c) among the rules, institutions and personalities (d) that comprise our legal system.

(d) *comprise* should be *compose.* The whole comprises the parts; the parts compose the whole.

16. (a) Floor coverings will cost $37351 (b) to replace while (c) finish-
    ings and fixtures will cost (d) at least another $43,000 to replace.
    (a) $37351 needs a comma—$37,351. In four-digit numbers, you
    have the option—$1200 or $1,200. There's no option with five
    and above.

17. (a) It wasn't the subfreezing playing (b) conditions or a matter of
    being (c) outplayed, the game was decided (d) by puck luck.
    (c) A compound sentence, it needs a semicolon after *outplayed*.

18. (a) A combination of the aging Walt Jones, (b) a rash of injuries,
    and a new generation of uncooperative talent (c) are (d) primarily
    responsible for the poor season.
    (c) The correct verb is *is,* which would agree with the sentence's
    subject, *combination.*

19. (a) The 15 bears he has shot (b) represent an unusual hunting
    record, "that's (c) pretty good for Montana," (d) the game warden
    said.
    (b) Drop the comma after *record.* Commas are not used between in-
    dependent and restrictive clauses or between paraphrased quota-
    tions and direct quotations.

20. (a) Orange County Judge Ralph E. McFarland (b) ordered the
    Joneses to keep their farm reasonably clear (c) of manure and (d)
    the removal of the manure piles near the fence.
    (d) Parallel construction requires that *the removal* function the same
    as *to keep* in (b). Thus "Orange County Judge Ralph E. McFarland
    ordered the Joneses to keep their farm reasonably clear of manure
    and to remove the manure piles near the fence."

21. (a) The further away I walk (b) the better (c) that painting looks
    (d) to my untrained eye.
    (a) *further* should be *farther* because you can measure the distance
    the speaker in the sentence walks.

22. (a) He is a registered (b) dietition and a (c) member of the Min-
    nesota and American (d) Dietetic Associations.
    (b) *dietition* is misspelled; *dietitian* is preferred. The word is also
    sometimes spelled *dietician.*

23. (a) Last seen in the vicinity of Bowe Street, police say (b) the sus-
    pect is dangerous (c) and could assault anyone (d) without provoca-
    tion.
    (a) Technically dangling modification, the error can be corrected in
    one of two ways—move the modification or move the attribution

police say. "Police say the suspect, last seen in the vicinity of Bowe Street, is dangerous and could assault anyone without provocation" or "Last seen in the vicinity of Bowe Street, the suspect is danger-ous and could assault anyone without provocation, police say."

24. (a) Sears, the largest department store (b) in the area, is (c) putting their best (d) merchandise on sale.

(c) The possessive pronoun *their* should be *its. Sears* is a singular noun, not a plural one.

25. (a) She implied from what he said (b) that he was (c) ill and would not (d) attend the party.

(a) *implied* should be *inferred.* The listener infers, the speaker im-plies.

26. (a) Five persons—Wildavsky, Jones, Phalan, Emerson and me— were (b) chosen to research and write (c) the Herald-Republic's first series of articles (d) on nursing home care.

(a) *me* should be *I. Me* is objective case and appears only in objects of verbs and prepositions.

27. (a) I took it (b) as a complement when (c) he told me I have teeth (d) as white as chalk.

(b) *complement* is misspelled; *compliment* is correct.

28. (a) If you want to observe (b) Congress, you (c) must go to Wash-ington, D.C. the capital (d) of the United States.

(c) A very common error; put a comma after *D.C.*

29. (a) The facts of the Watergate (b) scandal (c) will not be learned until each (d) major and minor figure write his own book.

(d) *write* should be *writes,* the tip-off being *each.*

30. (a) The secretary (b) is in charge of (c) ordering the stationery (d) for the office.

(e) No error, although you may have thought *stationery* was mis-spelled. Station*ery* is pap*er*.

31. (a) The woman on the stage (b) is a professor of child teaching; she's (c) considered by many (d) to be a child teaching expert.

(d) Put a hyphen between *child* and *teaching* so we know the profes-sor's a *child-teaching expert.*

32. (a) Plato said Atlantis was situated (b) beyond the Pillars of Hercu-les, (c) which is 200 miles (d) the east of the Strait of Gibraltar.

(c) *is* should be *are* to agree with the pronoun *which* which agrees with *Pillars,* a plural.

33. (a) Traditional espionage, such as the penetration (b) of the in-telligence agencies of other countries and the covering up (c) of

clandestine information is the (d) CIA's function, according to Tressler.

(c) Missing is a comma after *information*.

34. (a) Jones noted further (b) that the two city's zoos (c) are comparable, but that Cadbury has nothing (d) equivalent to Clive's public parks.

(b) The plural of *city* is *cities;* the plural possessive, then, is *cities'*.

35. (a) Neither the environmental nor the drug issue hold (b) the promise for controversy (c) the way the food (d) issue does.

(a) *hold* should be *holds. Neither . . . nor* constructions rely on the second noun, not both, to determine the number of the verb.

36. (a) "This is a good budget (b) for our investigation," the congressman said; (c) "any cut in my opinion will weaken what (d) we are trying to do."

(c) Commas are needed after *cut* and *opinion; in my opinion* is an aside and should be set off by commas. Otherwise you'll cut the congressman's opinion.

37. (a) Irregardless of what people say, (b) most of them (c) are opposed to restricting (d) industrial pollution.

(a) *Irregardless* is considered nonstandard usage; *regardless* is preferred.

38. (a) The following afternoon, (b) which was a Wednesday an (c) Air Force transport landed in an (d) abandoned dirt strip that once was the Clive airport.

(b) A comma is needed after *Wednesday* to complete setting off the non-restrictive clause.

39. (a) Since—if not because—Hayes (b) left, advertising linage has dropped (c) disasterously, to little more than half (d) the 1,280 pages the magazine had in 1973.

(c) *disasterously* is misspelled; it should be *disastrously*.

40. (a) It is possible that the widely-publicized (b) and twice-canceled meeting between the dictator and all Britons in his country (c) was a device to divert (d) world attention from the three deaths.

(a) Dump the hyphen in *widely-publicized*. There's no reason to hyphenate a compound modifier made out of an adverb and a participle.

41. (a) When he saw the fire damage, (b) he exclaimed: (c) "That must have been (d) some fire!

(d) End the direct quotation that begins in (c) with quotation marks.

42. (a) Packard suggested closing (b) the loopholes for the rich (c) and rejection of salary increases (d) for government officials.

(c) Parallel construction error; change *rejection* to *rejecting* so it's parallel with *closing*. "Packard suggested closing the loopholes for the rich and rejecting salary increases for government officials."

43. (a) When your nerves are frazzled, (b) there's nothing like a (c) soothing tranquilizer (d) to make everything seem right.

(c) *soothing tranquilizer* is redundant.

44. (a) The news media is (b) the major source of information (c) in this country (d) and in other democracies.

(a) *media* is plural; thus, *is* must be *are*.

45. (a) Pamela Rubin, who once (b) worked for a local newspaper, (c) now works for one (d) of the wire services.

(e) No error.

46. (a) One of every five (b) of the state's residents (c) live in the sort of poverty (d) that forced Bert Collins to leave the area.

(c) *live* should be *lives* to agree with the subject of the sentence, *One*.

47. (a) The fourth annual conference which (b) was held after the disaster, (c) left the participants as confused and discouraged (d) as before the disaster.

(a) A comma is needed after *conference* to set off the non-restrictive clause *which . . . disaster.*

48. (a) A newspaper or magazine without advertising (b) is a phenomena not often seen (c) in a media system (d) that depends so heavily on advertising revenues.

(b) *phenomena* is plural; it should be *phenomenon.*

49. (a) All of the animals (b) in the zoo are fed (c) at the same time so that the workers (d) can stay on a regular schedule.

(e) No error.

50. The petition (b) alledges (c) that the privately owned road (d) is unfit for use.

(b) *alledges* is misspelled; it should be *alleges*—no *d.*

51. (a) The psychiatrist (b) wanted to know (c) the affect the drug had (d) on his patients.

(c) *affect* is incorrect; the correct word is *effect.*

52. (a) Budget limitations (b) of a newspaper this size (c) prevents the hiring (d) of a staff for investigative reporting.

(c) *prevents* should be *prevent* to agree with the subject, *limitations.*

53. (a) The project requires cleaning (b) and reconstruction of a water channel, repairing dikes (c) and complying with (d) anti-pollution measures.

(b) Parallel construction error; change *reconstruction* to *reconstructing* so it's parallel with *cleaning*. "The project requires cleaning and reconstructing a water channel, repairing dikes and complying with anti-pollution measures."

54. (a) During that time, (b) a passing motorist saw the (c) fire in the Garber Mansion (d) and called the fire department.

(b) *passing motorist* is redundant.

55. (a) The survey conducted by two nationally known testing authorities show (b) that only one of 50 students (c) finds college less demanding (d) than high school.

(a) *show* should be *shows* to agree with *survey*, the subject of the sentence.

56. (a) He says he does not (b) like basketball, I doubt (c) that he has seen two games (d) in his life.

(b) This is a compound sentence so it needs a semicolon in place of the comma after *basketball*.

57. (a) He saw a dog (b) who's coat he described (c) as being as stiff as (d) a wire brush.

(b) *who's* is the contracted form of *who is*. To be correct, substitute *whose,* the possessive form of the pronoun who.

58. (a) Neither Cadbury nor Pilsdon are (b) the kind of city (c) I would like (d) to raise children in.

(a) *are* should be *is. Neither . . . nor* constructions rely on the second noun, not both, to determine the number of the verb.

59. (a) James Stein of Cambridge was (b) promoted by Harvard College, (c) his alma mater, (d) two weeks ago.

(e) No error although you may have mistakenly wanted to set off *of Cambridge* in commas.

60. (a) If you think she's (b) intelligent, you (c) should meet her (d) 5 year old sister.

(d) A compound modifier is hyphenated, making the correct form *5-year-old sister.*

61. (a) While the likelihood of (b) such an occurence is small, (c) care must still (d) be exercised by everyone.

(b) *occurence* is misspelled; the correct spelling is *occurrence.*

62. (a) Pressures that result from arguments and mistrust (b) between

local conservative and liberal groups—as well as (c) the influence of various local political (d) leaders—brings about this scrutiny.

(d) *brings* should be *bring* to agree with the subject, *pressures*.

63. (a) To criticize him however is (b) to hold him accountable to a high standard—indeed (c) one beyond most journalists, most researchers (d) and most college professors.

(a) *however* should be set off with commas.

64. (a) Maybe it's the black (b) jersies the Oakland Raiders (c) wear that make them appear (d) formidable to their opponents.

(b) *jersies* is misspelled; the correct spelling is *jerseys,* based on the convention that with *y*-ending words in which a vowel precedes the *y* do not change *y* to *i* and add *es*—just add *s*.

65. (a) Its very odd (b) how a person can have (c) so many different feelings about (d) something he plans to do.

(a) *Its* is the possessive form of the pronoun *it;* to be correct the sentence needs *it's,* the contracted form of *it is*.

66. (a) While in Lexington, (b) the Parnells only saw one house (c) they really liked (d) enough to consider buying.

(b) Misplaced modification; the adverb *only* modifies *house* not *saw*. "While in Lexington, the Parnells saw only one house they really liked enough to consider buying."

67. (a) The North Carolina senator, (b) an expert on government relations and services, (c) eluded to the growing gap between what the government receives in taxes (d) and what it provides in services.

(c) *eluded* is misused; the correct word for this sentence is *alluded*.

68. (a) A proposal to rezone part of Schuylkill Avenue (b) may be voted on by council (c) tonight or the proposal may be (d) remanded back to the planning commission for further discussion.

(d) *remanded back* is redundant.

69. (a) Hopefully, City Council will pass (b) a human relations ordinance (c) before the students (d) return to the Bakersfield College campus in September.

(a) *Hopefully* is misused. "City Council hopes it will pass a human relations ordinance before the students return to the Bakersfield College campus in September."

70. (a) Required mandatory (b) conservation measures must be (c) followed if we (d) are to conserve energy.

(a) *Required mandatory* is redundant.

71. (a) Forty hours of work (b) a week tires anyone (c) who has never worked (d) that much before.

(e) No error, although you may believe *tires* should be *tire* to agree with *hours*. Not so; plural numbers considered in a collective sense are treated like singular nouns. Hence, they take singular verbs.

72. (a) The writing of both authors (b) continue to (c) reflect their contrasting (d) basic philosophies on history.

(b) *continue* should be *continues* to agree with *writing*, the subject of the sentence.

73. (a) Occaisionally children will watch (b) a long program on television, (c) but it has to be a program (d) with special appeal.

(a) *Occaisionally* is misspelled; it should be *occasionally*.

74. (a) The city's recently formed (b) transit system (c) comprises 35 formerly independent (d) rail and bus lines.

(e) No error; this sentence shows the correct use of *comprise*.

75. (a) Studies indicate that (b) a word commonly mispelled (c) by college students is (d) occurrence.

(b) *mispelled* is *misspelled*. Prefixes don't alter spelling.

76. (a) Twain's stories are (b) very interesting, (c) they represent several (d) styles of writing.

(b) A compound sentence needing a semicolon, not a comma, after *interesting*.

77. (a) He took the dead soldier's (b) helmet because (c) he wanted a (d) momento of the war.

(d) *memento*, not *momento*. Think of *memory*.

78. (a) The judge ruled (b) that University of Florida students have (c) the legal right to vote in the (d) district where they attend college.

(c) *legal right*, at least in a sentence about a court decision, is redundant.

79. (a) The value of all of Mexico's exports (b) to the United States (c) are given as (d) 183 million pesos.

(c) *are* should be *is* to agree with the subject, *value*.

80. (a) Timothy R. Klingaman, (b) assistant superintendant of instruction, said (c) he is pleased with (d) the committee's work.

(b) *superintendant* is misspelled; the correct spelling is *superintendent*.

81. (a) The new faculty member (b) proposed the following changes, (c) discontinue two writing courses, add three theory courses (d) and increase the length of class sessions.

(b) The comma is masquerading as a colon or a dash. "The new faculty member proposed the following changes: discontinue two writing courses, add three theory courses and increase the length of class sessions."

82. (a) The intelligence unit tried to illicit (b) as much information as possible (c) from the spy who (d) had been captured during the last coup.

(a) *illicit* is misused; it should be *elicit*.

83. (a) The good old (b) days of (c) free enterprise (d) are over.

(e) No error, although you may have wanted to put a comma between *good* and *old*. However, only adjectives of equal rank get commas.

84. (a) Studying is (b) one of those chores (c) that makes college life (d) more than just one big party.

(c) *makes* should be *make* to agree with the pronoun *that* which agrees with its antecedent, *chores,* a plural noun.

85. (a) Nebraska Attorney General, Joseph Dalton, (b) argued that it doesn't cost (c) the Postal Service 15 cents to deliver (d) a first-class letter.

(a) Titles in front of names are not set off by commas. Had the title been used as the subject of the sentence, then the name would be in apposition to it and commas would be needed. "The Nebraska attorney general, Joseph Dalton, argued that it doesn't cost the Postal Service 15 cents to deliver a first-class letter."

86. (a) The organization needs (b) someone who (c) can provide liason (d) with other community groups.

(c) *liason* is misspelled; it should be *liaison*.

87. (a) The system did not seem (b) to be working on this day, it kept (c) rejecting the (d) operator's instructions.

(b) This is a compound sentence; it needs a semicolon instead of a comma between *day* and *it*.

88. (a) William K. Steigerwalt, (b) president of the Missoula National Bank has (c) announced the promotion of two officers from (d) the bank's main office.

(b) Missing is a comma after *bank* to set off *president of the Missoula National Bank,* which is in apposition to *William K. Steigerwalt*.

89. (a) He has three sisters; (b) his sister Judy (c) is a registered nurse (d) who just received a college degree.

(e) No error, although you may have wanted to set *Judy* off with commas. *Judy,* however, is restrictive and cannot be set off with commas, which would mean *Judy* could be dropped from the sentence without damaging the meaning. In this case, the person has three sisters and *Judy* is needed to make it clear which sister the sentence is about.

90.   (a) Sally another one of his sisters (b) is licensed by the (c) state of
      Indiana as (d) an x-ray technician.
      (a) *another one of his sisters* is in apposition to *Sally* and must be set
      off by commas.

91.   (a) His third sister, Lyn, (b) is a old hand (c) at reporting on inter-
      mediate (d) school units.
      (b) *a* should be *an*. *a* is used before consonant sounds; *an* is used
      before vowel sounds.

92.   (a) One of his brothers-in-law covers (b) high school and college (c)
      sports for a medium-sized (d) newspaper in Alabama.
      (e) No error, although you may have thought brothers-in-law,
      which is plural, was the subject of the sentence. *One* is.

93.   (a) The president of the (b) company puts (c) alot of trust in the
      old-fashioned (d) common sense of his workers.
      (c) the preferred spelling is *a lot,* not *alot.*

94.   (a) The principle of our high school (b) has three college degrees,
      (c) including one (d) from Wayne State University.
      (a) *principle* is misspelled; it should be *principal.*

95.   (a) Although he had followed (b) all of the proper proceedures, (c)
      the student could not persuade the registrar (d) to change his
      grade.
      (b) *proceedures* is misspelled; the correct spelling is *procedures.*

96.   (a) The jury was convinced to find (b) the man not guilty, (c) al-
      though some people had (d) their doubts.
      (a) *persuaded,* not *convinced. Convinced* is never followed by an in-
      finitive.

97.   (a) He found the (b) book a 950-page volume, (c) very difficult to
      read (d) to himself or to his children.
      (b) Missing is a comma after *book* to open the apposition, *a 950-
      page volume.*

98.   (a) This sentence may be (b) all right with you, (c) but its not (d)
      all right with me.
      (c) *its,* a possessive pronoun, should be *it's,* the contracted form of
      it is.

99.   (a) A professor of renowned scholarship, the faculty (b) entrusted
      Wentzel with the chairmanship (c) of the department in an effort
      to raise (d) the department's standards.
      (a) Misplaced modification, in which you have two choices to cor-
      rect it—move the modification or move the word modified. "The
      faculty entrusted Wentzel, a professor of renowned scholarship,

with the chairmanship of the department in an effort to raise the department's standards" or "A professor of renowned scholarship, Wentzel was entrusted by the faculty with the chairmanship of the department in an effort to raise the department's standards." The second version is poor because of the passive voice followed by the piling up of four prepositional phrases.

100. (a) On the platform were (b) two people—a former FBI agent, who is a (c) 1941 graduate of Oregon (d) State and the moderator.

(d) *who . . . State* is a non-restrictive clause. Such clauses are set off by commas, meaning a comma is needed after *State,* in addition to the one after *agent.*

101. (a) The reform-minded (b) government's nationalization (c) of some U.S. businesses had strained (d) relations between the United States and Chile.

(e) No error.

102. (a) Some social workers prefer (b) to work with young juveniles (c) rather than (d) adults.

(b) *young juveniles* is redundant.

103. (a) Numerous researchers have (b) complained about the time and effort (c) that has been wasted trying (d) to replicate shoddy experiments.

(c) *has* should be *have* because the subject *that* agrees with *time and effort,* which is plural.

104. (a) Only Barnhart considered what (b) the adverse national publicity would do (c) to the players' careers athletically and academically and (d) to the players psychologically.

(c) *athletically* is misspelled. *ly* adverbs are formed by adding *ly* to the adjective, which in this case is *athletic,* not *athletical.*

105. (a) The accomodations (b) were insufficient (c) to house everyone (d) at the conference.

(a) *accomodations* is misspelled; the correct spelling is *accommodations.*

106. (a) In the American system of justice, (b) judges are (c) trained to be (d) uninterested observers during trials.

(d) *uninterested* should be *disinterested.* If judges are *uninterested,* it means they don't care about their duties at all. If they are *disinterested,* it means they have no interest in the outcome of a particular court action; they are impartial.

107. (a) "It's going to be a long time (b) before I learn how to spell," (c) John Streeter, a student (d) told his teacher.

(c) *a student* is in apposition to *John Streeter* and should be set off by commas: ". . . John Streeter, a student, told . . ."

108. (a) Not one of (b) the members of the team (c) were able to explain the loss (d) to the satisfaction of the fans.

(c) *were* should be *was* to agree with the singular subject *not one*.

109. (a) There were less jellybeans (b) in the jar than (c) we had first (d) imagined.

(a) *less* should be *fewer*.

110. (a) When we had (b) finished eating (c) John opened the beer (d) we had brought on the picnic.

(b) Missing is a comma after *eating*. The comma makes it clear the people are not eating John.

111. (a) Because the legislature is concerned (b) with safety, their members (c) approved the new school (d) bus code.

(b) *their* should be *its* to agree with *legislature*.

112. (a) Hussey said the resolution is "unecessary (b) legislation that is (c) designed to force our (d) police department to hire homosexuals."

(a) *unecessary* is misspelled; the correct spelling is *unnecessary*. Prefixes don't alter spelling.

113. (a) Staunton police allege (b) that the man, who was not identified broke (c) into the Smiths' house (d) shortly after midnight.

(b) A comma is needed after *identified* to properly set off the nonrestrictive clause *who . . . identified*.

114. (a) The candidate told his supporters (b) he is confident he will win the (c) farm bloc and hold (d) his own among urban voters.

(e) No error.

115. (a) Eleven units (b) from the Oklahoma Panhandle (c) is scheduled to appear (d) in the Bicentennial parade.

(c) *is* should be *are* to agree with *units*.

116. (a) The Cougars, who in their initial year (b) of conference play handed Texas Tech (c) its first loss, 27–19, (d) needs only to beat Rice to gain the title.

(d) *needs* should be *need* to agree with *Cougars*.

117. (a) Women having handstand contests and wheelbarrow races is (b) far from the concept of collegiate (c) gymnasts getting ready (d) to go to the Nationals.

(a) *is* should be *are* because of the plural subject.

118. (a) Police arrested a total of (b) 15 terrorists, 9 Lebanese, (c) 3 members of the IRA, (d) 2 Algerians and a Brazilian.

(b) The first comma is masquerading as a colon or a dash, leaving the number of people arrested as 30 when it should be 15. "Police arrested a total of 15 terrorists—9 Lebanese, 3 members of the IRA, 2 Algerians and a Brazilian.

119. (a) Collective nouns take a singular verb (b) when considered as one unit (c) and a plural verb when (d) considered by its individual parts.

(d) *its* should be *their* because the word refers to the plural word *nouns* at the beginning of the sentence.

120. (a) The tax collector said that (b) the new tax law, with its many exceptions and qualifications, (c) make the tax forms (d) difficult to understand.

(c) *make* should be *makes* to agree with *law*.

121. (a) At twelve noon (b) many university employees (c) go downtown (d) to eat lunch.

(a) *twelve noon* is redundant.

122. (a) The student and professional chapters (b) of Sigma Delta Chi is sponsoring (c) the interview with (d) the candidates for the Senate.

(b) *is* should be *are* because of the plural subject, *chapters.*

123. (a) Not only are the schools not doing what they should be doing. Higher education is (b) also falling short because some professors are supposed to be training (c) the teachers who go into (d) the elementary and secondary schools.

(a) You can consider the error from at least two viewpoints. One is that the period should be a comma; another is that *Not . . . doing* is a sentence fragment.

124. (a) While the Senate took action in the conspiracy case, (b) discussions were under way (c) to modify the president's (d) proposed secrecy legislation.

(e) No error, although you may have wanted to make *under way* one word. It's two.

125. (a) Born in Germany in 1922, Jacob Schmidt's literary activities (b) began after he came (c) to this country with his uncle (d) and settled in California.

(a) Misplaced modification, best fixed this way: "Jacob Schmidt, born in Germany in 1922, began his literary activities after he came to this country with his uncle and settled in California."

126. (a) The administration is seeking to (b) help the farmers of this country (c) by increasing price supports, and (d) stepping up foreign sales.

(c) There's no need for the comma after *supports*. The sentence is not compound, in which case you might want to use a comma; it contains a compound predicate.

127. (a) When the candidate completed (b) his speech, the audience was given (c) by his campaign aides (d) copies of his literature.

(b) Unnecessary shift in voice, from active to passive. Better written: "When the candidate completed his speech, his campaign workers gave the audience copies of his literature."

Bibliography

The Associated Press Stylebook, Rev. ed. The Associated Press, New York, 1970.

The Associated Press Stylebook, Rev. ed. The Associated Press, New York, 1977.

Babb, Laura Longley, ed. *The Editorial Page.* Houghton Mifflin Company, Boston, 1977.

Baker, Sheridan, *The Practical Stylist,* 3d. ed. Thomas Y. Crowell Company, New York, 1973.

Barnett, Lincoln. *The Treasure of Our Tongue.* A Mentor Book. New American Library, New York, 1967.

Barzun, Jacques. *Simple & Direct, A Rhetoric for Writers.* Harper & Row, New York, 1975.

Baskette, Floyd K., and Jack Z. Sissors. *The Art of Editing,* 2d. ed. Macmillan Publishing Company, 1977.

Bernstein, Theodore M. *The Careful Writer, A Modern Guide to English Usage.* Atheneum, New York, 1973.

Brown, Charles H. *Informing the People.* Henry Holt and Company, New York, 1957.

Charnley, Mitchell V. *Reporting,* 3d. ed. Holt, Rinehart and Winston, New York, 1959.

The Compact Edition of the Oxford English Dictionary. Oxford University Press, New York, 1971.

Copperud, Roy H. *Words on Paper.* Hawthorn Books, New York, 1960.

Dillard, J. L. *American Talk.* Random House, New York, 1976.

Farb, Peter. *Word Play, What Happens When People Talk.* Alfred A. Knopf, New York, 1973.

Final Harvest, Emily Dickinson's Poems. Selection and introduction by Thomas H. Johnson. Little, Brown and Company, Boston, 1961.

Flesch, Rudolf. *The Art of Readable Writing.* Collier Books, New York, 1949.

Flesch, Rudolf, and A. H. Lass. *A New Guide to Better Writing.* Popular Library, New York, 1947; 1949 by Harper & Brothers.

Fowler, H. W. *A Dictionary of Modern English Usage.* Oxford University Press, New York, 1944.

Fowler, H. W. *Fowler's Modern English Usage,* 2d. ed. Revised by Sir Ernest Gowers. Oxford University Press, New York, 1965.

Gilmore, Gene, and Robert Root. *Modern Newspaper Editing.* The Glendessary Press, Berkeley, Calif., 1971.

Greene, Harry A., and Walter T. Petty. *Developing Language Skills in the Elementary Schools.* Allyn and Bacon, Boston, 1967.

Hayakawa, S. I., ed. *The Use and Misuse of Language.* Fawcett Publications, Greenwich, Conn., 1962.

Hayakawa, S. I. *Language in Thought and Action,* 3d. ed. Harcourt Brace Jovanovich, New York, 1972.

Hepburn, James G. *College Composition.* The Macmillan Company, New York, 1964.

Hough, George A., 3rd. *News Writing.* Houghton Mifflin Company, Boston, 1975.

House, Homer C., and Susan Emolyn Harman. *Descriptive English Grammar,* 2d. ed. Revised by Harman. Prentice-Hall, Englewood Cliffs, N.J., 1950.

Knightley, Philip. *The First Casualty.* A Harvest Book. Harcourt Brace Jovanovich, New York, 1975.

Langacker, Ronald W. *Language and Its Structure, Some Fundamental Linguistic Concepts.* Harcourt, Brace & World, New York, 1967.

McCrimmon, James M. *Writing with a Purpose,* 4th ed. Houghton Mifflin Company, Boston, 1967.

Mencken, H. L. *The American Language,* 4th ed. Alfred A. Knopf, New York, 1936.

Mencken, H. L. *The American Language, Supplement I.* Alfred A. Knopf, New York, 1945.

Morris, William, ed. *The American Heritage Dictionary of the English Language.* American Heritage Publishing Co., New York; Houghton Mifflin Company, Boston, 1969.

Myers, L. M. *The Roots of Modern English.* Little, Brown and Company Boston, 1966.

Neal, R. M. *News Gathering and News Writing,* 2d. ed. Prentice-Hall, Englewood Cliffs, N.J., 1949.

Newman, Edwin. *Strictly Speaking, Will American be the Death of English?* The Bobbs-Merrill Company, Indianapolis/New York, 1974.

The New York Times Manual of Style and Usage. Revised and edited by Lewis Jordan. Quadrangle Books, Chicago, 1976.

O'Hara, John. *My Turn.* Random House, New York, 1967.

Rank, Hugh, ed. *Language and Public Policy.* National Council of Teachers of English, Urbana, Ill., 1974.

Roberts, Paul. *Understanding English.* Harper and Brothers, New York, 1958.

Rubinstein, S. Leonard, and Robert G. Weaver. *The Plain Rhetoric.* Allyn and Bacon, Boston, 1964.

Sale, Roger. *On Writing.* Random House, New York, 1970.

Shaw, Harry. *Errors in English and Ways to Correct Them,* 2d. ed. Barnes and Noble, New York, 1970.

Skeat, Walter W. *A Concise Etymological Dictionary of the English Language.* Capricorn Books, New York, 1963. First Edition, 1882.

Stein, Jess, ed. *The American Everyday Dictionary.* Random House, New York, 1949.

Strunk, William, Jr., and E. B. White. *The Elements of Style.* Revised Edition by White. The Macmillan Company, New York, 1959.

Strunk, William, Jr., and E. B. White. *The Elements of Style.* Second Edition revised by White. Macmillan Publishing Co., 1972.

U.S. Government Printing Office Style Manual, Rev. ed. U.S. Government Printing Office, Washington, D.C., 1973.

Watson, Winifred, and Julius M. Nolte. *A Living Grammar.* Revised. Avenel Books, New York, 1956.

Westin, Alan F., ed. *The Supreme Court: Views from Inside.* W. W. Norton & Company, New York, 1961.

Westley, Bruce H. *News Editing,* 2d. ed. Houghton Mifflin Company, Boston, 1972.

Wimer, Arthur, and Dale Brix. *Workbook for Radio and TV News Editing and Writing,* 3d. ed. Wm. C. Brown Company, Dubuque, Iowa, 1970.

Index